M000251640

WHO AM I?

AND WHAT AM I DOING HERE?

DAVID WEBB & JOHN HAY

Who Am I? (And What Am I Doing Here?):
Biblical Worldview of Self-Image

Published by
Apologia Educational Ministries, Inc.
1106 Meridian Street, Suite 340
Anderson, Indiana 46016
www.apologia.com

Copyright © 2010 John Hay and Apologia Educational Ministries
ALL RIGHTS RESERVED

Fourth Printing: March 2019

ISBN: 978-1-935495-08-6

Cover Design: Sandra Kimbell
Book Design: Doug Powell

Printed by Asia Printing Co., Ltd. Seoul, Korea

Girl at Mirror printed by permission of the Norman Rockwell Family Agency.
Copyright © 1954 Norman Rockwell Family Entities.

Unless otherwise indicated, Scripture quotations are from:
The Holy Bible, New International Version © 1973, 1984 by International Bible Society,
used by permission of Zondervan Publishing House.

Other Scripture quotations are from:
Holy Bible, New Living Translation (NLT) © 1996. Used by permission of Tyndale House
Publishers, Inc. All rights reserved.

The Holy Bible, King James Version (KJV)

The Holy Bible, English Standard Version (ESV) © 2001 by Crossway Bibles, a division of Good
News Publishers. Used by permission. All rights reserved.

New American Standard Bible® (NASB) © 1960, 1977, 1995 by the Lockman Foundation.
Used by permission.

The Holy Bible, New Century Version (NCV) © 1987, 1988, 1991 by Word Publishing.
Used by permission.

International Children's Bible, New Century Version (ICB) © 1986, 1988 by Word Publishing

Contemporary English Version (CEV) © 1995 by American Bible Society

The Holy Bible, New King James Version (NKJV) ©1984 by Thomas Nelson, Inc.

For Jeffrey, James, Emma,
William, Virginia, and Aubrey,
my beloved grandchildren
and God's image-bearers.

For Abigail, Elizabeth, Hannah,
David, Michelle, and Philip
in whom I see God every day.

TABLE OF CONTENTS

Table of Contents

Table of Contents

HOW TO USE THIS BOOK

Thank you for choosing the What We Believe series and the second volume, *Who Am I? (And What Am I Doing Here?)*. As with every Apologia textbook, you will find this Bible curriculum easy to use for your whole family. The text is written directly to the student, making it appealing for children from six to fourteen. The material is presented in a conversational, engaging style that will make the study of God's Word exciting and memorable for your students, thereby creating an environment where learning is a joy.

Each lesson contains a great deal of information and is formatted to allow the child to learn at his or her own pace. The course was designed so that you may customize the amount of time you spend on each lesson, depending on your child's interest level and attention span. We do, however, recommend that you present the lessons in order, as each lesson builds on ideas previously discussed. Although most of the lessons can be covered in two-week segments, some will go a little more quickly, while others may take longer. Older students can read and do the activities on their own. Younger students will enjoy an older sibling or parent reading along with them.

Please note that the Bible verses in each lesson are taken primarily from the New International Version (NIV), although a number of translations are employed. For the sake of clarity, the authors have also made extensive use of the New Living Translation (NLT) and the New Century Version (NCV) as these versions use vocabulary more accessible to younger students. We recommend, however, that your student use your family's preferred translation for the purpose of memorizing selected passages.

NOTEBOOKING

Notebooking is a fun tool that enables kids to personalize and capture what they have learned in an artful keepsake. In each lesson in this book, you will find a number of passages under the heading "Make a Note of It." In these sections, students are asked to write in their notebooks about what they've learned in the lesson or about an experience they've had that relates to the lesson. We find notebooking is a more effective method for helping children to retain and internalize the teaching than simple fill-in-the-blank worksheets. As kids think about their lives in light of the lesson, the spiritual truths of the lesson will come alive for them and make real-life application easy.

Notebooking also allows children to customize the work to meet their individual needs. Younger children might enjoy drawing their responses, for example, or writing a letter to a grandparent about what they are learning.

To help you and your child construct a notebook, several formatted notebook pages are available on the Apologia website. Some of these pages will correspond directly to notebooking activities listed in the book. Others contain thought-provoking activities or Bible readings that supplement the main text.

LESSON STRUCTURE

Each lesson in *Who Am I? (And What Am I Doing Here?)* contains several key components.

The Big Idea. Each lesson opens with an introduction to the main topic of the lesson and a brief overview of what the student has learned up to this point.

What You Will Do. This section states the learning objectives for the lesson.

Short Story. Each of the lessons contains a short story featuring characters about the same age as your children. These stories give the student a glimpse into the lives of characters with differing worldviews and integrate concepts taught in the lesson that follows. As the story's characters work through their differences, minister to one another, and seek counsel from the Bible and their parents, students see what a worldview looks like in action.

Think About It. These thought-provoking questions dig deeper into the short stories and can be used to check the student's comprehension. You may choose to supplement or adapt these questions to better suit your child's age and reading level. More than reciting information back about the story itself, these questions probe the student's understanding and provide great dinner-table talking points.

Words You Need to Know. Important vocabulary words in each lesson are defined in the Words You Need to Know section. Kids should write these definitions in their notebooks. These are words that will be used and examined during the lesson and throughout the book. As children familiarize themselves with these words, not only will church services become more meaningful, but kids will be better prepared to express their faith to others.

Hide It in Your Heart. Although the Bible is quoted extensively throughout the book, each lesson identifies two specific Bible memory verses to be written in the child's notebook. The first of these expresses the main theme of the lesson. Your student will know by memorizing this verse that the theme of the lesson is biblical and something God desires us to know. The second pertains to a character trait that you will want your child to internalize and demonstrate as a result of the lesson. These verses are ideal for Bible memorization or copy work. The verses have been chosen carefully for the clarity of the concepts they communicate, but you may prefer to use your family's favorite translation of these verses.

Integrated learning. Throughout the text we have provided interesting articles with an age-appropriate approach to interdisciplinary topics related to the main text. Some of these topics are specifically related to elements in one of the short stories, while others are tied directly to the lesson. These articles are designed to help you and your child to pursue the book's ideas and concepts across the fields of art, math, science, history and more. The beauty of the integrated learning approach is that it gives the student a broader understanding of the main subject while exposing the student to new interests, skills, and experiences.

What Should I Do? This section highlights a specific godly character trait that the child should demonstrate as an appropriate response to what he or she has just learned. Here the student is given tools to consider how the lesson applies to his or her own life. Knowing the information provided in each lesson is good, but giving the child tools to put the information to use in daily life creates growth.

Prayer. The main body of each lesson concludes with a prayer that enables the child to acknowledge the gifts of God and to thank Him for all He has done. You may also choose to adapt these prayers for use as a family.

Worldviews in Focus. The final portion of each lesson is part of an ongoing study that introduces the child to the concept of differing worldviews. Worldview studies help us understand how people perceive the world around them. While the main body of each lesson focuses on components of the Christian worldview, the Worldviews in Focus passages will help children begin to understand why others believe as they do. Each of these passages depicts a typical day in the life of a child being raised in a different culture with a different worldview. Help your child understand that although the characters and events in these stories are fictional, the locations, lifestyles, and beliefs depicted are very real and common to families like the ones your child will meet in these stories.

What's the Difference? These discussion questions allow children to compare and contrast in a non-judgmental way their own worldview with the one portrayed in the preceding story.

House of Truth. Four of the lessons end with the addition of a new part of the House of Truth. Intended to be a hands-on memory aid, the House of Truth is a visual model constructed one step at a time. As new concepts are learned, the foundation, walls, and roof of the house are constructed, giving the child a concrete way of thinking about his life within the kingdom of God. In *Who Is God? (And Can I Really Know Him?)*, we erected the foundation and first wall of the House of Truth. In this book, the student will complete the second wall of the house. A new wall will be added in both the third and fourth volumes of the series.

The House of Truth can be used figuratively, drawn in the student's notebook, or built with items you have on hand. A three-dimensional, build-as-you-go model is also available for purchase separately from Summit Ministries. This colorful, durable House of Truth is constructed block by block as each affirmation of the biblical Christian worldview is developed lesson by lesson. The model forms a visual, tactile framework to help children understand these truths and integrate them into their lives. You can purchase the model at www.summit.org.

LESSON PLAN

Each lesson is designed to be flexible and adaptable to your family's needs. Organize the lessons into a schedule that works for you and your child. Here is a sample lesson plan to consider based on a schedule of three weeks per lesson, two days per week:

WEEK ONE

Day One:
Read "The Big Idea" and "What You Will Do"
Read the Short Story and discuss
Discuss the questions in "Think About It"

Day Two:
Study "Words You Need to Know"
Memorize "Hide It in Your Heart" verses
Read sidebar articles and do activities
Write or draw in notebook about what was studied

WEEK TWO

Day Three:
Read and discuss first half of the main lesson
Notebook the "Make a Note of It" activities
Write or draw in notebook about what was studied

Day Four:
Read and discuss second half of the main lesson
Notebook the "Make a Note of It" activities
Write or draw in notebook about what was studied

WEEK THREE

Day Five:
Read and discuss "What Should I Do?" for character development
Read and use the prayer for spiritual development
Write or draw in notebook about what was studied

Day Six:
Read the Worldviews in Focus section
Discuss the questions in "What's the Difference?"
Construct or draw the next phase of the House of Truth

ADDITIONAL TEACHING MATERIALS

Some lessons contain activities that require advance planning. A list of materials for these activities has been provided with each activity. Nearly all the materials are household items or are easily obtained. You will find the Apologia website to be a valuable source of information and materials to help you in teaching this course.

WHY SHOULD YOU TEACH WORLDVIEW?

When a particular worldview is held by a large number of people, it becomes highly influential, swaying many through media, entertainment, education, and corporate behavior. Some of the more widely held worldviews of the twenty-first century include secular humanism, socialism and Marxism, New Age, postmodernism, and Islam. Not to be excluded is the biblical Christian worldview, the focus of this curriculum.

People develop their worldviews based upon beliefs they perceive to be true. Obviously, not all beliefs are true. If they were, we would not see the wide diversity of behaviors that stem from different interpretations of the same reality. For example, the beliefs of secular humanists that permit abortion cannot be equally true with the beliefs of conservative Christians that do not permit abortion. Nor can the beliefs of cosmic humanists that identify all existence as part of a universal consciousness be equally true with the beliefs of Christianity that affirm that creation is dependent upon one transcendent God.

Diverse beliefs about reality fill the marketplace of ideas in the emerging global village. Many ideas are competing for dominance, and this competition is producing conflict and confusion in cultures long held together by traditional worldviews. Christian-based cultures are awakening to find mosques standing next to churches and Bible-based laws swept from the books by a simple majority vote of humanist legislators and judges.

Within this global arena of conflict and change, Christians are faced with at least two critical questions: "How do we know what is true?" and "How must we live our lives in relation to the truth we come to know?" This curriculum is designed to address questions like these. It is based on the biblical Christian worldview, which affirms that truth is absolute and knowable through the revelation of God. It affirms that knowledge of God is the beginning of wisdom and the key to understanding the world around us.

You have the privilege and responsibility of leading your child not only in the paths of truth, but also to a knowledge and fear of the One who is the Truth, Jesus Christ. With the lessons contained in this, the second book in the What We Believe series, you will lay several essential foundational truths upon which the biblical Christian worldview is built. Lay these stones of foundational truths well. Pray that God will continually reveal and confirm the truths of His Word in the hearts of your student and that your child will respond in obedience to them.

We think you will find this to be an important course of study. Many eternal truths are presented that can change the way your child looks at the world every day. Minor points of doctrinal difference have been avoided in order to focus on the larger issues that make up our faith. As Christians we are asked to be ready to give an account of the hope that is in us. We hope this book brings your faith into clearer focus and your family ever closer to the Lord.

COURSE WEBSITE

The Apologia website contains additional resources to help you teach this course. Visit www.apologia.com/bookextras and enter the following password: madeinHisimage. Capitalize the *H*, and be sure the password contains no spaces. When you hit "enter," you will be taken to the course website.

WHAT ARE WE DOING HERE?

> THE SPIRIT OF GOD HAS MADE ME; THE BREATH OF THE ALMIGHTY GIVES ME LIFE.

JOB 33:4

THE BIG IDEA

How many questions do you suppose all the people in the world ask every day? Would you guess millions? Billions? Trillions? What we do know is that almost every person from every race and culture ask many of the same questions—very personal, very important questions. One question everyone asks at some time in their lives is "Where did I come from?" But what do we really mean when we ask this question? Most of us know the names of our mothers and fathers and when and where we were born. Some people have even made a hobby of tracing their ancestry back hundreds of years. But knowing who came before us still doesn't answer the question of where we come from.

When we ask this question, what we're really asking is this: Where did people come from in the first place? How did we all get here? Are we the result of a cosmic accident? Did humans come here from another planet? Or did someone actually design and create us? While many people search a lifetime to find the answers to these questions, the truth is really not all that difficult to find. Thousands of years ago, God revealed to us *exactly* where people come from.

Does it sound like we as people spend a lot of time thinking about ourselves? We do! Much of what we think about our lives is trivial and rather boring. *Do I want Cheerios or oatmeal for breakfast? Should I wear the green shirt or the blue one? When I become rich and famous, should I drive a sports car or ride around in a limousine with a built-in swimming pool?* But we also ask more important questions: *Who am I? Why am I here? Where will I go after I die?* In order to answer these questions correctly, we must first understand that God created us in His image. This means that God made you and me to be like Him in many ways. Of course, you and I are not God and can never be exactly like Him. But when we understand that He made us to "look" like Him, it's not hard to see that we are very precious to Him indeed.

Who are you and why are you here? In this book you will learn that you are not what you do or the place where you live. You are not the clothes you wear, the things you own, the friends you make, or the grades or honors you earn in school. You are much, much more. And it's only when you understand what it means to be made in God's image that will you truly know who you are and why you were put on this earth.

WHAT YOU WILL DO
» You will identify the attributes of God.
» You will identify the characteristics that identify you as a person created in God's image.

BABY, IT'S COLD OUTSIDE!

Tanks on a frozen Russian battlefield during World War II. Photo: Tannenberg.

In terms of sheer size, Russia is the largest country in the world. It's also the coldest, with an average temperature of just 22.1 degrees Fahrenheit, or –5.5 degrees Celsius. Because of Russia's vast size, its climate differs dramatically depending on where you are located. Yet even in Moscow, Russia's capital, winter temperatures only occasionally peak above zero during the daytime. *Brrr!*

While the living conditions may sound harsh, the cold winter weather has actually protected Russia from being conquered. In 1812, the French general Napoleon tried to invade Russia. But the cold weather slowed his army and made it hard to get supplies and food to the soldiers. Many thousands of men became sick or died because of the cold. In fact, more soldiers died from exposure, sickness, or starvation than were killed in battle! Accounts of this epic defeat vary, but as many as 685,000 men marched into Russia with Napoleon. Fewer than 70,000 made it out alive.

More than a hundred years later, during World War II, Hitler's Germany tried to conquer Russia with a force of more than 3.5 million troops. But heavy rains followed by the onset of winter left much of the German war machine frozen in the mud, slowing their advance. In the end, the same problems that plagued Napoleon led to Germany's defeat by the Russian people.

The Bible says that God causes nations to rise and fall (Daniel 4:17). With the geography of a nation and its weather also under His control, He can choose to protect and provide for its people using something as simple as snow and cold weather to stop a seemingly invincible army.

SASHA'S CHOICE

"The snows will come early this year." Anna Petrova set the tea kettle on the stove. "Look at little Kiska," she said, nodding toward the cat. "Her fur is already so thick. I believe we're going to have a very cold winter."

"Winters are always cold in Dmitrov, my precious Anya. You just forget from year to year," her husband teased.

"Oh, Misha, I know they are, but I was hoping this year would be different. I don't want such cold weather when our little one arrives. Our cottage is never very warm, and the thought of going outside with a new baby in the winter—oh, I shiver just thinking about it."

Mikhail Petrov rose from his chair and put his arms around his wife. "Don't you worry, my dear Anya. I'll make sure the fire keeps us warm, and we'll have plenty of blankets for the sleigh when we go to the market or to church. Now, let's have some hot tea."

As Anya poured the tea, she said, "If it's a girl, I would like to name her Antonina."

"I like that name," Misha replied. "But of course we would call her Tonya for short. And what if it's a boy?"

"Well, I do like the name Aleksandr very much. It would be nice to name him after your grandfather, don't you think?"

"Then Aleksandr it will be. The footsteps of a little Sasha would be a precious blessing to this home," Misha said with a smile.

Winter did come early that year. By November, the village of Dmitrov was a snowy wonderland. The boughs of fir trees drooped under the snow's weight, and the villagers spent many hours clearing paths from their cottages to the main village road. Darkness covered the countryside by three o'clock every afternoon, and sunlight never touched the snow until after eight in the morning. It was indeed going to be a long, cold Russian winter.

"Do you know what day it will be one month from today?" Anya asked one snowy morning as she set a bowl of hot kasha on the kitchen table.

"Why, Christmas, of course," Misha replied. "And you've already got my present, haven't you?"

"Oh, Misha," Anya said, "I haven't even thought about Christmas with the baby on the way. Besides, we won't have any extra money for gifts this year. We'll be a family of three, not two."

"I was only teasing about my gift," Misha said. "Besides, our little one will be the most precious gift we could ever hope to receive."

After breakfast, Mr. Petrov gave his wife a gentle hug and headed outside to prepare the sleigh. "I'll go to the market by myself today," he said. "You stay by the fire. It's really too cold for you to be outside."

Just as Misha closed the door, Anya took a deep breath. "Oh, my," she gasped. "Could it be?" She sat down at the table and then took another breath. "Oh, my," she said again. "I think, I think I'd better . . ." She hurried to the door and flung it open, allowing a gust of wind and snow to swirl into the little cottage. "Misha!" she called with urgency. "Misha!"

"What is it, my love?" her husband asked as he hitched the horse to the sleigh. "What's wrong?"

"Nothing's wrong. But instead of going to the market, I think you'd better go and fetch Doctor Raskov." She gasped again and clutched the doorframe, trying to catch her breath.

"Is it—? Is it time, Anya?" Misha dropped the harness and rushed to his wife's side.

"I think so," she whispered.

"I'll get Mrs. Yarsky to come stay with you while I go into the village. I'll bring the doctor as quickly as I can," Misha shouted as he climbed into the sleigh.

"Yes, yes. Please hurry!" Anya pushed the door against the wind to close it.

Within an hour, Misha had returned.

"Now just stay calm, Mikhail," instructed Dr. Raskov. "Mrs. Yarsky and I have everything under control."

After what seemed a very long time, Dr. Raskov returned from the bedroom to the small living room.

"You have a son, Mr. Petrov. He looks quite healthy, but . . ."

"But what?" Misha asked, beginning to worry.

"Come into the bedroom. I want to discuss this with both of you together."

Anna Petrova held little Aleksandr in her arms. She smiled as she saw Misha, but tears in her eyes also revealed a deep concern and even fear.

"What is it?" Misha asked again as he approached the bed.

"Your son has a crippled foot," the doctor replied. "Oh, he seems to be quite healthy otherwise, but we'll have to see how he grows before we'll know how well he'll be able to walk."

Misha sat on the side of the bed. Tenderly he picked up his newborn son and looked into his eyes. "You are God's special creation," he said with tears of joy. "You are God's gift to us. You are God's gift to this village and to this world. You are our son, our precious Sasha. God is giving you to us, and we promise to raise you in His ways and for His glory." He kissed Sasha's red, wrinkled face and then laid him back in his mother's arms. Then he kissed Anya gently, held her hand, and smiled. "Thank you for carrying our child," he said with tears in his eyes. "What joy he will bring to us. What joy he will bring to God!"

Through the cold winter months, Misha kept his promise to Anya: The cottage was never cold, and by the time Sasha was old enough for his first outing to the village, Mr. Petrov had collected more than enough blankets to keep all three of them warm in the sleigh.

"I'm worried about taking Sasha into the village," Anya said as she bundled him in a warm blanket.

"Why, Anya? We have plenty of blankets."

"Oh, it's not the cold I'm worried about," she replied. "I just know that the old babushkas in town have nothing better to do than sit around and gossip. I'm sure they've already heard about Sasha, and by now everyone in the village knows."

"Of course they know—everyone knows when a baby's born in Dmitrov," Misha replied, pretending not to understand Anya's worry.

"That's not what I mean," Anya said. "I mean that everyone probably knows about his foot, and they're no doubt thinking he's not a normal boy."

"My dear Anya," Misha said as he cracked the whip to let the horses know it was time to go, "it doesn't matter what people say. We know who our Sasha is. God knows who he is. Let them gossip. It will make no difference to our family."

But it did make a difference to the Petrov family.

For a long time little Sasha could do no more than crawl, and only with great difficulty.

"Oh, Misha," Anya cried one day just after Sasha's second birthday, "will our little boy ever learn to walk?"

"In time, my dear," Misha assured her. "In time."

And in time Sasha did learn to walk. Of course, he couldn't walk like children who had two perfect feet. He had a noticeable limp, but it didn't keep him from getting into the same mischief all young boys get into.

One day, as he toddled unsteadily toward a low bookshelf, his mother warned, "Sasha, don't pick up that vase! You might drop it and break it." But it was too late. Before Anya could reach him, the vase was in his little hands. He then lost his balance and his grip, and the vase shattered on the tile floor.

"Oh, my Sasha! I should scold you, but I'm so happy you can walk to the shelf that I can't bring myself to be angry," Anya said as she scooped up her son. "You sit here while I pick up the pieces."

As Sasha grew, his mobility improved. He still couldn't run fast or walk as steadily as other children, but there was no place he couldn't go if he tried hard enough.

One summer day, when he was six, Sasha was helping his parents in the vegetable garden when his father announced, "Sasha, in only one month the new school year will begin. You're old enough now to learn to read and write. Are you ready?"

"I am, Papa," Sasha replied eagerly, for he had as yet spent very little time with children his own age. This was partly because he lived outside the village and partly because his parents had chosen to keep him close to home until he was older and stronger.

That evening, after Sasha was asleep, Anya confided her fears to her husband. "I'm worried, Misha. I'm worried for Sasha that the children at school will not be kind to him."

"Everything will be fine," Misha said. "Sasha is strong. Besides, everyone will love him. He's kind, intelligent, and . . . well, quite handsome, you know. The young girls will certainly like him." He laughed.

"Oh, Misha, there you go again, trying to make me laugh to keep me from worrying. But I can't help it. I just don't want someone to say or do anything cruel to our precious Aleksandr."

Photo: Hugin-barnaul.

On the first day of school, Mr. Petrov hitched up the family wagon. Anya packed a small lunch in a cloth sack and gave it to Sasha along with a thin composition book and two pencils.

"Enjoy your first day of school. And remember—be friendly to everyone," she said with a smile and a few tears. "Papa will fetch you and Sveta after school." Sveta's family, the Romanoffs, lived on the small farm next to theirs, and she and Sasha had often played together growing up.

As Anya Petrova watched the wagon disappear over a small hill, she prayed, "Dear God, please watch over Sasha. Please help him to make good friends and to be a good friend to others."

The schoolyard was already filled with children when Sasha and Sveta arrived. Mr. Petrov helped both children down from the wagon and hugged Sasha. "I love you, my son. Be a good boy and enjoy your first day of school. I'll meet you and Sveta right here this afternoon at two when school is finished."

As his father drove away, Sasha swallowed and took a deep breath, trying not to cry. Then he limped slowly over to a group of children he thought might be about his own age. "Hi," he said nervously. "I am Aleksandr Mikhailovich Petrov. My family lives just outside the village on a small farm."

"We know who you are," said a boy named Ivan.

"But how do you know me?" Sasha asked with surprise.

"Everyone in Dmitrov knows about the crippled boy with the bad foot," Ivan scoffed. "I see you still haven't learned to walk properly."

Sasha didn't want to believe what he was hearing. He wanted to run away and hide. "I walk just fine," he finally replied with as much courage as he could gather.

"It's okay," said Sveta, who had heard the whole conversation. "Come on, Sasha. It's time to go inside."

Sasha took his assigned seat and looked around the room at the other children. Everyone seemed to know everyone else in the class, but the only student he knew was Sveta.

As class began, the teacher announced, "I'm Mrs. Lushenko. Now before we begin our first lesson, I want each of you to come up, one by one, to the front of the room and introduce yourself to the other students. Tell us a little bit about your family and what you did this summer."

Sasha's heart raced and his faced flushed. *I can't walk to the front of the class. Everyone will laugh at me*, he thought. Then he closed his eyes and put his head on his desk to hide his tears.

"Aleksandr. Aleksandr Petrov. It's your turn. Please come to the front and introduce yourself," Mrs. Lushenko said without emotion. "And do sit up straight in your chair and listen when the other students introduce themselves."

Sasha lifted his head, wiped his tears on his sleeve, and stood. Slowly and with a noticeable limp he made his way to the front of the class. Some of the children snickered.

"We'll have none of that," Mrs. Lushenko said. "Now, Aleksandr, tell us something about yourself and your family."

"I . . . I . . ." But he couldn't speak. His stomach knotted with fear as the other children stared at him. Then he turned and walked as quickly as he could out of the classroom, down the hall, and out into the schoolyard.

"Oh, Papa," he cried aloud, "please come now and take me home!"

Mrs. Lushenko had followed Sasha outside. "What is the matter, Aleksandr? Please come back inside. I will not allow the other children to tease you or make fun of you. So please, you must come back in."

The rest of the school day passed very slowly for Sasha. He kept to himself at lunch and recess, and only Sveta came to talk with him. "Sasha, it's okay," she said. "I am your friend. Just ignore what the other kids are saying."

Sasha didn't answer, nor did he say anything the rest of the school day.

On the way home, his father asked, "So, my son, how was your first day of school? Did you make new friends? Do you like your teacher?"

But Sasha would not talk to his father either.

"Sasha, did you hear me?"

Still Sasha did not answer.

Sveta explained, "Some of the children were not kind to Sasha. Ivan was especially cruel. But I told Sasha to ignore them."

Wisely, Mr. Petrov didn't ask any more questions on the way home. "Thank you, Sveta, for being Sasha's friend," he said as they approached her house. "I'll take you both to school again tomorrow."

"I'm not going to school tomorrow," Sasha said angrily. "I'm never going back to school. You can take Sveta, but I'm not going."

Mr. Petrov put his hand on Sasha's shoulder. "We'll talk about it tonight with your mother," he said softly.

When they arrived home, Sasha jumped down from the wagon, hurried into the house, and ran straight to his room. He didn't even notice his mother walking in from the garden.

"What's wrong with Sasha?" she asked anxiously.

"It seems that some of the children made fun of him at school today," Misha replied.

"I knew it. I knew it!" Anya said angrily. "People are so cruel. And those old gossiping babushkas—if I see any of them in the village I'm going to give them a piece of my mind."

"Now, Anya, calm down," Misha said. "After supper, we'll all talk about this. This is something Sasha will have to face many times in life, even when he's older."

Sasha ate very little that evening and said nothing.

Finally his father said, "Sasha, let's all go and sit outside. We need to talk about what happened today. It's not good for you to hold it all inside."

"It's not right, Papa," Sasha cried. "I can't help it if I walk funny. But I bet I can beat up any of those kids who teased me!"

"Well, maybe you could," his father replied. "But what would that accomplish? You can't make friends that way, and fighting will only bring you trouble."

"But why did God make me this way?" Sasha blurted out. "Why can't I walk like all the other kids? It's not fair!"

His mother put her hands on Sasha's cheeks and began to cry. "No, it may not seem fair to you, my dear son. But God did not make a mistake when He created you. You are an answer to our prayers. You have brought your father and me more joy than you could ever imagine. And you are very special to God."

"If I was so special to God, I'd be able to walk just like everyone else," Sasha said.

"My son," said Sasha's father affectionately, "I know it may not seem fair to you right now. But you are one of God's unique creations. In fact, every person God creates is unique. No two people are exactly alike. But every one of us is made in God's image. Do you know what that means?"

"No, Papa," Sasha sobbed.

"It means that God created you to be like He is in many ways. Oh, you certainly aren't a god, but God gave you a mind—a very good mind, I might add. Do you know why?"

"No, Papa," Sasha said, wiping his face.

"Because God has a mind. He thinks and shares His thoughts with us. And because He created us with minds, we can think and share our thoughts with Him and with others. Of course, God's thoughts are much higher than our thoughts, but He gave us minds so we could know Him and enjoy a wonderful relationship with Him as our heavenly Father."

"But God can't understand how I feel," Sasha protested. "He didn't go to school today and get teased by all the other children. He doesn't know what it feels like to look different."

"Sasha," his mother said with understanding, "God does know how you feel. He has feelings just like we do. He loves us very much, but He also is angered when people disobey Him. And He certainly understands what it feels like to be rejected. Remember, many people hated His Son, Jesus, and nailed Him to the cross."

"Sasha," his father said, "why do you think you feel hurt and angry about what happened at school today?"

"Because it wasn't right," Sasha replied. "It's not right to make fun of other people."

"How do you know it's not right?" his father asked, encouraging Sasha to think more deeply about what he had just said.

"Well, I just do. Don't you?"

"Of course. But the reason we know that being unkind to others is wrong is because God made us in His image. God knows right from wrong, and He created us with the ability to know right from wrong. You see, Sasha, your mother and I didn't really need to teach you that it's wrong to be unkind to others. You would have known that the first time anyone was unkind to you. Now let me ask you a question, my son. Have you ever done something you knew wasn't right, even though your mother and I never specifically told you it was wrong?"

"Probably," Sasha said sheepishly.

"You already know certain things are right or wrong because you have a conscience, and your conscience will tell you in your heart if what you are doing is right or wrong. Oh, our consciences aren't perfect, and we need God's Word to teach us more perfectly. But if you listen to your conscience, you'll usually know if you're doing right or wrong. Now my son, let's talk about what happened at school today. Would it be right or wrong to get into a fight with Ivan and the other children who teased you? Would it be right or wrong to tease them or call them names?"

Sasha sat quietly for a minute, knowing the correct answers to his father's questions but still wanting to get back at the other children. Finally he admitted, "No, it wouldn't be right to fight with them or call them names."

"That's right. So what is the right thing to do?"

After another long silence, Sasha replied, "I think I should forgive them and still try to be friendly. But that would be too hard!"

"I didn't ask whether the right thing would be easy or hard," Mr. Petrov responded seriously. "I asked what would be the right thing to do."

"Forgive them," Sasha mumbled under his breath, not looking up at his father.

"So what are you going to do? You really have only two choices. You can try to get even, or you can forgive and try to be friends with them."

"Do I have to make a choice?" Sasha asked, still not sure he wanted to do the right thing.

"You will be making a choice whether you want to or not. If you don't forgive, that's a choice. If you do forgive, that's also a choice," his father said. Although Sasha did not respond immediately to what his father said, he clearly understood that he had a decision to make.

"Now," Mr. Petrov said, "it's been a very long and difficult day for you. It's time to say your prayers and get ready for bed."

Sasha smiled. "May I pray now?"

"Of course," his mother said.

"Dear God," Sasha prayed aloud. "Thank you for hearing my prayers. Please help me to forgive Ivan and the other children who made fun of me. Please help me to make new friends and to like school. And please bless Mama and Papa and Grandma and Grandpa. Oh, and please bless Sveta, who is my best friend. In Jesus' name. Amen."

Misha and Anya Petrov walked Sasha to his room, tucked him into bed, and kissed him good night.

"Remember, my precious Sasha," said his father, "God loves you very much. You are made in His image. That's who you are. Nothing anyone says or does can ever change that."

"I love you, Papa. I love you, Mama," Sasha replied sleepily.

THINK ABOUT IT

» Where does this story take place? Do you think the story takes place in a modern place and time? Why? Why not?

» What kinds of problems does Sasha face by the time he's ready for school?

» After the family discussion about bearing God's image, do you think Sasha will ever again struggle with his handicap? Why? Why not?

MAKE A NOTE OF IT

Keep a notebook or journal in which you write about what you have learned. When you see the "Make a Note of It" box, you will be asked to record in your notebook your thoughts and answers to important questions.

In the story "Sasha's Choice," Sasha learned that he was created by God to be unique and that neither his birth nor his lame foot was an accident. What is it about the way you were made that you've sometimes wished you could change? Have you ever thanked God for making you this way? Write about a time you were teased for something. How did it make you feel? How did you respond? Have you ever teased someone? If so, how do you think you made that person feel?

WHAT'S IN A NAME?

The boy in our story introduces himself to his classmates as Aleksandr Mikhailovich Petrov. Yet his parents and best friend call him Sasha. His father's name is Mikhail, but his wife calls him Misha. His mother's name is Anna, but her husband calls her Anya. No, you haven't gone mad. Nor has the spell-check function on the authors' computers gone on the blink.

The Russian language has a remarkable capacity for transforming words and giving them new shades of meaning and emotional color. The same is true of personal names. Let's start with Aleksandr (the Russian form of Alexander). The name comes from two Greek roots: *alex*, which means "defense," and *andros*, which means "of a man." Therefore, the meaning of the name is "defender of people." A shorter, or diminutive, form of Aleksandr in Russian is Sasha. The name Sasha is used in informal conversations between people of the same age or between close relatives. The familiar form of Mikhail is Misha, while Anya is the familiar form of Anna. These familiar forms are like nicknames in America, where a man in Ohio named Joseph is often called Joe by his friends and family.

So why does Sasha introduce himself as Aleksandr Mikhailovich? Because Mikhailovich means "son of Mikhail." If Sasha were to someday have a baby sister named Maria, she would be called Maria Mikhailovna, which means "daughter of Mikhail." In Russia, the father's name is used with the person's full first name in polite conversation. This is a way of honoring a person's father as well as recognizing his or her heritage.

For much the same reason, the followers of Jesus Christ identify themselves as *Christians*. In doing so, we honor our Father in heaven whose Son has set us free from sin. As the apostle Peter wrote, "Praise God for the privilege of being called by his name!" (1 Peter 4:16, NLT).

WORDS YOU NEED TO KNOW

» **Parable:** A short story that contains biblical truths for our lives
» **Image:** A visual representation of something or someone
» **Image-Bearer:** A person who carries, or bears, the likeness of God
» **Christlike:** Being like Jesus Christ in character, spirit, or deed

HIDE IT IN YOUR HEART

For we are God's masterpiece. He has created us anew in Christ Jesus, so we can do the good things he planned for us long ago. (Ephesians 2:10, NLT)

And the Lord—who is the Spirit—makes us more and more like him as we are changed into his glorious image. (2 Corinthians 3:18, NLT)

THIS IS A JOB FOR . . . YOU

In the 1930s, in Cleveland, Ohio, high school friends Jerry Siegel and Joe Shuster teamed up to create a character for a popular new kind of magazine called comic books. After considering and discarding several different ideas, Siegel and Shuster eventually settled on the story of an orphaned child from a dying planet who is sent to Earth in a spaceship built by his father. The child is found in a Kansas cornfield by a childless couple that takes him in, names him Clark, and raises him as their own son. As the boy grows, he discovers that he has powers and abilities far beyond those of humans—including super strength, super speed, super hearing, x-ray vision, and in later versions, the ability to fly. Raised according to the traditional values of his foster parents, he grows to adulthood and chooses to use his amazing abilities to fight for truth, justice, and the good of all mankind. Wearing red-and-blue tights and a cape beneath a business suit, this "super man" establishes a secret identity as Clark Kent and lives among us as an ordinary person, his extraordinary abilities unknown even to those closest to him. He takes a job as a reporter at a city newspaper where he is able to learn immediately when Superman's unique services are required anywhere in the world.

Photo: Paramount Pictures and Fleischer Studios.

Superman first appeared in the magazine *Action Comics* in 1938, and the mighty hero was a huge success, eventually becoming one of the most popular and enduring fictional characters of all time. Since his debut, the Man of Steel has appeared in numerous comic books, novels, radio programs, songs, movies, and television shows, not to mention countless Superman games, posters, T-shirts, lunch boxes, and action figures. He's even had his own Broadway musical!

So what is it about this character that has captured the imaginations of several generations of boys and girls, both young and old? Some point to the idea that this incredibly powerful being is selfless and heroic.

Photo: Marjory Collins (Office of War Information).

Superman statue outside of Metropolis, Illinois City Hall. Photo: flickr.com user PhotoDu.de.

After all, he could rule the world if he wanted to, but he uses his powers only to help others. Others point to the similarities between the story of Superman and the story of Jesus—a miraculous child is sent to Earth to become the savior of humanity. Some have even suggested that Superman's popularity demonstrates that mankind needs a savior and knows it.

What is certain is that Superman is a wish-fulfillment fantasy. We all have a basic desire to be more than what we seem to be. Who among us hasn't imagined himself to be a humble, mild-mannered citizen who is secretly stronger, faster, smarter, and destined for greater things?

Well, I have good news for you: You *are* more than you appear to be. Much more. You're not just *any* person. You are the amazing, wonderful, unique creation of Almighty God, the all-knowing, all-present, all-powerful ruler of the universe Himself:

"The Spirit of God has made me; the breath of the Almighty gives me life." (Job 33:4)

You made my whole being.
You formed me in my mother's body.
I praise you because you made me
in an amazing and wonderful way.
What you have done is wonderful.
I know this very well.
You saw my bones being formed
as I took shape in my mother's body.
When I was put together there,
you saw my body as it was formed.
(Psalm 139:13–16, ICB)

"Sure," you might say, "but God made everybody. I'm nobody special." Wrong! You are one of a kind. There has never been and never will be anyone quite like you. No one who has ever lived has possessed your combination of talents and abilities, friends and family, joys and sorrows, resources and opportunities. God designed you, molded you, and breathed life into you—and then He broke the mold! The Bible calls you "God's masterpiece" (Ephesians 2:10, NLT).

You don't have to pretend to be a superhero or anyone else to feel important. You weren't meant to be like someone else. You see, God knew what He was doing when He created you. You were part of His plans from the beginning of the world:

You saw me before I was born.
Every day of my life was recorded in your book.
Every moment was laid out
before a single day had passed.
(Psalm 139:16, NLT)

He made you to be precisely who you are, and He selected this exact time and place for you to live (Acts 17:25–26). Not Ancient Egypt. Not England in the Middle Ages. Not a space colony circling Alpha Centauri in the year 3000. You were meant to live here and now. God even knew you would be reading these words at this very moment! He knew every person you would ever meet and every situation you would ever encounter, and He chose YOU to live this life.

Why? To do the good things God has specifically prepared YOU to do.

Since the time of the original sin, when Adam and Eve first disobeyed God, the world has not always been a very nice place. People hunger for food and for love and too often go without. Some people hate their neighbors because of what they believe or how they look, while others desire the land or riches their neighbors possess and will go to war to take these things for their own. Other people do things to hurt themselves because they don't understand that God made them with a purpose in mind. So with all of these terrible things happening around us, what can just one person do to help? What can YOU do?

From the time you were born, God has given you a special set of gifts—your talents, your personality, your experiences—that no one else possesses. And when you give your life to His Son, Jesus, He sends the Holy Spirit to live inside you to guide you and help you understand His Word. Then God places you in specific situations and introduces you to specific people—some who need your help, others who have been sent to help you—so that you can bring Him glory by doing good works in His name:

> *He has created us anew in Christ Jesus, so we can do the good things he planned for us long ago.* (Ephesians 2:10, NLT)

> *I can do all things through Christ who strengthens me.* (Philippians 4:13, NKJV)

Sin has made the world a dark place, and people need the light of God's glory in their lives. They need to know that God is real and that He has a plan for each and every one of us. They need to hear that God's Son has made a way for people to once again enjoy harmony with God, harmony with one another, harmony with themselves, and harmony with God's creation, just as God intended when He created the world. When you first believe that Jesus is the one and only Son of God and that He gave His life to pay the price for your sins, He gives you the right to be called a child of God (John 1:11–13). As a child of God, you represent your Father on earth. When people meet you, when they talk with you, when you show them God's love, they should be able to see His glory reflected in you.

How is this possible? How can people see God when they see you?

That's what this book is about.

MAKE A NOTE OF IT

Like Clark Kent, do you have a special gift or talent that few people know about? What can you do better than anyone you know? Have you thanked God for this gift? Write down several ideas for how you can use this gift to reflect God's glory and show His love to others.

THE GIRL AND THE MIRROR

Norman Rockwell was a twentieth-century painter and illustrator who enjoyed tremendous popularity in the United States. Rockwell was most famous for his depictions of everyday life in America, especially in works he created for covers of *The Saturday Evening Post* magazine. His distinctive style and subject matter captured the optimism and can-do spirit of his time.

When Rockwell was growing up in New York City, his pastor encouraged his interest in drawing and painting and even asked young Norman to tutor other boys in art. As a teen, his illustrations were published in *St. Nicholas Magazine* and *Boys' Life*, the monthly magazine of the Boy Scouts of America. When he was twenty-two, Rockwell painted his first cover for *The Saturday Evening Post*, then the most popular weekly magazine in America. He would go on to paint more than 300 covers for the *Post*.

For the March 6, 1954 issue, Rockwell painted "Girl at Mirror," one of his most enduring images. In this picture, a young girl sits and studies herself in a large mirror propped up against a chair. On the child's lap is a magazine open to a full-page photo of the movie star Jane Russell. Nearby are a tossed-aside doll, a comb, a hairbrush, and cosmetics. There's a bitter sweetness and humor to the image of a little girl coming to terms with the hard fact that the mirror refuses to give her back the same glamorous image shown in the magazine.

But the girl is also asking an important question: Who am I going to be? The mirror and the magazine represent a choice you, too, must make. Will you try to please the world and live up to an impossible standard of beauty and success as portrayed in TV shows and movies? Or will you please God by allowing Him to make you into the person He created you to be?

IF YOU ARE MADE IN GOD'S IMAGE, WHY CAN'T YOU LEAP TALL BUILDINGS IN A SINGLE BOUND?

In order to understand who you are and why you are here, the first thing you need to know is that you were made in the image of God. An **image** is something that is a representation of something else. An image can be inanimate, or nonliving, such as a portrait or painting: *This painting is a striking image of my grandmother.* Or an image can be a person who looks like someone else: *She is the very image of her mother.* The Bible tells us, "God created man in his own image, in the image of God he created him; male and female he created them" (Genesis 1:27). He made you in His likeness, then He crowned you with glory and honor (Psalm 8:5). You are a masterpiece indeed!

So what does it mean to be made in God's image? Are your eyes like His? Do the two of you have matching birthmarks on your shoulders? Do both of you have brown, curly hair that frizzes when it rains? No, being made in God's image does not mean that you physically resemble God. After all, God is spirit (John 4:24) and cannot be seen (1 Timothy 6:16).

Instead, being made in God's image means that He created you with certain characteristics, or attributes, that God Himself possesses. This does not mean that you are God, nor will you ever be a god. In some ways you are like God; in other ways you are not. So let's look at some of the things we know about God.

GOD IS ETERNAL

God has always existed. He has no beginning and no end. We cannot know how old God is because He exists outside of time as we know it, so He never grows older and He will never die:

> *The Lord is the God who lives forever. He created all the world. He does not become tired or need to rest.* (Isaiah 40:28, ICB)

> *Before the mountains were brought forth,*
> *or ever you had formed the earth and the world,*
> *from everlasting to everlasting you are God.* (Psalm 90:2, ESV)

You are made in God's image, but does that mean you are eternal? No. You were created. You had a very definite beginning. You were born to a mother and a father who existed before you. But God was not created. God existed before anything that now exists, and He will exist forever.

GOD IS IMMUTABLE

God never changes. His attributes are immutable, meaning they never change. God is always God. He will never grow old, He will never leave you or forsake you, He will always keep His promises, and He will always remain the same:

> *In the beginning you laid the foundations of the earth,*
> *and the heavens are the work of your hands.*
> *They will perish, but you remain;*
> *they will all wear out like a garment.*
> *Like clothing you will change them*
> *and they will be discarded.*
> *But you remain the same,*
> *and your years will never end.*
> (Psalm 102:25–27)

Jesus Christ is the same yesterday and today and forever. (Hebrews 13:8)

You are made in God's image, but does that mean you are immutable? No. Your clothes change, your hairstyle changes, your tastes change. (Someday you may even like lima beans!) You no longer listen to the same music or read the books you enjoyed when you were younger. Every day you grow a little older and, hopefully, a little wiser. Did you know the outer layer of your skin, the epidermis, replaces itself every thirty-five days? You live in an almost constant state of change, but God never changes. He will always be who the Bible says He is, and you can always count on Him to be there for you.

GOD IS OMNIPRESENT

God is everywhere. There is never a time or place where He is not present. The word that describes this attribute of God is *omnipresent*. (The prefix omni- means "all.") God fills all of time and space, yet the laws of time and space do not limit Him. He is omnipresent through-out creation, yet He exists apart from creation. He is unique—there is nothing and no one like Him anywhere:

> *"Am I a God who is only close at hand?" says the LORD. "No, I am far away at the same time. Can anyone hide from me in a secret place? Am I not everywhere in all the heavens and earth?"* (Jeremiah 23:23–24, NLT)

> *Where can I go from your Spirit?*
> *Where can I flee from your presence?*
> *If I go up to the heavens, you are there;*

if I make my bed in the depths, you are there.
If I rise on the wings of the dawn,
if I settle on the far side of the sea,
even there your hand will guide me,
your right hand will hold me fast.
(Psalm 139:7–10)

You are made in God's image, but does that mean you are omnipresent? No. Wherever you go, there you are. You cannot be in two places at once. Nor can you occupy the exact same space currently occupied by another person. Also, you exist within the confines of time and, outside of science fiction, can only travel in one direction through time: forward (and slowly at that). God, on the other hand, is everywhere at all times simultaneously. So take comfort in the knowledge that wherever you go, our loving God is there with you.

GOD IS OMNIPOTENT

Jesus said, "With God all things are possible" (Matthew 19:26). Why? Because God is omnipotent (om-NI-po-tent), meaning "all powerful." We sometimes call Him "the Almighty" or "Almighty God." God created all things simply by speaking them into existence, and He sustains all things, from providing food for the smallest creature to keeping order in the universe:

"It was my hand that laid the foundations of the earth, my right hand that spread out the heavens above. When I call out the stars, they all appear in order." (Isaiah 48:13, NLT)

This image from the Hubble Space Telescope shows thousands of galaxies in various stages of development. Photo: NASA, ESA, R. Windhorst, S. Cohen, M. Mechtley, and M. Rutkowski (Arizona State University, Tempe), R. O'Connell (University of Virginia), P. McCarthy (Carnegie Observatories), N. Hathi (University of California, Riverside), R. Ryan (University of California, Davis), H. Yan (Ohio State University), and A. Koekemoer (Space Telescope Science Institute).

"Ah, Sovereign LORD, you have made the heavens and the earth by your great power and outstretched arm. Nothing is too hard for you." (Jeremiah 32:17)

You are made in God's image, but does that mean you are omnipotent? No. After all, you can't change the course of mighty rivers or bend steel with your bare hands like Superman, and even he isn't *all* powerful. There are limits to what you can do or even choose to do. But God has no such limits. The only thing God cannot do is to go against His nature, which means you can always count on God to love you and provide for you because that's who He is.

GOD IS OMNISCIENT

You already know that God exists outside of time and can therefore observe all events throughout the course of our history as if they were all happening at the same time. You also know that God exists in all places all the time. So it's not too difficult to figure out that God also *knows* everything. He is omniscient (om-NISH-ent), meaning He knows everything that has happened or will happen in the past, present, and future. More importantly, He can see everything that goes on *inside* of us. He even knows your thoughts before you think them:

> *O LORD, you have searched me*
> *and you know me.*
> *You know when I sit and when I rise;*
> *you perceive my thoughts from afar.*
> *You discern my going out and my lying down;*
> *you are familiar with all my ways.*
> *Before a word is on my tongue*
> *you know it completely, O LORD.*
> (Psalm 139:1-4)

For God is greater than our hearts, and he knows everything. (1 John 3:20)

You are made in God's image, but does that mean you are omniscient? No. You can't know what someone else is thinking, as much fun as that may sound. You don't know what will happen next week, tomorrow, or even ten minutes from now. You may not know the capital of Uzbekistan, but there is nothing that God does not know or understand. And there is nothing that can be hidden from Him (Hebrews 4:13). So He always knows exactly what you need in every situation. All you have to do is ask (Mark 11:24).

GOD IS HOLY

God is perfect. His thoughts, His emotions, and His ways are always holy. This means He always does what is right. God has never sinned and cannot sin because it would be against His nature:

He is the Rock, his works are perfect, and all his ways are just. A faithful God who does no wrong, upright and just is he. (Deuteronomy 32:4)

"As for God, his way is perfect; the word of the LORD is flawless." (2 Samuel 22:31)

You are made in God's image, but does that mean you are holy? This question is more complicated, and we will closely examine the answer in a later chapter. Have you ever sinned? Of course. The Bible tells us that everyone has sinned and fallen short of God's glory (Romans 3:23). But God's Word also commands us to be holy because He is holy (Leviticus 11:45). So follow His example. Remember, God will never cheat or lie to you. He will always be fair, and He will always keep His promises. Will you?

GOD IS A PERSON

God is not a mystical field of energy like the Force in *Star Wars*. He is a personal being. A person has a mind, emotions, a will, a conscience, creativity, and a spirit. Does God have these things? Let's see:

- God is creative (Genesis 1:1; Revelation 4:11).
- God has thoughts (Isaiah 55:8–9; Psalm 139:17–18).
- God has feelings (Genesis 6:5–6; Zephaniah 3:17).
- God makes choices (Deuteronomy 7:6–8; John 6:38).
- God knows right from wrong (Genesis 3:22; Job 34:12).
- God is a spiritual being (John 4:24; Romans 8:16).

You are made in God's image, but does that mean you are a person? Yes! This is what it means to be created in God's image. As a person, you have the ability and desire to create, you can think and know things with your mind, you can feel emotion, you make choices, you know the difference between right and wrong, and you have a spirit, created by God, that will live on for all eternity. These qualities separate people from the animal kingdom and set us above all other creatures on earth.

Being made in God's image means that you were created to have those characteristics that make God a personal being. In each of the lessons that follow, we will examine one of these characteristics and look at how you can use it to give God glory and reveal His presence and His love to other people.

WHAT SHOULD I DO?

Because God is holy, because He is without sin or imperfection, He exists in perfect harmony with Himself. Likewise, He created people to be sinless and live in perfect harmony with themselves. Before the Fall, Adam and Eve were both at ease with themselves and with their bodies. However, once they chose to disobey God, everything changed. Sin entered the world, and immediately Adam and Eve became unhappy with their appearance and began making decisions motivated by fear and shame. People have been making these kinds of ill-advised decisions ever since.

However, the moment you first believe that Jesus is the one true Son of God and that He died to pay the price for your sins, you become a "new creation" (2 Corinthians 5:17). You begin to live a new life—a life in which you become more and more like the One who made you (Colossians 3:10). And as a new creation, you must begin thinking differently about yourself. Being God's **image-bearer** means that you carry, or bear, His likeness with you wherever you go. But it also means that you are committed to becoming more like God's Son, Jesus, every day. God's Word says that, as a follower of Christ, you "show the Lord's glory" and you're "being changed to be like him" (2 Corinthians 3:18, ICB). As you become more **Christlike**, as you think, act, and love more like Jesus did, then you will experience the kind of peace and harmony with yourself that God intended when He created you.

Of course, every person is made in God's image, though not every person has accepted God's free gift of salvation. As you read this book, remember that every life is a gift from God. God creates every life, so every life is sacred from the moment it begins. Because God creates every life, we must respect, protect, and care for each one from its beginning to the end of its time on this earth. And we must follow Jesus' command to tell others about Him and what He has done for us so that others can also experience the kind of peace that only comes from knowing and trusting God.

So the next time you find yourself in the middle of a crowd and you wonder where all the people around you came from, remember that you already know the true answer to this question.

Make a Note of It
Instead of becoming more like Jesus, people often look for other ways to feel better about themselves and find lasting peace. Will money bring you personal harmony? Will the right clothes? Will shinier hair, a prettier face, or bigger muscles give you peace? Will the number of friends you have? Why can't these things bring you the lasting personal harmony God created you to enjoy?

A Prayer
Dear God, thank you for creating me in your image. Thank you for the plan that you have for my life. Help me to follow your plan so that I become everything you made me to be. Help me to grow to be more like Christ every day. Help me to reflect your glory so that when people see me, they see you and the love you have for them. In Jesus' name. Amen.

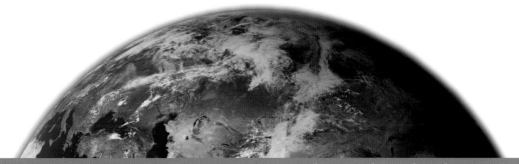

Photo: NASA.

WORLDVIEWS IN FOCUS

MEET AMIRA

People are often confused about who they are. This doesn't mean that they don't know their own names or they fail to recognize that they're human beings. What people are confused about is what makes them valuable, or even if they have any worth at all. Have you ever wondered what makes you valuable?

Perhaps you've felt inferior to some of your friends. Maybe you don't play sports very well, or you have difficulty doing math even though you study hard. Perhaps you don't have as many friends as somebody else does, or you think you're not very handsome or pretty. If you've ever felt this way, you're not alone. In fact, most people at some time in their lives struggle with their own sense of value and worth. Sadly, as people struggle to find out who they are and what they are worth, they may try to create value for themselves in wrong and even harmful ways.

Some people join the wrong crowd in order to be accepted by others and to feel important; they associate with people who are involved in activities that are not only sinful but also harmful to themselves and others. Some people dress or talk in a certain fashion to try to fit in. Some simply pretend to be superior and treat others unkindly. Some try to prove their worth by winning medals and awards. Others try to find their worth by collecting money and possessions. Sadly, some people just withdraw from society—feeling alone and inferior, they try to find comfort by staying away from people they believe will reject them.

However, the biblical Christian worldview sees all people as valuable. In God's eyes, a person's value is not based on whether he or she is male or female, black or white, talented or untalented, attractive or unattractive. Everyone's value is based on one thing and one thing only: All people are valuable because God created all people in His image. We read this truth in the very first chapter of the first book of the Bible.

Near the end of each lesson in this book, you will meet a person with a different worldview. Together, we will discover what his or her worldview has to say about what gives a person value or whether people have any value at all. As you read about these different worldviews, keep in mind what the biblical worldview says about people: People of all races, all ages, all shapes and sizes, even those who hold differing worldviews, are God's image-bearers. Therefore, all people have equal worth and value!

First, let's meet Amira, a young Muslim girl living in London, England.

Amira lives in Waltham Forest, a northeast suburb of London. Her father first came to England from Pakistan to go to school and liked it so much he decided to stay. Amira has just celebrated her twelfth birthday.

Amira wakes up before dawn each morning. She washes her hands and face and gets dressed. Like most Muslim girls, she wears a knee-length tunic over loose pants so she will always be modest. Amira says a short Arabic prayer, or *dua*, when she enters the bathroom, then another dua when she leaves. There are many small prayers that she needs to recite before or after daily tasks.

Her mother says that "making dua" is an important part of the Islamic religion. Her mother works hard to be a good Muslim and does her best to train her children to be good Muslims too. She says that wearing modest clothing, including a headscarf, helps her feel safe wherever she goes. But Amira knows that her mother is secretly glad that her husband hasn't asked her to wear the traditional *burkha*, long robes that cover a woman from head to toe so that only her eyes are visible to others.

Ready for her day, Amira joins her family downstairs for morning prayers. Not every Muslim girl needs to participate in prayers, but Amira's father wants her and her younger sister, Layla, to learn as much as their older brother, Rashid. Rashid will one day be the head of his own household, so he is required to learn all the prayers and rituals by heart. Amira kneels and listens as her father and Rashid recite the prayers in the Arabic language. She knows that Muslims around the world are reciting the same prayers at the same time, and all are bowing in the same direction—toward the Saudi Arabian city of Mecca, Islam's holiest city.

After morning prayers, Amira eats breakfast, saying a dua before she starts. She eats only with her right hand because Muslims believe that the right hand is clean, while the left hand is not. Before she leaves the table, she says another dua, helping Layla (who is still learning the prayers) recite it with her.

Amira puts on her headscarf, making sure her hair is modestly covered, and leaves with her sister for school. Their father walks with them to see that they arrive safely. Either he or Rashid is with the girls and their mother whenever they leave the house. Sometimes Amira can tell that this irritates her mother, but neither of them would ever say anything about it to her father. He says that it is the responsibility of the head of the household to watch over and protect the women of his family.

Amira's school is near the mosque, the Muslim place of worship, which is a few blocks away from her house. As Amira arrives at school, she greets the other girls in her class. In Muslim schools, girls and boys in the school have separate classes, and most of Amira's teachers are women. Amira learns math, history, and science, but she also studies Arabic and memorizes verses from the Qur'an, which is the holy book of Islam. She has learned that the word *Islam* means "to submit," and a

The shahada as it appears on the flag of Saudi Arabia.

Muslim is "one who submits." Amira is considered a true Muslim because she has recited the confession of faith and follows the teachings of the prophet Muhammad. The confession of faith, called the *shahada*, says, "There is no God but Allah, and Muhammad is his prophet." This is the most important belief of Islam and the first of five foundational beliefs called the Five Pillars of Islam.

At noon, Amira hears the call to prayer. Although the boys in her school must stop class and bow to pray, Amira and her female classmates instead close their books and eat the lunches they have brought with them. Today Amira's mother has given her a piece of flatbread wrapped around chicken and vegetables and a juicy orange for dessert. When Amira and her classmates have finished their lunch, they return to their studies. Amira's teachers encourage her to always be on time for school and to do her homework with a good attitude. They say that behaving properly is an important part of being a Muslim.

After school, Amira and Layla walk home with their father. They arrive just in time for the third prayer of the day. Washing their hands again, they join their parents and listen while their father prays. He kneels on a special prayer rug to make sure that the area where he is praying is clean. Muslims pray five times throughout the day. Prayer, or *salah*, is the second pillar of Islam. The daily prayers are very important to her father, and he makes sure that the entire family observes them carefully.

Amira and her family live in an area populated mostly with Muslim families. Her neighbors go to the same mosque as her family, and many work at the same businesses. Often the families gather together to celebrate a wedding or the birth of a baby. On social occasions such as these, women and girls are usually separated from the men and boys. Muslims believe that separating men and women will protect them from inappropriate contact or desires.

Amira's father owns a store on a street near the edge of the Muslim neighborhoods. Most of the people who shop there are Muslim, although a few non-Muslim families shop there as well. Once, when Amira's father had to stop at his store while walking the girls home from school, Amira saw an English mother and her daughters come in to shop. They didn't wear head-scarves or modest tunics and pants, and they didn't have a father or brother with them. Although the mother smiled at her, the girls just looked at her strangely. Amira's father later told her that some people in London are afraid of Muslims because some Islamic terrorists set off bombs in the London underground, or subway. Her father explained that not all Muslims are terrorists and not all English people are afraid of Muslims.

On Fridays, Amira and her family go to the mosque for special prayers. Amira likes going to the mosque because she gets to see all her friends, including those who don't attend the Muslim school. When they arrive, Amira takes off her shoes and follows her mother to the women's section. Women and men are separated during prayers so that they don't distract one another. They wash their hands and faces, kneel on the floor, and listen as the *imam*

Fazl-Mosque in London. Photo: Ceddyfresse.

(teacher) prays. The imam tells them to bow with their foreheads touching the ground. This shows respect and devotion to Allah.

After mosque, the family returns home to eat dinner together. Once, when Amira's parents took her shopping and to a movie in London's famous Piccadilly Circus, they walked past a restaurant serving bangers and mash, a dish made with mashed potatoes and sausage. She was intrigued by the smell, but she knows that Muslims

Piccadilly Circus in London. Photo: Matthias Prinke.

must not eat anything made with pork because pigs are unclean animals. Tonight, Amira's mother has made falafel balls out of chickpeas, a dish that reminds her of her childhood home in Pakistan. Her father declares that this is the best falafel he has ever tasted, and Amira's mother smiles because he says the same thing every time she makes it.

At sunset, Amira's father gathers everyone again for prayers. After washing her hands again, Amira kneels and whispers some of the prayers along with her father. She is trying to learn enough Arabic to understand the words of the prayers. Muslims believe that Arabic is the language of heaven and only prayers said in Arabic are holy.

In the evening, Amira and Layla study passages from the Qur'an with their father. He says it is a gift to study the Qur'an and learn about how Islam came to be a religion. Many Muslim girls are not allowed to study at all. This is one reason Amira likes living in England, where she is much freer to learn and be a part of the Muslim community than in stricter Islamic countries like Saudi Arabia. Amira's aunt, who lives in Riyadh, the capital of Saudi Arabia, says that where she lives there are much harsher restrictions on what women can wear, what they can learn or do, and where they can go. Her aunt has never even seen a movie! Amira is grateful that

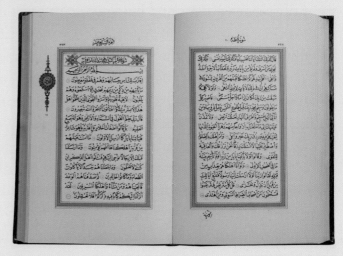

An old copy of the Qur'an.

her father wants his daughters to learn as much as they can. Although sometimes he is gruff, Amira can tell that he loves her very much because of the things he does for her.

Amira's father teaches her that Allah is the one true God and that he created the universe and rules over everything he made. He says that Allah is all-powerful, all-knowing, and eternal. The Qur'an teaches that Allah is completely unlike the people he created. Amira's father says that Allah is so far above his creation that no one can know him or have a relationship with him. Allah does not reveal himself to people, only his will and commands. Learning about Allah and his laws makes Amira a little uneasy. Because Allah is so different from the people she can see and relate to, she is afraid she will break a law and make him angry.

Her father says that there will be a time of judgment in the future when everyone's good deeds and bad deeds will be weighed. To get to heaven, people must have done more good deeds than bad ones while they were alive. Good deeds can be small things, like saying prayers and reading the Qur'an, or they can be big things like making a pilgrimage to the holy city of Mecca. Amira's father tells her to obey Allah's laws, to show respect for her parents and teachers, and to live a good life. He also teaches her that it's important to give money to the poor. Amira helps her father count up the alms he gives each year to help provide for poor or sick people. Alms-giving, which Muslims call *zakat*, is the third pillar of Islam. Muslims try to teach themselves to be content with what they have by giving away part of their money each year.

Because Amira is now twelve years old, her father says she is old enough to participate in the Muslim practice of fasting during the month of *Ramadan*. For this one month of the year, Muslims do not eat or drink anything during the day. While the sun is shining, they fast. But after the sun sets, they eat a big dinner. Fasting during Ramadan helps Muslims understand what poor people experience every day so that they will be more generous in giving to the poor. Ramadan is also a time to practice being nicer to other people, watching more carefully what you say, and being content with the things you have. Layla is still too young and Amira's mother is pregnant, so they won't fast like the rest of the family. Fasting, which Muslims call *sawm*, is the fourth pillar of Islam.

Learning about Islam and participating in the Muslim rituals that show devotion to Allah make Amira feel like she is part of the worldwide family of Islam. Every day, in many countries around the world, Muslims are doing the same things she is. But Amira sometimes worries that she won't be able to do enough good things in her life to get to heaven. She talked with her cousin Hassan about this, and he told her that boys have many more duties than girls, like memorizing the daily prayers and studying Islamic law. Then he made her angry by boasting that boys are also freer to do things and go places by themselves.

Hassan told her his father wants him to find a good profession when he is older so that he can marry and raise a family. Amira knows that although she could choose to go to a university and even have a career of her own, her father would prefer that she marry instead. He says that taking care of a husband and family is the best way she can contribute to the spread of Islam throughout the world. Her mother agrees and is teaching Amira how to cook and take care of a house. The marriage of Amira's parents was arranged by their parents. Although they had met only once, Amira's mother

Pilgrims at the Kaaba in Masjid al-Haram, Mecca, Saudi Arabia. Photo: omar_chatriwala.

married her father in Pakistan and then moved to England with him. Amira can see that her parents love each other, even though they sometimes argue. (Amira has noticed that her father wins most of the arguments.)

But Amira won't have to think about marriage for a while. On this evening, after prayers, she is helping Rashid prepare for his first pilgrimage to Mecca. Once in every Muslim's life, he or she must visit the holy city. After arriving in Mecca, pilgrims change into white clothes and cut their hair. Then they spend three days performing rituals to honor Allah and the prophet Muhammad, who founded Islam in the seventh century. Pilgrimage, which Muslims call *hajj*, is the fifth pillar of Islam.

Amira has learned in school that the people of Mecca in Muhammad's time didn't want to learn about Islam and persecuted the early Muslims, so Muhammad and his followers escaped to Medina. This escape, called the *hijrah*, took place in September 622 according to the Christian calendar. Today, Islamic calendars mark how many years have passed since the hijrah. The Muslim calendar is a lunar calendar, meaning most years have only 354 days. Amira's calendar at school says the current year is 1431.

Before Amira goes to bed, she and her family wash their hands and gather one last time to kneel and recite the evening prayers. Then Amira climbs into bed and makes one last dua before falling asleep.

WHAT'S THE DIFFERENCE?

- How is the way Amira lives different from the way you live? How are your lives similar?

- Why do you think Amira is so careful to make dua, eat the right foods, and participate in the ritual prayers throughout the day?

- What do you think visiting a mosque would be like? What would Amira think of your church if she visited it?

- How is Amira's view of Allah different from the biblical Christian view of God?

- How is the way Amira sees herself different from the way you see yourself as a child of God?

THE HOUSE OF TRUTH: THE FIFTH PILLAR

Throughout the What We Believe series, you will be building a House of Truth to help you remember what God says in the Bible about Himself, who you are, and how God expects you to live. This is a special house, not one built with lumber and other ordinary building materials. The plan for building your House of Truth is the Bible. Each part of this worldview model represents an essential truth from God's Word. Just as we build strong houses with good materials on strong foundations, so we must build our lives with the truths God gives us in the Bible. These truths will be displayed on the foundation, walls, and roof of the House of Truth.

In the first book, *Who Is God? (And Can I Really Know Him?)*, you learned that if you are wise, you will build your life on the Rock that is God and His Word. You also learned that wise people build a foundation of wisdom for their lives by knowing and loving God and obeying His commands. You then built on your foundation and constructed the first wall of your house with these eight important biblical truths:

1. God always tells me what is right and true.
2. God is the only true and almighty God.
3. God is God the Father, God the Son, and God the Holy Spirit.
4. God is the Creator.
5. God created me to be His child and to give Him glory.
6. God created me to need Him for everything.
7. Sin causes separation and disharmony between me and God.
8. Jesus died to restore fellowship and harmony between me and God.

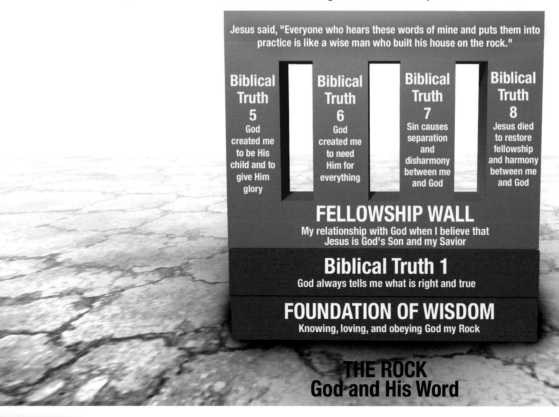

Jesus said, "Everyone who hears these words of mine and puts them into practice is like a wise man who built his house on the rock."

Biblical Truth 5 God created me to be His child and to give Him glory

Biblical Truth 6 God created me to need Him for everything

Biblical Truth 7 Sin causes separation and disharmony between me and God

Biblical Truth 8 Jesus died to restore fellowship and harmony between me and God

FELLOWSHIP WALL
My relationship with God when I believe that Jesus is God's Son and my Savior

Biblical Truth 1
God always tells me what is right and true

FOUNDATION OF WISDOM
Knowing, loving, and obeying God my Rock

THE ROCK
God and His Word

THE IMAGE-BEARING WALL: YOUR RELATIONSHIP WITH YOURSELF

The first wall in your House of Truth was the Fellowship Wall, which represents your relationship with God when you believe Jesus is God's only Son and your Savior. As you work through this book, together we will build the second wall in your house—the Image-Bearing Wall. This wall represents your relationship with yourself as you become more like Jesus Christ.

The Image-Bearing Wall will consist of the next four pillars in your house. In the first lesson, you erected the first pillar in your Image-Bearing Wall:

BIBLICAL TRUTH 9

God created me in His image.

Biblical
Truth
9
God
created me
in His image

IMAGE-BEARING WALL
My relationship with myself as I become more like Jesus

Biblical Truth 2
God is the only true and almighty God

FOUNDATION OF WISDOM
Knowing, loving, and obeying God my Rock

THE ROCK
God and His Word

WHAT WILL YOU MAKE TODAY?

> Sing to the Lord a new song, for he has done marvelous things.
>
> ## Psalm 98:1

The Big Idea

Our home is often a beehive of activity. One child likes to draw and paint. One likes to design clothes and sew. Another enjoys cooking and working in the garden. One has written three novels and is working on a fourth. One is a musician, and another will sing and dance at the drop of a hat. What do you like to do? Play an instrument? Crochet? Take photographs? Write and perform skits? Keep a scrapbook? Compose songs? Origami?

Why do you suppose you and your friends enjoy these kinds of activities? It's because God has given His children a desire to make something beautiful! Open your Bible to the very first verse of the first chapter. What does it say? "In the beginning, God created . . ." But what does it mean when it says God "created"? The dictionary tells us that to create means to cause something to come into being that would not naturally happen on its own. The resulting creation can be described as an expression of a person's imagination.

When we first encounter God in the Bible, He isn't parting the Red Sea or handing down the Ten Commandments to Moses or commanding legions of angels. No, we first meet God as an artist who is creating a work of astounding beauty. With infinite love and boundless imagination, He speaks a wondrous array of shapes, textures, and colors into existence and then proceeds to paint the universe. At the end of each day He steps back, considers His work, and says, "Good."

God is an artist. The Bible calls Him a potter (Isaiah 64:8) and an author (Hebrews

How Tall Will I Be?

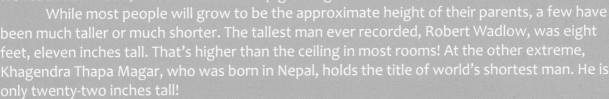

Do you ever wonder how tall you will be when you grow up? Your adult height may be strongly influenced by the height of your parents or even *their* parents. Your height can also be influenced by other factors, such as how much nutritious food you eat and how much you exercise. In general, boys will grow to be taller than girls.

We all start life being measured in inches, but we grow quickly for the first couple of years. Throughout childhood, our growth slows to a steady pace. Later, during the teen years, we grow quickly again until we reach adulthood, when our bones stop growing.

While most people will grow to be the approximate height of their parents, a few have been much taller or much shorter. The tallest man ever recorded, Robert Wadlow, was eight feet, eleven inches tall. That's higher than the ceiling in most rooms! At the other extreme, Khagendra Thapa Magar, who was born in Nepal, holds the title of world's shortest man. He is only twenty-two inches tall!

So how tall you will be? Try the following formula:

Step 1. Figure out the height of both of your parents in inches.
Step 2. Add the two numbers together.
Step 3. Divide this total by 2.
Step 4. If you're a boy, add 2.5 inches. If you're a girl, subtract 2.5 inches.
Step 5. Convert the total back to feet and inches.

Remember, this formula will only give you an estimate. Your actual results may vary.

Height can be a touchy subject, especially when you're young. You may feel like you're too tall or too short or just awkward at times as you are growing. Don't worry. Everyone has felt like that! More important than how you look on the outside is the kind of person you are inside. Do you try to keep a cheery disposition? Do you make people laugh? Are you helpful and kind toward others? You can't make yourself any taller, but you can work to develop wonderful qualities inside that will last your whole life.

12:2). He sings (Zephaniah 3:17) and He knits (Psalm 139:13). He is an architect (Job 38:4–7), a landscaper (Genesis 2:8–9; Job 38:25–27), a perfumer (Exodus 30:34–38), and a fashion designer (Exodus 28:2–41). He is the Great Artist, and we are His works of art (Ephesians 2:10), fearfully and wonderfully made in God's own image (Psalm 139:14).

God created all things for His enjoyment, but people were specially made to reflect God's glory. One of the ways we reflect His glory is when we create things. Almost from the beginning, people have expressed themselves by making music (Genesis 4:21). God also gave to certain people artistic skills and selected them to perform specific jobs (Exodus 31:1–6). King David was a fearsome warrior, but he was also a poet and a musician who sang and danced before the Lord.

The Bible doesn't tell us whether David was a good dancer or a clumsy one, but we do know he danced with all his might (2 Samuel 6:14–15). That's because creativity is not about what you can do or what you're good at. Creativity is a response. It is a way of worshiping God and who He is, a way of worshiping His infinite beauty and love. When you read His Word, when you see the magnificence of all He has created, you may be moved to write a poem, paint a picture, sing out loud, or dance with all your might. It's a way to demonstrate your love to someone who positively adores you.

WHAT YOU WILL DO
» You will examine God's creative nature and how it is reflected in your own life.
» You will identify the intended purpose of your creative gifts.
» You will be encouraged to use your talents and abilities to serve others in a way that will glorify God.

THE POCKET KNIFE

"How tall am I now, Papa?" Sasha asked, standing as straight as he could against the frame of the front door.

"You're exactly the same height you were last night," his father laughed.

"But I want to grow *tall*."

"You will, my son, but it won't happen overnight. Let's wait until school begins in the fall. Then we'll measure you again."

By the end of that summer, Sasha had grown a little but not enough to satisfy him. He had always been the shortest boy in his class. He was now in fifth grade and felt increasingly self-conscious not only about his height, but also about his limp. And although none of the students except Ivan, the class bully, teased him anymore, Sasha kept more and more to himself, preferring solitary activities such as studying and reading.

"Papa," he asked one Sunday morning as the Petrov family was on the way to church, "do you think I'll ever grow tall and be able to walk like other people?"

Keeping one hand on the reins, Mr. Petrov turned and put his other hand on Sasha's knee. "I don't know, my son. Perhaps you won't. But that won't keep you from doing and becoming all God wants you to do and be. Remember, you're not just a person made in God's image; you are one of a kind."

One of a kind, Sasha thought. *That's the truth. I'm the only crippled boy in my whole village.*

"And how is the Petrov family this fine Sunday morning?" Father Yakov asked as Mr. Petrov led his family into the churchyard. Father Yakov was the priest at the village's small but beautiful Russian Orthodox church.

"Quite well," Misha replied.

"And Sasha, how are you enjoying fifth grade this new school year?"

"Okay, I guess. But I'd like it better if I weren't the shortest boy in my class," Sasha replied despondently. "And even if I weren't the shortest, I'd still look different because of how I walk."

"You know, young man," Father Yakov said, stroking his long beard, "it just may be that God has a special message for you this morning. Listen carefully and tell me what you think after the service."

Although Sasha usually tried to listen to the priest's sermons, he made a special effort to do so on this day.

"This morning I want to read from the eighth Psalm," Father Yakov began. He then read:

> *I look at the heavens,*
> *which you made with your hands.*
> *I see the moon and stars*
> *which you created.*
> *But why is man important to you?*
> *Why do you take care of human beings?*
> *You made man a little lower than the angels.*
> *And you crowned him with glory and honor.*

After he finished reading, the priest said,

"Not only are we made in God's image, but we are the most important part of God's earthly creation. God made human beings just a little lower than the angels. Then He crowned us with glory and honor. What does this scripture mean? First, it means that in God's earthly creation, only men and women were created in God's image. Only people were given the privilege to worship God and to have fellowship with Him, to enjoy His presence in everything we do wherever we are.

Church of Transfiguration, Suzdal, Russia. Photo: Alex Zelenko.

"You can worship God in your work whether you are a farmer or a doctor. You children can worship and honor Him by doing your best in school. And everyone has a special talent that God has given them. Some of you have musical talent. Others are gifted athletes or artists. Some of you have the ability to write beautiful poems or stories. Still others have special talents for taking care of others. Whatever your talent, the Bible tells us to do everything for God's glory."

Sasha tried to pay attention to the rest of the sermon, but all he could think about was what Father Yakov had said about God giving everyone a special gift or ability. *I sure don't have any special abilities,* he thought. *I can't even walk well, and I'm shorter than all the boys in my class. What could I ever do to bring God glory?*

As Sasha's family was leaving the church, the priest asked, "So Sasha, did you listen well? Did you learn that God crowned you with glory and honor by creating you to bear His image? Did you understand that God has given you gifts and abilities that He wants you to use for His glory and to bless others?"

"I heard what you said," Sasha replied. "But I'm not sure that God gave me any special ability. If I could just walk and grow like other kids—that would be the best gift I could ever receive."

"Sasha," the priest replied, "glory and honor are not reserved for those who stand tall or run like the wind. You have the privilege of knowing God and receiving His promises. One day you'll discover your gift, and when you do, I hope you'll use it to glorify and honor God."

Sasha smiled politely, although he wasn't convinced that this was true for him. He limped off toward the wagon.

"Thank you, Father," Mr. Petrov said. "In time, he will understand. Right now, he's going through a very difficult time. We're praying that God will soon show Sasha that he is loved for who he is and that he does indeed have unique gifts."

After supper that evening, Sasha's mother asked him, "Was everything okay at church today?"

"Yes, Mother. The sermon was very interesting."

"What about Sunday school? Were you paying attention in class, Sasha?" his father asked.

"Of course," Sasha replied defensively. "I always do."

"Then why do you think Brother Pavel asked your mother and me to visit him before vespers this evening?"

"Um . . . uh . . ." Sasha avoided looking at his father.

"What is it, my son? Have you done something wrong?"

"Uh . . . I took the pocket knife you gave me for my birthday to church," Sasha confessed, still not looking up at his father.

"I told you not to take your knife to church," Mr. Petrov replied sternly.

"But I didn't show it to anyone! I just kept it in my pocket."

"Then how did Brother Pavel know you had it with you?" his mother asked.

"I . . . I was sitting under a tree after church, by myself, just cutting on a piece of wood. Brother Pavel took the knife from me and said he would have to talk to you about it."

"All right, Sasha. Go to your room. We'll discuss it this evening with Brother Pavel," Mr. Petrov said with authority.

For Sasha, the day passed much too quickly. When he heard the clanging of the beautiful church bells calling the faithful to evening prayer, a sound that usually filled him with happiness, he felt only shame and dread.

"Thank you for coming," Brother Pavel said as Sasha's parents entered his office. "First, I want to tell you what a wonderful student Sasha is. He is one of the brightest students in the class. And he's always most courteous to the other students."

These words calmed Sasha considerably, and the smile on Brother Pavel's face gave him reason to hope that the trouble he was in might not be so serious after all.

"What I am concerned about is that Sasha seems to stay mostly to himself, especially after services. This morning, I saw him sitting under a tree in the churchyard carving a piece of wood with a small knife. As I approached him, I saw him quickly fold up this pocket knife and put it in his pocket. When I asked him about it, he said he knew that he wasn't supposed to bring it to church."

Sasha looked down, knowing that his father was staring sternly at him.

"I took the knife," continued Brother Pavel, as he gave the knife to Sasha's father.

"I'm sorry, Papa. I'm really sorry," Sasha whispered, trying not to cry.

After a brief silence, Brother Pavel continued. "I don't think we need to worry about Sasha bringing his knife to church again. What I really want to discuss with you is this." He opened his cupboard, reached in, and took out a beautifully carved wooden lamb.

"Sasha carved this lamb with his pocket knife," Brother Pavel said.

"Why, it's beautiful," Mrs. Petrova breathed. "However did you do that, Sasha?"

"I just did," Sasha replied with a hint of a smile. "I found a broken tree limb on the ground, and I wanted to see how well the knife would cut wood. Then I just kind of started carving."

"My goodness," Mr. Petrov said. "That's quite incredible, my boy!"

Sasha smiled again, pleased, but still not sure what kind of trouble he was in.

"Sasha seems to have a real talent here," Brother Pavel said. "And this is the real reason I asked you to come in. I am suggesting that you encourage Sasha to pursue this talent. In fact, I've gone so far as to ask a friend of mine in the village who is a master woodcarver if he would be willing to work with Sasha after school. His name is Sergei Kerensky. Perhaps you've heard of him. He's carved some of the beautiful altars in our village churches. He said he would be most happy to help Sasha develop his skill."

"Oh, yes, I've heard of him," Mr. Petrov replied. Then he turned to Sasha. "Would you like to learn to carve from Mr. Kerensky, Son?"

"I would, Papa. I really would," Sasha replied eagerly.

"Mr. Kerensky said he could begin working with Sasha tomorrow afternoon, if you like. If it works out, Sasha could go to his shop every Tuesday and Friday for lessons," Brother Pavel added.

"Thank you. Thank you very much," Anya said. "We certainly approve, don't we, Misha?"

"Of course we do. But on one condition: Sasha must never take his pocket knife to church again. He may leave it with Mr. Kerensky."

The master carver Sergei Kerensky worked patiently with his new student week after week, and young Sasha Petrov developed a fine talent for woodcarving.

One cold, snowy December afternoon, at the end of his lesson, Sasha said, "Mr. Kerensky, all the kids at school are talking about what they want Father Frost and the Snow Maiden to bring them on New Year's Day."

"And what do you want, Sasha?" Mr. Kerensky asked.

"Well, I know that Father Frost and the Snow Maiden are only make-believe," Sasha replied as he made a delicate cut in the piece of wood he was carving. "But it's fun to pretend. I've asked my parents for another carving knife—you know—a real carving knife like this one." He held up the knife in his hand. "I know that if they do buy me the knife, we'll all pretend it's from Father Frost, but I'll know it's really from them."

"Sasha," Mr. Kerensky said in a serious tone, "with all of the excitement about Father Frost on New Year's Day, don't forget that on Christmas Day we remember the greatest gift ever given to anyone. You do know what that gift is, don't you?"

"Oh, yes," Sasha said. "On Christmas we celebrate the day God gave us His Son, Jesus. My family always celebrates Christmas. We go to church on Christmas Day, and we invite friends to our house for dinner. Then we sing and tell stories and, of course, my father reads us the Christmas story."

Photo: Malene Thyssen.

"I'm very happy to hear that your family celebrates the real meaning of Christmas, Sasha," Mr. Kerensky said with a smile. "The holidays are not all about receiving gifts. This is a time to think about giving—to think about how much God gave us and how we can show our appreciation by giving to others. Oh, receiving gifts is wonderful, but I hope you'll never forget that giving is at the very heart of Christmas."

Sasha heard the bells of his father's sleigh approaching and began putting away the tools. Suddenly, his eyes lit up and a big smile spread across his face. "Mr. Kerensky, I have an idea. Do you think I could give a gift to Jesus this Christmas?"

"Why, what do you mean, Sasha?"

"I was just thinking that at Christmas time everyone's always asking for things. What if I carved something to give to Jesus for His birthday on Christmas?"

"And what do you think you might want to carve for Him?"

"I think I'd like to carve a crèche. You know, a nativity scene. I could carve Mary and Joseph, the baby Jesus, the manger, animals, wise men—everything!" Sasha said, his excitement growing.

"Why, I think that's a splendid idea, Sasha. But do you think you can carve an entire set before Christmas?" Mr. Kerensky asked. "Christmas is only four weeks away."

"I can. I know I can. Especially with your help. But we'll have to keep it a secret so everyone will be surprised—well, everyone except Jesus, I guess." Sasha laughed.

"I'll help you, Sasha. And your secret is my secret," Mr. Kerensky said with a sparkle in his eye. "Now hurry along. Your father's waiting in the sleigh, and it's quite cold out this evening."

Sasha found it hard to concentrate on his schoolwork that month because his mind and heart were always on the nativity set he was carving. Nevertheless, he managed to keep up and do all his assignments.

"Today's the last day of school and your last lesson before Christmas," Sasha's mother said as she stood stirring a pot of delicious-smelling borscht. "Mr. Kerensky told your father that you would need some extra time with him after school today. Is there a problem?"

"Oh, no problem. No problem at all," Sasha replied, trying to keep from grinning. "I just need to finish what I'm working on before Christmas."

That afternoon, Sasha hurried to Mr. Kerensky's shop. He loved the smell of sawdust and wood shavings on the floor. "We'll finish today, won't we?" Sasha asked with apprehension.

"We *must* finish today, young man," Mr. Kerensky replied. "We'll wrap the pieces here in the shop, and I'll bring them to the Christmas Day service. I've already talked to Father Yakov, and he's very excited. Our secret is his secret as well."

Photo: Andreas Praefcke.

Sasha worked with great determination, sanding each piece—the stable, the manger, Mary, Joseph, the shepherds, the wise men, and of course, the animals. Then he picked up the piece he had been most careful in carving, the figure of the infant Jesus. He sanded it carefully and placed it reverently in the tiny manger.

"You've created a beautiful nativity set, young man." Mr. Kerensky smiled. "I'm quite proud of you."

"Do you think Jesus will like it?" Sasha asked.

"Dear Sasha, Jesus has already received this gift with much joy," Mr. Kerensky replied. "You know, of course, that it's not so much the actual piece as what it represents—a gift of your heart to Him. Sasha, don't ever stop giving your heart to Jesus. Give him your life. Give him your talents. When you do, you give God glory—and that's what He created you to do."

Sasha and Mr. Kerensky carefully wrapped each piece of the nativity in scraps of soft cloth. Then they laid them inside a wooden box and closed the lid.

"You're a fine young boy, Sasha Petrov," Mr. Kerensky said as he put his arm around Sasha's shoulder. "You're a fine young boy."

Christmas Day dawned with bright sunshine revealing a fresh snowfall from the night before. Smoke swirled from the village chimneys as horses with steaming breath pulled sleighs to the church. Almost everyone in Dmitrov went to church on Christmas. Sveta Romanoff's family was there, and even Ivan, the school bully, was there with his family.

"Merry Christmas, Sveta. Merry Christmas, Ivan," Sasha shouted as he climbed down from his family's sleigh and hobbled toward the church.

"Merry Christmas, Sasha," Sveta called.

Even Ivan managed an almost heartfelt "Merry Christmas, Sasha."

Inside the old church, everyone joined together to sing the traditional Christmas carols, and Father Yakov retold the Christmas story.

"And let us never forget," he said as he closed his sermon, "that Christmas is about giving. 'For God so loved the world that He gave his only Son.' And in that spirit of giving, I would like Sasha Petrov to come forward to the altar."

Sasha's parents looked surprised, as did everyone else in the congregation. Sasha stood and walked with his usual limp to the altar. This time, however, his limp didn't seem to bother him. In fact, he seemed completely unaware of his height or how he walked this day.

"Sasha, I think you have something you wish to say this morning. Is that right?" Father Yakov asked kindly.

"Yes, Father Yakov," Sasha began, then addressed the congregation. "Today I want to thank God for all the things He's given to me and my family. Of course, I want to thank Him most of all for sending Jesus to be our Savior. And because He's given me so much, I want to give something back to Him."

Then Sasha nodded at Mr. Kerensky, who stepped up to the altar with the wooden box in his hands. People began to whisper with anticipation as Sasha opened the box and began to unwrap the pieces of the nativity set. Carefully, he arranged the pieces on a small table that Father Yakov had placed in front of the altar.

Then Sasha said simply, "Thank you, Mr. Kerensky, for helping me make this gift for Jesus. And thank you, God, for sending Jesus to be our Savior."

Oohs and *aahs* filled the small church. At the priest's invitation, the people came to the altar to see Sasha's Christmas gift to Jesus.

Sasha felt embarrassed by all the attention he received after the service. But he was happy, too, hearing how much the people appreciated his gift to Jesus. As he was climbing into his sleigh, he saw Ivan walking toward him.

"Did you really carve that whole nativity set by yourself, Sasha?" Ivan asked.

"Yes, I did. Mr. Kerensky is a good teacher, and with his help, I was able to do it."

Ivan stood awkwardly for a moment, then said, "I wish I could carve like that. Do you think you could you teach me how sometime?"

Sasha was surprised. But he smiled and said, "Sure, if you really want me to."

"I really do," Ivan replied. "And, uh . . . Merry Christmas, Sasha."

"Merry Christmas to you too, Ivan," Sasha replied warmly.

"I think Ivan just gave you a wonderful Christmas gift," Anya Petrova whispered as she climbed into the sleigh next to Sasha.

"Yes. I think so, too," Sasha said. "Maybe he wants to be my friend. Maybe he's not really as mean as everyone thinks he is."

After the Petrovs' Christmas guests had left for their homes, more new snow began to fall. Misha placed two large logs on the fire while Anya prepared cups of hot raspberry tea.

As Sasha stared at the brightly burning logs, he said, "Papa, do you remember the Sunday when Father Yakov talked about God crowning us with glory and honor?"

"Yes, I do," his father replied.

"Well, when I heard him explain what that meant, I thought for sure I didn't have a crown like that because I'm crippled. I didn't feel very special to God, and I kept wondering why He would create someone like me."

"Oh, my precious Sasha," his

Painting: Nikolaj Alexejewitsch Kassatkin.

mother said as she put her arms around him, "being crowned with glory and honor has nothing to do with what you look like or how you walk. Being crowned with glory and honor means you are created in God's image so you can have fellowship with Him and give Him glory."

"That's what Father Yakov told me after church that Sunday. He said that God gives us talents that we should use to give Him glory."

"And have you discovered a talent God gave you, my son?" his father asked.

"I think so, Papa."

"And when did you discover it?"

"It was the day Brother Pavel saw me carving that lamb at church with my pocket knife," Sasha replied. "Instead of scolding me, he told me my carving was beautiful."

"And when did you decide to use your talent to carve the nativity set for Jesus?"

"The day Mr. Kerensky and I were talking about the real meaning of Christmas. He told me to never forget that Christmas is about giving—about God giving Jesus to be our Savior.

That's when I decided that I wanted to carve a nativity set and give it to Jesus for His birthday. Do you think He likes it?"

"Is it a gift of love from your heart?"

"Oh, yes, Papa," Sasha replied sincerely.

"Then I'm quite sure Jesus is pleased, my son." Misha Petrov smiled at his son. "I'm sure He is very pleased."

THINK ABOUT IT

» How does Brother Pavel show wisdom in the way he responds to Sasha's taking his pocket knife to church?

» In what way is Mr. Kerensky, the master woodcarver, more than just a teacher to Sasha? How does Sasha begin to change as a result of the time he spends learning to carve wood?

» If you were to give a Christmas gift to Jesus, what might it look like?

» How do you think this experience will affect the way Sasha thinks of himself, especially his height and his crippled foot? Will he ever worry about such things again? Why or why not?

WORDS YOU NEED TO KNOW

» **Creativity:** The ability to express my thoughts and imagination for the glory of God
» **Christian:** A follower of Jesus Christ
» **Calling:** God's purpose for your life, for which He has gifted you and chosen you
» **Humility:** An attitude in my heart that I am not better than any other person, each of whom is created in God's image and needs to know Him

HIDE IT IN YOUR HEART

Whatever you do, work at it with all your heart, as working for the Lord, not for men, since you know that you will receive an inheritance from the Lord as a reward. (Colossians 3:23–24)

Each of you has received a gift to use to serve others. (1 Peter 4:10, NCV)

An Ugly Duckling Becomes a Swan

Anna Pavlova (usually pronounced Pav-LO-vuh) was a Russian ballet dancer born in 1881. As a child, she was frail and often sick because she had been born prematurely. One day, her mother took her to see Tchaikovsky's ballet *The Sleeping Beauty*. Anna was fascinated. She wouldn't rest until her mother took her to audition for the Imperial Ballet School. The first time Anna auditioned, she was refused because of her age and sickly physique. But Anna kept trying, and two years later, at age ten, she was accepted as a student.

Anna wasn't like the other young ballerinas. Her legs were too long, her feet were too arched, and her ankles were weak. She was so thin, her fellow students taunted her by calling her "the broom." But Anna loved to dance. So she worked very hard, practicing for hours and taking extra classes. After eight years as a student, Anna graduated from the ballet school and became a featured dancer in the Imperial Ballet of Russia.

Even as a professional, Anna Pavlova did not have perfect technique. She danced with her knees slightly bent and struggled to strengthen her ankles. But she became famous partly because of these flaws. People loved her frail, feminine style, especially in ballets like *Giselle*, which tells the story of a peasant girl who dies for love. Her most famous role, the Dying Swan, was created just for her.

After several years as a prima ballerina in the Imperial Ballet, Anna began to travel, performing her favorite ballets and sharing her intense love of dance with people around the world. Audiences adored her because she danced with feeling and emotion rather than worrying about perfect technique. Some of the twentieth century's most successful dancers first took up ballet because they were inspired by the great Pavlova's dedication, hard work, and love for her art.

Called by God

Was there anything Bezalel couldn't do? The man was an artist's artist, skilled in all sorts of craftsmanship, including woodcarving, cutting precious stones, and engraving precious metals. Bezalel also kept many apprentices whom he instructed in the arts. He supervised the manufacture of furniture, fabrics, decorations, clothing, and perfumes—all of which had to meet the most exacting standards. He was the greatest artist of his generation.

What's that? You've never heard of Bezalel? Perhaps you're familiar with some of his work. Ever hear of the Ark of the Covenant? How about the Tabernacle, the dwelling place on earth for the Most High God?

Bezalel was once a mere slave, one of six hundred thousand Israelite men who, along with their wives and children, made bricks out of Egyptian mud, worked in Egyptian fields, and built cities and monuments for the Pharaoh. But God heard the cries of His chosen people and sent Moses to deliver the children of Israel from bondage. Now God desired to dwell among His children. However, no one could look upon the Lord's glory and live, so He commanded that a special place be built, a tabernacle, to be a house for His glory.

In order to serve its purpose, God's holy dwelling would need to be made by the finest craftsmen using only the best materials. And it had to be built *exactly* according to

A replica of the Ark of the Covenant. Photo: Ben Schumin.

God's specifications (Exodus 25:9). But who could be trusted with such an assignment? God knew just the man for the job:

> Then the LORD said to Moses, "See, I have chosen Bezalel . . . and I have filled him with the Spirit of God, with skill, ability and knowledge in all kinds of crafts—to make artistic designs for work in gold, silver and bronze, to cut and set stones, to work in wood, and to engage in all kinds of craftsmanship." (Exodus 31:1–5)

So what made this man, a former slave, worthy to take on the awesome job of building a house for Almighty God? This passage from Exodus identifies three very important qualifications that set Bezalel apart from other candidates:

1. God chose him for the task.
2. God filled him with the Holy Spirit.
3. God gave him special skills and abilities.

Let's take a closer look at each of these qualities and what they mean for you and me.

GOD CHOOSES US FOR A PURPOSE

Those who believe that Jesus Christ is God's Son, that He died to save us from our sins, and that He has risen from the dead and reigns forever as King of all creation, they are called by His name—**Christians**, which means "followers of Christ." God's Word tells us that every Christian has been chosen by God:

But you are a chosen people, a royal priesthood, a holy nation, a people belonging to God, that you may declare the praises of him who called you out of darkness into his wonderful light. (1 Peter 2:9)

Every believer has been hand-picked by God, and each one shares a common purpose—to sing His praises. Another translation says, "God chose you to tell about the wonderful things he has done" (ICB). Of course, there are many ways to tell people about God. You can talk to a friend or neighbor about Jesus, or you might grow up to become a pastor or minister and preach His Word. You can show the love of God to others by volunteering at a homeless shelter, or you may become a missionary and share the good news of His salvation with people halfway around the world.

Whatever your gifts or talents may be, you can be sure of this: God has a special purpose for your life, a purpose for which He has gifted you and chosen you so that you will be in a unique position to tell others about Him. We refer to this as a **calling**, or the call of God on your life. Like Bezalel, you too are called by God, and you need to be ready to accept the work He gives you to do. God may call you to be a singer of songs or a writer of books, or He may call you to be a keeper of accounts or a seller of appliances. He may call you to work with your hands as a sculptor or as a plumber. Or He may call you to be a teacher or a parent—or both!

Be ready and willing to obey when God calls, and He will work in you and through you, "giving you the desire and the power to do what pleases him" (Philippians 2:13 NLT). Whatever He calls you to do, remember to "work at it with all your heart, as working for the Lord, not for men, since you know that you will receive an inheritance from the Lord as a reward" (Colossians 3:23–24).

GOD FILLS US WITH THE HOLY SPIRIT

Bezalel is the first person in the entire Bible who is said to have been filled with the Holy Spirit. An artist! Why did God choose *this* man to receive the Holy Spirit? God wants nothing more than to be with His children, and Bezalel was equipped by the Spirit to play an important part in fulfilling the deepest desire of God's heart.

When you become a new creation, the Holy Spirit comes to live inside you for the same reason: God wants to be near you and build a relationship with you. God also gives you His Spirit to help you understand and remember His instructions (John 14:26) and to equip you to tell others about Him and show them His love (Galatians 5:22–23).

GOD GIVES US SPECIAL SKILLS AND ABILITIES

You now know that you have been given a unique set of talents and abilities so that you can bring God glory by doing good works in His name. We see in the story of Bezalel that "all kinds of crafts" can be used to tell others about the great things God has done. Just as there are many different kinds of art, so God gives many different kinds of gifts. You probably have not yet discovered all of your own talents. What's the best way to discover your God-given abilities? Lessons? Practice? Certainly these things are important, but the Bible says the surest recipe for success is prayer + faith + obedience to His Word. Walk with God every day, and He will reveal His gifts to you. Hebrews 11:6 says that He "rewards those who earnestly seek him." Jesus said it this way: "Seek first his kingdom and his righteousness, and all these things will be given to you" (Matthew 6:33).

In the twenty-fifth chapter of the Gospel of Matthew, Jesus tells the parable of the talents. In this parable, a talent is not an ability but a unit of money worth more than a quarter-million dollars. Nevertheless, the principle Jesus taught also applies to the gifts and abilities God has given you. In the parable, the master of a house is preparing to take a journey, and he calls his servants together and gives each of them one or more talents to invest in his absence. Two of the servants use their talents well and, upon their master's return, present him with the money they earned from their investments. The third, however, buries his money in the backyard, afraid of what his master might say about the way he used the talent he was given. When the frightened servant returns the talent unused, his master becomes very angry. The master takes the talent away from him and tells the others,

"Throw that worthless servant outside, into the darkness" (Matthew 25:30).

You see, God's gifts must never be hidden. You have been given certain abilities, and God expects you to use these abilities to lead people to Him and to bring Him glory. The Lord equipped Bezalel with great skill, and in exchange, Bezalel had to be willing to use his gifts for the glory of the Lord. Of course, you don't have to be a great artist in order to bring God glory. God has entrusted you with your own set of gifts, and you need only to be obedient, responsible, and excited about the calling God has placed within you. Whether you grow up to become a painter or a cook or a secretary or an athlete, don't worry if everything you produce isn't a masterpiece. You are not called to succeed all the time. You are called to do your best, to be faithful with your talents, and to be obedient to the call of God on your life.

MAKE A NOTE OF IT

God is the Great Artist, and His technique is visible in the essence of everything we see. Indeed, His very image is in every person we meet. Take a moment to look around you today and enjoy the beauty of His creation. Then draw or paint a picture or take a photograph of someone or something that reveals His glory to you.

WHOSE GLORY?

In 1498, the artist Michelangelo Buonarroti was asked to create a life-sized sculpture for a tomb to be located at the ancient church of St. Peter's Basilica in Rome. His contract called for the sculpture to be the most beautiful work of marble in Rome, one that no living artist could surpass. The Pietà (pee-ay-TAH), as it would be known, would depict the seated Virgin Mary holding the lifeless body of the crucified Christ across her lap. Two years later, the sculpture was installed in St. Peter's for a celebration of the year 1500. The Pietà was widely praised for the beauty and power of its imagery, and Michelangelo's fame spread throughout Europe as visitors to Rome returned home.

One day, the artist was visiting St. Peter's when he overheard a conversation among a group of tourists. One person said to another that the Pietà had been carved by one of their own artists from Milan. Angered by this, Michelangelo returned to the chapel at night and, by the light of a candle, carved these words in Latin on the sash across Mary's chest: *Michelangelo Buonarroti, Florentine, made this*. However, he later regretted his outburst of pride and vowed never again to put his name on his work. The Pietà is the only piece of art that Michelangelo ever signed.

You see, most artists in the fifteenth century did not sign their work. They understood that their art was a gift and that its purpose was not to win glory for themselves but, rather, to point people toward the Great Artist. These men of faith knew they had been entrusted with a sacred task—to use their talent to win praise for God. Today, people often spend enormous amounts of time and money strengthening and developing their talents, and there's nothing wrong with that. And there's nothing wrong with being successful in your chosen career. (An artist or musician is no different from a

The Pietà by Michelangelo. Photo: Stanislav Traykov, Niabot.

laborer, businessperson, merchant, or athlete who has been called by the Lord to do a specific kind of work—artists are simply people whose God-given talents require that they work in the arts.)

But if you discover you have an extraordinary talent, you must use it to tell others where the gift came from. "What do you have that was not given to you?" Paul asks. "And if it was given to you, why do you brag as if you did not receive it as a gift?" (1 Corinthians 4:7, NCV). Even the most talented artist is completely dependent on God for his colors, his raw materials, his abilities, even his very existence! After all, only God can create something out of nothing. King David certainly knew where his psalms came from:

He has given me a new song to sing, a hymn of praise to our God. (Psalm 40:3, NLT)

Your gifts are not your own; they come from God. And when He gives you a talent, you must use it to glorify Him (1 Corinthians 10:31). Remember, your purpose is to reflect God's beauty and the wonder of everything He has made, not to win glory for yourself. Nevertheless, if you obey the Lord and keep His commands, He promises to bless the work of your hands:

The LORD your God will then make you successful in everything you do. He will give you many children and numerous livestock, and he will cause your fields to produce abundant harvests, for the LORD will again delight in being good to you as he was to your ancestors. The LORD your God will delight in you if you obey his voice and keep the commands and decrees written in this Book of Instruction, and if you turn to the LORD your God with all your heart and soul. (Deuteronomy 30:9–10, NLT)

The Tower of Babel by Hendrick van Cleve.

The book of Genesis tells the tragic story of a people who used their creativity for the sole purpose of gaining fame and power for themselves. In the years following the Great Flood, the descendants of Noah began to multiply, and they still spoke one common language. A number of the people moved east and settled in a plain called Shinar. Once there, someone had the bright idea to build a city—not just any city, mind you, but the greatest city the world had ever seen. The people thought this was a splendid idea and said to one another, "Let's build a city and a tower for ourselves, whose top will reach high into the sky. We will become famous. Then we will not be scattered over all the earth" (Genesis 11:4, NCV).

Just a few generations before, God had unleashed a flood to wipe nearly all of mankind from the face of the earth because of their constant wickedness (Genesis 6:5–8). Yet these people did not build a city to honor God, to reflect His magnificence, or as a memorial of His mercy toward Noah and his family.

> *True genius without heart is a thing of naught. For not great understanding alone, not intelligence alone, nor both together make genius. Love! Love! Love! That is the soul of genius.*
> **Nikolaus Joseph von Jacquin, as quoted in Wolfgang Mozart's personal souvenir album**

Instead, they acted out of selfish ambition—they planned to rob God of the praise and glory. So God did not bless the work of their hands, and He scattered them to the ends of the earth and confused the language of people everywhere. From that time the place was called Babel,

BACH TO BASICS

Johann Sebastian Bach is one of history's most famous composers. More than 250 years after his death, there are numerous Bach societies, Bach festivals, and entire orchestras dedicated to performing his works. Yet in his day, Bach was virtually unknown as a composer, at least outside of the German towns where he quietly lived and worked.

Bach was never attracted to fame or fortune. Although clearly a genius, he was refreshingly modest and humble. He once told a student, "Just practice diligently, and it will go very well. You have five fingers on each hand just as healthy as mine."

For a while he served as *Kapellmeister*, or master of music, to the court of Prince Leopold, but such grand surroundings were a distraction to him. He left to accept a position at a church in Leipzig, where he devoted himself fully to church music. The brilliant composer spent the last twenty-seven years of his life at St. Thomas Church, not building his reputation, but simply teaching music and getting ready for Sunday. He composed a new cantata for the choir nearly every week for two years.

Bach composed music for the glory of God and to inspire others. He once said, "The aim and final end of all music should be none other than the glory of God and the refreshment of the soul." At the end of many of his scores he wrote the initials *SDG*, which stood for *Soli Deo Gloria*, or "To God alone be the glory." Today, this hard-working servant is considered one of the greatest composers ever known. But for many years he was simply a good man who went about his daily work with all his might. Whatever you choose to do with your life, creative or otherwise, you may never achieve greatness. But you can be good, and you can do your best every day, working as though you are working for the Lord (Colossians 3:23).

because the people no longer understood one another (Genesis 11:9). Today, even with satellites and cell phones and the Internet at our fingertips, we still experience the effects of this curse every time we attempt to communicate with someone who speaks another language or comes from another culture.

MAKE A NOTE OF IT

Write a poem, a song, or a short story about two friends, both of whom are extremely talented. They might be singers or dancers or musicians or another kind of performer. One uses his or her gift for the glory of God; the other uses his or her gift to pursue fame and fortune. Write about which of the two has chosen the best path. Which of them ends up happier? Why?

WHOM WILL YOU BLESS?

Recently, I found my youngest daughter tossing an odd-looking, squishy toy from one hand to the other. When asked about it, she said it was a "stress ball" and that she had made it herself. A stress ball is a squeezable "toy" normally used by office workers to help relieve tension or exercise the muscles of the hand. They're often made into fun shapes and filled with gel or foam rubber. My daughter made hers from an old sock and some dry rice. "Wow," I said. "That's very creative." A few minutes later, she brought me a selection of her socks that no longer had matches. I chose a blue sock adorned with orange flowers, a green frog, and the words *Toadily Cool.* A few minutes later she presented me with my very own stress ball. I keep it on my desk next to the computer.

Some people want nothing more than to see their name in lights. They sing or write or paint because they crave the approval of their parents or friends or the public. But as we have seen, people are given talents in order to glorify God. Being creative is about honoring Him and giving happiness to others. You may have already discovered that you've been given a serious artistic talent, or you may be just a beginner taking lessons. Or you may simply enjoy singing songs, dancing, writing stories, or drawing pictures. Whatever your skill level, you can bless others by sharing the things you create. Write a poem for a friend who is feeling down. Make a card for a neighbor who is sick. Bringing people joy and peace by showing them God's love does not require you to have perfect pitch or professional training or nimble fingers. In fact, it doesn't require anything at all except being willing to give your time, your talents, and your love. Master painter Vincent van Gogh, who studied to be a pastor, once said, "The more I think it over, the more I feel there is nothing more truly artistic than to love people."

Self-portrait of Vincent van Gogh. Photo: flickr.com user Pachango.

MAKE A NOTE OF IT

Sometimes we write and sing songs or paint pictures or take photographs to help us remember important truths that we tend to forget over time. King David did this often and called them psalms. Write a psalm that reflects three or more of the attributes of God you learned about in lesson 1.

WHAT IF YOU DON'T HAVE A "SHOWY" GIFT?

Even if you never become the world's greatest actor or wood-worker or cartoonist or inventor, you can still enjoy making art for the Lord. Sing in the bathtub and forget the public. You don't need an audience of thousands to sing or dance before the Lord. As Big Bird once sang, "Don't worry that it's not good enough for anyone else to hear." God doesn't mind if your technique is not perfect. After all, even the greatest works of art ever made—the *Mona Lisa*, Beethoven's Ninth Symphony, and the Taj Mahal included—are worth infinitely less in God's eyes than the people who made them.

Take a look at the person in the picture on the left: This photo depicts a young woman who makes her living as a fashion model. What might she think makes her important or valuable? Yes, she is able to earn a good income because of the way she looks. But what will happen as she grows older and her looks begin to fade and she is no longer able to work as a model? Will she still feel important? Does her value to God depend on what she wears, how she styles her hair, or what she looks like? The Bible tells us:

Don't be concerned about the outward beauty of fancy hairstyles, expensive jewelry, or beautiful clothes. You should clothe yourselves instead with the beauty that comes from within, the unfading beauty of a gentle and quiet spirit, which is so precious to God. (1 Peter 3:3–4, NLT)

What about this sports team that has just won a championship? What do you suppose these young men think makes them important or valuable? Their athletic skill? The cheering crowds? Perhaps it's the money they are being paid, the fancy cars they drive, or the products they endorse. Maybe it's the trophy they are hoisting in victory. But what happens when their feet begin to slow or they sustain a few injuries? When their cars begin to rust and the trophies lose their luster, will these men still feel important? Does their value to God depend on how many goals they score or how many games they win? No. The Bible says:

Photo: Steindy.

For the world offers only . . . pride in our achievements and possessions. These are not from the Father, but are from this world. (1 John 2:16, NLT)

The LORD does not look at the things man looks at. Man looks at the outward appearance, but the LORD looks at the heart. (1 Samuel 16:7)

Many people try to prove their worth by piling up achievements, social status, fashion, wealth, or fame. Yet these things mean nothing to God. Your true worth lies in the fact that you are made in God's own image, and that makes you very special indeed. As a child of God, you can be sure that you are infinitely loved whether you are the world's greatest athlete or the last kid picked when choosing sides for basketball. You are so highly valued, in fact, that God chose to die on a cross rather than live without you. You are worth more to Him than all the trophies and jewelry and money in the world.

WHAT SHOULD I DO?

Have you ever noticed how quiet and "unmiraculous" many of the miracles of Jesus were? His very first miracle, turning water into wine, was noticed only by His mother, His disciples, and a few servants at the wedding feast in Cana. When Jesus fed thousands of people with a couple of fish and a few loaves of bread, He didn't wave His arms and shout or call down thunder from heaven; He simply prayed and told His disciples to pass out the food. Jesus never called to the crowds, "Hey! Look what I did! Isn't that cool?" In fact, He did nothing to call attention to Himself but instead told people to look to His Father in heaven. And indeed, when Jesus healed the sick, as in Luke 5:24–25 and 18:42–43, those who witnessed the miracle often went about afterward praising God.

As we have seen, you and I have each been given unique talents, and at times we might be tempted to look at our own gifts and abilities and think we are somehow greater or more privileged than others. Yet as the apostle James points out, we do not have any gifts that were not given to us by God (James 1:17). Even Jesus said He could do nothing by Himself, but did only what He saw His Father doing (John 5:19). We need to follow Christ's example and, with humility, use our gifts to point people toward the Giver of all good gifts.

Humility is an attitude that says, "I am not better than anyone else." After all, every man, woman, and child is made in God's image. And God does not want anyone to be destroyed but wants everyone to know Him and choose Him (2 Peter 3:9). The Bible says that each of us has received a gift "to use to serve others" (1 Peter 4:10, NCV). So instead of using our abilities to win praise for ourselves, we need to win praise for our heavenly Father by showing God's infinite love to those who believe and to those who don't. Remember, whatever God has chosen you to do, whatever gifts He has given you, your true work is to know and love God and to help others know Him.

A PRAYER

Dear God, thank you for the talents and abilities you have given me. Help me to discover my gifts and my calling. Help me to do my best at whatever work you give me to do. Show me how I can best use my talents to serve others and bring glory and honor to you. In Jesus' name. Amen.

Photo: NASA.

WORLDVIEWS IN FOCUS

MEET REMY

Remy is a twelve-year-old boy who lives in Montreal, the largest city in the Canadian province of Quebec. Remy's parents are both teachers at McGill University in downtown Montreal. His father teaches history and loves studying the Renaissance and Leonardo de Vinci. His mother is a plant biologist and is very concerned with reversing global warming and saving the earth through recycling.

Remy's father came to Montreal from France to go to college. While he was here, he met Remy's mother and, as she says, biology won out. They got married after college and five years later decided to have Remy. He doesn't have any brothers or sisters, though, because his parents believe that the earth is overpopulated already. Remy's parents take great pride in being responsible in caring for the earth.

Because they live in the province of Quebec, where the official language is French, Remy speaks French at school and with his friends. But because his mother's family was originally from Massachusetts, Remy speaks English at home. Remy's parents are proud that he is bilingual, and they want him to learn more languages as he grows older. The three of them take an international trip each summer, so Remy has traveled to most of the countries in Europe and several in Asia. Italy is his favorite country so far because of the many wonderful museums and the great food.

Because his parents are highly respected and well off financially, Remy can choose to do almost anything with his life. Remy's mother wants him to become a doctor, while his father is encouraging him to become an anthropologist and study the human race throughout history. But what Remy really wants to be is a musician. Although he took piano and violin lessons when he was younger, his favorite instrument is the cello. His teacher says he has real talent and is challenging him to play more difficult pieces. One day he hopes to join the Montreal Symphony Orchestra, so he goes as often as possible to hear them play. His favorite piece is *Boléro* by Maurice Ravel—the Montreal Symphony is famous for performing Ravel's compositions. His parents are very proud of his artistic talents, even if it means he probably won't go to medical school.

Remy's parents chose to live in Montreal because it is the cultural capital of Canada. The city is filled with museums, theaters, symphony halls, and opera houses. Remy's parents have season tickets to the ballet and the opera, so nearly every weekend, when

Place des Arts. Photo: flickr.com user Po Yang.

they aren't at the symphony, they attend a performance or see a new play. In fact, their apartment is closer to the Place des Arts—the major performing arts complex in Montreal—than it is to the university where Remy's parents work. The three of them enjoy the walk to the Place des Arts almost as much as they do the show. And every time the Cirque du Soleil presents a new acrobatic show, Remy's parents make sure they have front-row seats!

Remy's mother and father believe it is important to cultivate good taste in music and art. They make it a priority to expose Remy to as many new and different experiences as possible because they want him to be well-rounded and sophisticated. They believe that the world is moving toward a time when people will recognize the futility of war and join together in peace, so they want Remy to be as smart and as cultured as possible so he will thrive in this new world. Remy likes feeling sophisticated. Somehow he thinks that having good taste makes him a better, more interesting person. His parents even let him taste champagne last New Year's Eve!

Remy and his parents don't own a car, and they walk almost everywhere they go. Remy's mother says that not owning a car reduces the amount of pollution in the air, while his father says that he is glad not to have to drive in winter weather. Instead, they walk or take the underground (subway) wherever they need to go. Remy doesn't miss having a car, though on cold days he is grateful for the miles of underground walkways in Montreal. Besides, living

without a car makes him feel like he is doing something good for the environment.

Remy's parents are also careful to recycle cans and plastic soda bottles and to use as little paper as possible. They send their students assignments by e-mail instead of printing them on paper—Remy's mother jokes that she is saving at least one tree a week this way. Remy's dad has also replaced all the light bulbs in their apartment with environmentally friendly compact fluorescent bulbs. As a family, they try to use as little electricity as possible, and Remy gets scolded whenever he leaves a light on in an empty room or doesn't turn off the television after watching a show.

His mother says that all of these things help reduce their "carbon footprint" so the earth won't be harmed by the way they live. Living in Montreal helps them toward this goal. Recycling there is simple, just like putting the trash out on the curb, and so is composting. The city has even designated a day to donate used furniture and appliances so they don't end up in landfills. Remy's mother is passionate about the environment, so much so that it sometimes embarrasses him, especially if she starts one of her lectures in front of his friends.

Instead of going to public school, Remy's parents send him to an elite private school. As respected teachers at one of the oldest universities in North America, they can afford it. Remy studies math, science, and grammar, but he also takes advanced classes in literature, history, and languages. School is a lot of work, but his parents want him to challenge himself to succeed. Remy knows that his parents love him and want only the best for him, but sometimes their emphasis on learning more and more makes him feel like they don't appreciate how far he has already come.

Remy's parents also make him earn his allowance money. He must do chores around the house, like rinsing the dishes and washing and folding laundry. Remy's parents teach him that he will succeed in life only if he earns it. His father says that self-reliance is key—no handouts, no charity, just take on the world with your wits and your two hands and make it on your own. Remy wonders if his father has taken this philosophy from his favorite poem, "Invictus," which declares that every man is the master of his fate and the captain of his soul. Remy's father keeps a framed copy of the poem on his desk at work.

Remy's father also tells him "you are what you do" and that the only real way to feel good about yourself is to build a life and reputation that stays true to your principles, whatever they may be. (His father explains that each person sees truth a little differently, so no one should judge anyone else.) This philosophy makes Remy wonder, though, if there is anything about him that makes him valuable as a person. Is he only as good as the things he does? What about those people who are unable to contribute anything useful to society? Should they be pushed aside to make room for those who can accomplish big things? Remy knows his father says these things to encourage him to work hard, but deep down his advice makes Remy feel nervous. What if he doesn't succeed? What if in the end he's worthless?

Notre-Dame Basilica. Photo: Serdar Gurbuz Photography.

A recent experience has got him thinking more about who he is and where he is going. Last Christmas, Remy visited the famous Notre-Dame Basilica with Andre, a Catholic friend, to attend the Christmas Eve service. This was a rare treat for Remy, because his parents don't really celebrate Christmas. His father says Christmas is a pagan holiday that was later dressed up as a religious one, and that the historical Jesus, if he even existed, would have been born in spring, not winter. They do exchange gifts and have a special dinner on Christmas Day, but they don't place much importance on the holiday.

Remy loved the Christmas Eve service, with all the candles and incense and priests in robes. For some reason, the music touched him in a special way. That night the organist played a piece by Johann Sebastian Bach, and ever since, Remy can't get enough of Bach's church music. Although he would never mention it to his parents, the beautiful music and the lavish service struck a chord deep inside his heart. Since then, Remy has been secretly learning more about religion when he can, trying to figure out what it was he liked so much about the service. He has already asked Andre if he can go with him at Easter this year to hear the *St. Matthew Passion*, Bach's oratorio that tells the story of Christ's crucifixion from the Gospel of Matthew.

You see, Remy's parents don't believe God exists. They say that everything in the world came into being by accident and life evolved over millions and millions of years. His father says that people invented the idea of God out of fear and superstition. He says there is no higher power than humans. Remy's mother tells him that because people are the most advanced life form on the planet, they have a responsibility to take care of it. Even though Remy has questions about God, he would rather not ask his parents because he doesn't want to disappoint them.

Remy has been asking Andre questions about what his family believes, especially about what happens after a person dies. Remy's grandmother passed away about a year ago, and it made him very sad. If death is the end, as his father says, then Remy knows he will never see his grandmother again. But Andre told him that good people who die go to heaven. Remy wonders how good a person has to be to go to heaven, but he knows his grandmother was a good person, so he thinks she must have gotten in.

Once Remy asked his parents about heaven, but his father said it's a myth, just like God, and that people made it up to help themselves feel better about losing someone they loved. He said that as much as he wanted Remy not to feel sad over his grandmother's death, he wasn't going to lie to him. It's better in the long run, his father said, to face the truth than to believe a comfortable lie.

On another occasion, Remy asked his father how he knew that God wasn't real. His father said that the only way to know something is true is through scientific experimentation and by using our senses and mind. Remy's father said that only physical things—things that can be measured and categorized—are real. Anything that can't be measured—like God, heaven, angels, or even the soul—cannot be scientifically proven and therefore isn't real.

Unfortunately, these conversations have only made Remy more confused. His father's answers seem so rational and logical that he can't help but believe them. But he also knows what his heart feels when he listens to Bach's music. His heart tells him that there is something more, but he knows that feelings can't be measured or tested. When his brain gets tired of running in circles, he's glad he has many more years ahead of him to figure out all these puzzles!

Montreal skyline. Photo: Text2Texte.

In the meantime, Remy is determined to enjoy life. He loves weekends when the weather is nice, because it means that he and his parents will spend time together walking all over Montreal. Sometimes they walk past the many stores along Rue Sainte-Catherine, window shopping and watching the tourists, and they love trying out new food. Because

Montreal is built on an island, like New York City, fresh seafood is always available. Remy's mother prepares simple, healthy meals at home during the week because of their hectic schedules, but they always eat out on weekends. Montreal has more restaurants than almost any other city in the world, and Remy's parents seem determined to try them all.

During the summer, the family takes a bike trip every Sunday morning. Montreal has miles and miles of bike trails, and Remy thinks he must have seen every inch of the island by now. His parents say that even when he was a baby, they would go biking together. Maybe that's why he loves fresh air and sunshine so much! Because Montreal summers are short and the winters long, he and his parents try to make the most of every mild day.

Although Remy has many questions about who he is, how he should live, and what will happen to him after he dies, he tries not to let his quest for answers make him too serious. He expects to live a long time and believes he will one day make himself into the kind of scholar and musician that will make his parents proud.

WHAT'S THE DIFFERENCE?

- How is the way Remy lives different from the way you live? How are your lives similar?

- Remy works hard to develop his musical talent. What does he hope to do with this talent? Why does he want to be a successful musician? How is the way Remy sees his talent different from the way you see your gifts as a child of God?

- Remy's friend Andre tells him that good people go to heaven. Can a person be "good enough" to get into heaven? What does the Bible say we need to do to have everlasting life?

- What does Remy's father teach him about what makes a person successful? How is this different from what the Bible teaches about success?

- Although Remy's mother does not believe in God, what does she do to be a good steward of the earth God has given us?

- Why do you think Bach's church music speaks to Remy? What would Remy's parents think about his decision to learn more about God? Should Remy tell them what he is doing? Where can Remy find the answers to his questions about life and death and who he is?

THE HOUSE OF TRUTH: THE SIXTH PILLAR

In our story, "The Pocket Knife," Sasha learned that all people are made in God's image and that people are the most important part of His earthly creation. The Bible tells us God has crowned us with glory and honor. He has given us, His children, the privilege to worship Him and fellowship with Him, to enjoy His presence in everything we do, wherever we are. To help us honor Him, He has given each person unique gifts and talents to use for His glory.

In this lesson, you erected the second pillar in your Image-Bearing Wall:

BIBLICAL TRUTH 10

God has crowned me with honor and glory.

Biblical Truth 9
God created me in His image

Biblical Truth 10
God has crowned me with honor and glory

IMAGE-BEARING WALL
My relationship with myself as I become more like Jesus

Biblical Truth 2
God is the only true and almighty God

FOUNDATION OF WISDOM
Knowing, loving, and obeying God my Rock

THE ROCK
God and His Word

WHAT'S ON YOUR MIND?

> "LOVE THE LORD YOUR GOD WITH ALL YOUR HEART AND WITH ALL YOUR SOUL AND WITH ALL YOUR MIND."

MATTHEW 22:37

THE BIG IDEA

Your brain is a wonderfully complex organ. Every second millions of neurons are sending and receiving messages to and from every part of your body, making your brain an extremely busy place. Every waking hour you think hundreds of random thoughts, remember numerous facts and past events, make dozens of choices, and process several different emotions, all while making sense of the sights, sounds, tastes, and smells you're now experiencing. And yet the simplest things—what you eat and drink, what you watch on TV, even the kinds of games you play—can affect this amazing piece of precision machinery.

With so much going on in your head, it's no wonder the Bible has a lot to say about the care and feeding of your mind:

Don't copy the behavior and customs of this world, but let God transform you into a new person by changing the way you think. (Romans 12:2, NLT)

If a person's thinking is controlled by his sinful self, there is death. But if his thinking is controlled by the Spirit, then there is life and peace. (Romans 8:6, ICB)

Finally, brothers, whatever is true, whatever is noble, whatever is right, whatever is pure, whatever is lovely, whatever is admirable—if anything is excellent or praiseworthy—think about such things. (Philippians 4:8)

BUTTER WEEK

Pancakes are tasty, but have you ever thought of giving them their own holiday? In Russia, eating pancakes is one way the people welcome the return of spring after a long, cold winter. These pancakes, called *blini* (BLEE-nee), remind the Russian people of the summer sun because they are round and golden brown and can brighten any day.

Blini get their own week during a holiday called *Maslenitsa* (mos-LEN-ee-tsah), or Butter Week. Butter Week is a time of joy, feasts, gifts, and public celebrations. In the Russian Orthodox Church, Lent comes right before Easter. Lent is a time to avoid eating certain foods like meat, fish, and dairy and egg products so people can focus their attention on spiritual things to be ready for Easter. The forty days of Lent represent the time Jesus spent in the wilderness before the beginning of his public ministry. Because Lent is a time of doing without, Russian families celebrate Butter Week by enjoying their favorite foods, sledding, having snowball fights, going on sleigh rides, and visiting the homes of friends and relatives.

To use up any eggs, milk, and butter they might have before Lent, Russians make dishes like blini, which are similar to pancakes or French crêpes, but are very thin and not as sweet. Sometimes blini are eaten by themselves with butter, but most of the time they are stuffed with delicious fillings such as meat, salmon, mushrooms, caviar (fish eggs), fruit preserves, or honey. Then they are folded into pockets and enjoyed.

While it is appropriate to eat blini any time of day at any time of the year, it is still seen as a holiday tradition. Russian-Americans enjoy this treat when celebrating Thanksgiving in their new country, and it is a must at any Christmas celebration. Here's a simple recipe for making your own blini. (Remember, one pancake is a blin; two or more are called blini.)

2 eggs
1 tablespoon white sugar
1/3 teaspoon salt
½ cup all-purpose flour
2½ cups milk
1 tablespoon vegetable oil
1 tablespoon butter

Preparation

Whisk together the eggs, sugar, and salt in a medium-sized bowl. Sift the flour into the bowl, and stir it in as you add the milk. Mix until smooth and well blended. The batter should be thin.

Lightly oil a skillet or spray it with cooking spray, then heat the skillet over medium heat. Pour about 2 tablespoons of the batter into the pan, then tilt the pan to spread the batter out evenly. When the edges of the blin look crisp and the center appears dry, slide a spatula carefully under the blin. Flip the blin and cook it for about 1 minute on the other side, or until lightly browned.

Remove the blin to a plate. Put a little butter on it, then fold it in half and in half again to form a triangle. Makes 20 blini.

Na zdarOv'ye! (Enjoy!)

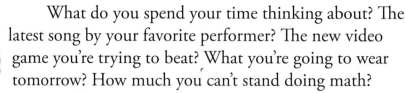

What do you spend your time thinking about? The latest song by your favorite performer? The new video game you're trying to beat? What you're going to wear tomorrow? How much you can't stand doing math?

Did you know God thinks about things too? As we've seen, one of the ways we know God is a person is that He has thoughts. And when God created you in His image, He gave you a mind so you can think about things, know things, and share your thoughts with Him.

He made people to think about the same kinds of things He does—things that are true, things that are right, things that are lovely. But when sin entered the world, people began to think about things that are untrue, cruel, and ugly. Today many people no longer think about the many wonderful things God has given them or what He has done for them. Instead, they spend time thinking about what they *don't* have, such as a shiny new car, a bigger television, or a famous name. This kind of thinking makes people woefully unhappy and causes them to sin.

God has given us many commandments to help us think and live in a way that will please Him and keep us free from sin. His Word, the Bible, teaches us how to love, how to spend our money, how to pray, even the kinds of things to think about. One day, a man came to Jesus and asked which is the greatest of all God's commandments. Jesus answered him, "Love the Lord your God with all your heart and with all your soul and with all your mind" (Matthew 22:37). *All* your mind. You may well ask, "With so much going on in my head, how can I love God with *all* of my mind? And what kind of stuff does He want me to think about anyway?" That's what this lesson is about.

The Thinker by Auguste Rodin. Photo: Taty2007.

WHAT YOU WILL DO

» You will recognize how your thoughts can lead you to do good or to do evil.
» You will examine what Scripture says about renewing your mind by changing the way you think.
» You will identify six things God wants you to think about every day.
» You will practice "meditating" on God's Word.

Photo: Wolfgang Sauber

THE WOODEN BIRD

"I said no, and that's my final answer," Ivan's father said angrily. "Now hurry up or you'll be late for school. And don't forget to fill the log bin before you leave." Mr. Yushenko had little patience with Ivan, who always seemed to be in trouble at home or at school. And the idea of taking the time after school to allow Sasha Petrov to show Ivan a few woodcarving skills was out of the question.

"So what did your father say?" Sasha asked Ivan the first day of school after the Christmas and New Year's holidays.

"He said no, just like I knew he would," Ivan replied with bitterness. "He never lets me do anything—except work, that is."

"Maybe my father could talk to your father," Sasha said, trying to be encouraging.

"That wouldn't help." Ivan was despondent. "Besides, I don't really need you to teach me how to carve. I can learn by myself."

As Ivan trudged off into the school building, he made no effort to be friendly to anyone. In fact, that day he lived up to his reputation as the class bully by pestering and teasing several of his classmates.

Sasha was disappointed. Ever since his conversation with Ivan on Christmas Day, he had been looking forward not only to teaching him how to carve wood, but also to becoming friends. Now neither seemed possible.

That afternoon, as Sasha entered the wood shop for his first lesson of the new year, Mr. Kerensky greeted him warmly. "Sasha Petrov! Happy New Year! It's good to see you again. And did you receive that carving knife you wanted?"

"I did, Mr. Kerensky," Sasha said with little enthusiasm. "I brought it with me. Of course, I told my teacher, Mr. Yavorsky, and he kept it safe for me until after school."

"Well, you don't sound too excited about your new knife or about being here for your lesson," Mr. Kerensky replied with a puzzled look on his face.

"Oh, I'm very happy with my new knife. And I always want to come for my lesson, you know that. It's just that Ivan . . . you know Ivan Yushenko, the boy in my class . . . ?"

"What about Ivan?"

"Well, after the Christmas Day service at church, he asked me to teach him how to carve wood. That really surprised me because . . . well, you probably know, Ivan's not much of a friend to anyone. He has a reputation as the school bully."

"It seems I've heard that from some of the folks in the village," Mr. Kerensky acknowledged.

"Well, when Ivan asked me to teach him, I said I would. But today at school he told me his father said he had too much work to do at home. He told Ivan he had no time to waste on carving lessons."

"Well, that's too bad. Perhaps the next time I see Mr. Yushenko, I'll have a talk with him. Now what kind of carving project do you think you'd like to begin working on this winter?"

"Can you teach me how to carve birds?" Sasha asked.

"I was thinking the very same thing," Mr. Kerensky said. "Why don't we begin with a dove?"

"Yes! Oh, yes," Sasha replied eagerly. "I can't wait to learn to carve the lines for feathers."

Photo: Peter Kammer.

One afternoon in early February, as Mr. Kerensky was teaching Sasha how to carve the delicate feather lines in the wings of his dove, a snow-covered man entered the shop.

"Good afternoon," Mr. Kerensky said as he looked up. "May I help you?"

"My wife has need of some new wooden spoons and a rolling pin," said the man gruffly as he removed his *shapka* and dusted the snow from his beard and coat. "Do you have any for sale?"

"Why, Mr. Yushenko, I didn't recognize you under all that snow. Do come in and warm yourself by the fire. Yes, I have plenty of spoons. And just yesterday I made three rolling pins. Please, take a look."

As Mr. Kerensky stood and shook the wood shavings from his apron, Sasha whispered, "Remember what you said about talking to him about letting Ivan take carving lessons?"

Mr. Kerensky nodded and went to help Mr. Yushenko. As he was wrapping the spoons and rolling pin, he said, "So, how is your boy Ivan these days? Keeping busy with his school-work, I suppose."

"Yes, he stays busy. Why, with schoolwork and home chores, he has time for little else. But work is good for him. Keeps him out of trouble. And getting into trouble is something he's very good at."

"I was thinking," Mr. Kerensky said as he wrapped up Mr. Yushenko's purchase, "I need someone to sweep my floors, fill the log bin, and keep the shelves tidy. What would you think of allowing Ivan to give me a hand after school a couple of days each week? Oh, I can't pay much, but—"

"Why that's a splendid idea!" Mr. Yushenko said, thinking only how a little extra money would help his family. "When could he start?"

"Well, as I was saying, I can't pay very much. But he can begin this Thursday. And if you don't mind, Sasha and I could teach Ivan a little about carving—just for fun, you know. After work."

"As long as he gets paid for working, then I suppose it's all right. I'll make sure he comes here right after school on Thursday."

On his first day at the shop, Ivan completed his responsibilities eagerly and quickly. He wanted to have as much time as possible for learning to carve. Sasha helped Ivan with his work so he could finish sooner, which seemed to bolster their tenuous friendship.

After just four lessons, Ivan had completed his first carving project—a large cooking spoon. "Take it home to your mother tonight," Mr. Kerensky said. "Give it to her as a gift. And here are your earnings."

"Thank you, Mr. Kerensky," Ivan said with a smile as he headed out the door.

Photo: Yan Schweizer.

A biting wind nipped at Ivan's nose as he hurried through the snow down the narrow village streets. As he opened the door to his family's tiny cottage, his father shouted, "Hurry up and close that door! It's cold enough in here without letting in all of frozen Siberia. Did you get paid today?"

Ivan was used to his father's gruff and impatient manner, so this did not bother him. "Yes," Ivan said as he took off his coat and cap. "Mr. Kerensky paid me one ruble for last week and one ruble for this week."

"Two rubles? That's quite a sum for just four afternoons of work," Mr. Yushenko replied. "Put them in the box on the table."

Ivan placed the two coins in the box, then walked over to the stove where his mother was making a stack of blini in preparation for the coming Butter Week celebration.

"I have a gift for you, Mother," he said with a shy smile.

"Why, thank you, my son! What ever could it be?" she asked as she unwrapped the wooden spoon.

"It's my first project," Ivan said.

"Oh, it's lovely!" she replied. "I can never have too many good spoons for all the cooking I do for this family. Go show it to your father."

Photo: Donovan Govan.

Ivan hesitated before walking across the room and handing the spoon to his father.

"Is that all you've been able to accomplish in four lessons?" he grumbled, hardly looking at the spoon. "Why I thought you'd be carving as well as Sasha by now. You know—sheep and oxen and mangers and all the rest."

Ivan took the spoon, turned, and handed it back to his mother. Tears filled his eyes, but he managed to keep from crying openly in front of his father. His mother gave Ivan an understanding hug but said nothing in his defense.

The next day at school, Sasha asked, "What did your parents think of the spoon you made? Did they like it?"

"Yeah, they thought it was beautiful," Ivan said sarcastically as he brushed past Sasha without stopping. "My father *really* liked it."

Sasha sensed something was wrong, but it wasn't until Tuesday afternoon at Mr. Kerensky's shop that he knew for sure.

"I want to learn how to carve birds like Sasha," Ivan announced after he had finished his chores.

"You're not quite ready for that, my boy," Mr. Kerensky said.

"Yes, I am," Ivan snapped. "I can carve just as well as Sasha can. All I need is a little help."

"Very well, if you think so," Mr. Kerensky answered kindly, also sensing that something was disturbing Ivan.

Ivan tried to follow Mr. Kerensky's patient instructions, but his unsteady hands yielded only crude results. In his frustration, Ivan grew more and more impatient and careless. Finally, realizing that he was not ready for such advanced work, he threw the carving tools and his block of wood on the floor. "I hate woodcarving!" he shouted. "And I hate working in this dusty old shop. And I don't need you or Sasha to teach me anything."

"Just a minute, young man," Mr. Kerensky said firmly. "Pick up the tools and the block of wood. Then put them both back on the table. I will not allow outbursts like that in my shop."

Ivan stared at Mr. Kerensky, then at Sasha. After what seemed a very long time, he began to cry. Finally, he picked up the knife and the wood block and set them on the table.

"What's really wrong, Ivan?" Mr. Kerensky asked. "I don't believe for one minute that you meant what you just said. You've learned to carve quite well after just four lessons. What is it, my boy?"

"My father didn't like the spoon I carved. All he wanted to know was if I got paid or not," Ivan cried. "He never likes anything I do—my chores, my school work, anything."

"I like your spoon," Sasha said.

"No, you don't," Ivan said bitterly. "And you don't really like me either. No one at school likes me. But I don't care. I'm the strongest kid in my class, and if anyone ever—"

"Ivan," Mr. Kerensky said, "I like you very much, and I'm sure others do too. I want you to continue working here after school. And I want you to continue learning to carve, if you wish. In time, I'm sure your father will be very pleased with the things you make."

Ivan continued working at Mr. Kerensky's shop throughout the spring, not because he wanted to, but because he was afraid of what his father would say if he stopped earning his weekly ruble. Although his carving skills improved, he no longer took any of his projects home to show his father. The only thing he showed his father or anyone else was a building anger and a quick temper. His belligerent attitude alienated him even further from his classmates. And the more they shunned him, the more unfriendly and unkind Ivan became toward everyone.

An old ruble. Photo: flickr.com user woody1778a.

Easter came and went. Then one April afternoon, Ivan's father asked, "Isn't it about time you showed us another woodcarving? I'm sure that by now you've learned to carve something more complicated than spoons. I heard from Sasha's father that he's learning to carve birds. Are you carving birds too?"

"Uh . . . sure, Father," Ivan stammered. "I'm carving a bird."

"Hmph. Then bring it home this week and show me. Did you get paid this week yet?"

"Yes, Father." Ivan turned and walked outside.

The following Thursday, Sasha hurried to Mr. Kerensky's shop after school without waiting for Ivan to walk with him as he usually did.

"Where's Ivan?" Mr. Kerensky asked.

"I think he's coming later," Sasha replied. "I didn't wait to walk with him. He's unfriendly to everyone at school these days. I don't think he really wants to work here anymore or learn to carve."

"I think you're right."

Just then, Ivan walked into the shop looking angry. "Why didn't you wait for me, Sasha? We always walk together."

"I, um . . . I don't know."

"Well, I don't care," Ivan said bitterly. Then as he picked up the broom and began to sweep the floor, he said, "And why don't you have to sweep floors, Sasha?"

Mr. Kerensky didn't say anything but opened the cupboard door and removed Sasha's dove. "I think you might finish this in a week or so," he said, handing the carving to Sasha. "Just a few more cuts around the beak, a little sanding, a few more feather lines, and I think you'll be ready to take it home. Let's get busy."

As Sasha began his work, Mr. Kerensky turned to Ivan. "I think the floor looks fine, and the shelves are in good order. Why don't we get started on your lesson? I think you're ready to try something a bit more difficult. What do you say?"

Ivan seemed surprised but readily agreed.

That afternoon Mr. Kerensky worked patiently with Ivan, assuring him that his carving skills were developing well. By the end of the lesson, Ivan had roughed in the shape of a bird.

"But it doesn't even look like a bird yet," Ivan complained impatiently as Mr. Kerensky told the boys to begin putting their supplies away for the day. "It's crude and kind of ugly."

"Patience, my boy," Mr. Kerensky said. "In time it will be a bird. You'll never create a beautiful piece without work and patience. Now put away your carving and the knives. It's time to close up shop and go home."

"My father's here," Sasha said. "Good-bye, Mr. Kerensky! Bye, Ivan!"

When Mr. Kerensky stepped outside to greet Sasha's father, Ivan's mind began racing. He had an idea. He went to the cupboard, quickly opened the door, and placed his wood block and knife on the shelf. Then he grabbed Sasha's nearly finished dove, slipped it into his school satchel, closed the cupboard door, and hurried outside.

"Bye, Sasha," Ivan said. "See you tomorrow at school."

As he hurried through the village streets toward his house, Ivan's heart began to fill with hope, fear, and guilt—hope that his father would compliment him on the carving, fear that his dishonesty would be discovered, and perhaps

Photo: flickr user Tom T.

84

most painful of all, guilt for stealing Sasha's carving, although he kept telling himself that he was only borrowing it for the evening.

That night, after supper, Ivan showed the dove to his father.

"Now that's more like it," Mr. Yushenko said. "Much better than a spoon. Maybe you're learning something after all. Good job, son."

For a moment, Ivan's heart leaped. He smiled at the words, but the warmth in his heart quickly faded as fear and guilt washed away the compliment he knew he didn't deserve. Ivan said, "I'm really tired after working today. Good night, Father." He then carefully placed the dove back into his satchel and slipped away to his room.

Ivan slept very little that night, for as hard as he tried, he could not make the fear and the guilt go away. What would happen if anyone should discover what he had done? Could he return the dove to Mr. Kerensky's cabinet before anyone noticed it was missing? Finally, after devising a plan to cover his misdeeds, Ivan fell into a troubled sleep.

At breakfast the next morning, Ivan said to his mother, "I didn't get to finish my chores at Mr. Kerensky's shop yesterday afternoon. He asked if I could come early this morning and finish sweeping before school. I need to leave right away."

"All right, Ivan," she replied. "But finish your breakfast first."

Ivan quickly ate his kasha, grabbed his satchel, and without even saying good-bye, hurried out the door. He knew that Mr. Kerensky always arrived at his shop early and hoped that this day would be no different. Indeed, as he turned the corner, he saw Mr. Kerensky sweeping the sidewalk in front of the shop. Ivan slowed to a walk, then took a deep breath.

"Good morning, Mr. Kerensky," he said.

"Why, good morning to you, Ivan! What brings you into the village so early this morning?"

"Well, yesterday you let me begin my lesson before I had a chance to finish my chores," Ivan said nervously. "I thought I'd better finish them this morning before school."

"That's not necessary, Ivan. I've just about finished sweeping."

"Oh, but I want to," Ivan insisted. "I wouldn't want you to have to do my job."

"Very well then," Mr. Kerensky replied. "Here's the broom."

Ivan hurried inside. He set his satchel near the cupboard, and as he began sweeping, he watched for an opportunity to return the dove unnoticed. When Mr. Kerensky

Photo: National Child Labor Committee.

walked to the front window to hang up his *OPEN* sign, Ivan reached into his satchel, took out the dove, and pulled on the cupboard door. To his shock, it wouldn't open. He pulled again. Still it wouldn't open.

"You'll need the key to unlock it," Mr. Kerensky said. "I always lock it at night. That's where I keep all of my knives. I also keep Sasha's and your carvings there."

Ivan stood horrified. Sasha's dove was in his hand. There was nothing he could do to hide it. He felt like running. He felt like crying. But all he could do was just stare in fear at Mr. Kerensky.

"Hand me the dove," Mr. Kerensky said kindly but firmly as he unlocked the cupboard. Then he replaced the dove on the shelf.

Realizing he could not cover what he had done, Ivan simply said with a trembling voice, "I'm so sorry."

Photo: Wolfgang Sauber.

"Sit down, Ivan," the woodcarver said. "I think I may know what you hoped to gain by taking Sasha's carving, but for now that is not the most important thing. What is important is for you to see and understand what is in your heart."

"But my father never likes the way I do anything," Ivan blurted out defensively. "And everyone likes Sasha better than me, and—"

"Stop!" Mr. Kerensky looked stern for a moment, but then his countenance softened. "I am not asking for excuses. What I want you to do is look at your own heart. You alone are responsible for what is there. Let me ask you a simple question: Was taking Sasha's dove home with you right or wrong?"

After a long silence Ivan admitted, "It was wrong."

"And how do you feel about what you did?"

"I feel bad," Ivan said, looking down at the floor. "And I'm afraid."

"What are you afraid of, Ivan?"

"I'm afraid of what people will think. I'm afraid of the punishment my father will give me. Please don't tell my father, Mr. Kerensky! I'll work much harder cleaning the shop, I'll—"

"Your father will need to know," Mr. Kerensky said kindly. "But I will talk to him. In fact, there is much I need to discuss with him. For now, it's important that you understand what is happening in here." The woodcarver tapped lightly on Ivan's chest. "Ivan, we all have evil thoughts sometimes. We do and say things God did not create us to do or say. And because of the sinful things we do, we experience shame, guilt, fear, anger, and other feelings God never intended for us to have."

Ivan looked up at Mr. Kerensky but said nothing.

"These bad feelings are like a warning bell," Mr. Kerensky continued. "They tell us that something is wrong. But sadly, most people don't really understand that the pain in their hearts is caused by their own sins. Instead, people try to cover up their sins with other sins, and this leads to even more bad feelings."

Ivan knew Mr. Kerensky was right. Already that morning he had lied to his mother about needing to finish his work at the shop before school, and this lie had increased the guilt he was feeling.

After a long silence, Mr. Kerensky reached into the cupboard. He took out Ivan's rough carving and placed it on the table. "Yesterday you said that you didn't think your carving looked like a bird yet," he said. "You said it was crude and ugly."

"It *is* crude and ugly!" Ivan said.

"Ivan, look inside yourself. Look at your own heart. What do you see? Is it something beautiful? Is it filled with peace and joy? Or is it something crude and ugly?"

Ivan looked again at his carving. Then he looked down at the floor. "I don't think my heart is very beautiful," he admitted. "I don't really like how I feel. I don't like feeling angry all the time. And I don't like feeling guilty about the things I've done."

Mr. Kerensky picked up the carving. "Do you think this roughly cut piece of wood can ever become a beautiful bird?" he asked.

"I don't think so," Ivan said, "unless you help me with it."

"Oh, I can help you with this. And if you work on it patiently, one day you will have carved a very beautiful bird."

Ivan allowed himself to smile for the first time since he walked into the shop that morning.

Then Mr. Kerensky asked another question. "Ivan, do you think your heart, which is now like this roughly cut piece of wood, could ever become something beautiful—a heart filled with peace, joy, and love for others, including your father?"

"Maybe. Maybe if I try really hard, and maybe if you help me."

"If you work hard and if I help, you may one day carve a beautiful bird. But neither your hard work nor my help will ever make your heart beautiful."

"Why not?" Ivan asked with puzzled look.

"Because only God can change a heart. Only He can shape our hearts into something beautiful and fill them with peace, joy, and love." Mr. Kerensky looked at the old clock on the wall, then he placed his hand on Ivan's shoulder. "It's almost time for school to begin. You'd better hurry, or you'll be late."

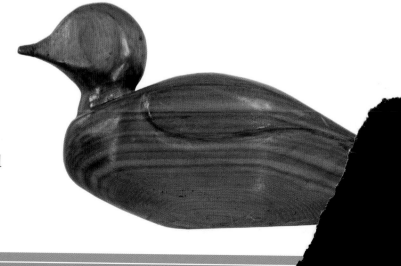

As Ivan stood to go, he asked, "May I still work in your shop, Mr. Kerensky? Will you still teach me how to carve?"

"Certainly! There's much I want to teach you about creating something beautiful out of a rough old block of wood. But more importantly, Ivan, I think there's much God wants to teach us both about what He wants to create out of our rough old hearts."

"Even *my* heart, Mr. Kerensky?" Ivan asked.

"Yes, even your heart," the old woodcarver replied with a reassuring smile.

THINK ABOUT IT

» How would you describe Ivan's relationship with his father? How does he respond to his father's criticism?

» Why does Ivan take Sasha's bird carving and pretend that it's his? How long does Ivan enjoy his father's compliment? Why?

» What do you think is beginning to happen in Ivan's heart and life? Why?

WORDS YOU NEED TO KNOW

» **Transform:** To change completely
» **Renew:** To make new again
» **Meditation:** Thinking deeply about God and His Word

HIDE IT IN YOUR HEART

Finally, brothers, whatever is true, whatever is noble, whatever is right, whatever is pure, whatever is lovely, whatever is admirable—if anything is excellent or praiseworthy—think about such things. (Philippians 4:8)

...ous for nothing, but in everything by prayer and supplication, with thanksgiving, let ...ests be made known to God; and the peace of God, which surpasses all understand- ...uard your hearts and minds through Christ Jesus. (Philippians 4:6–7, NKJV)

Photo: Dean Franklin.

MOUNT RUSHMORE

One of the world's most famous sculptures, Mount Rushmore National Memorial is located amid the majestic beauty of the Black Hills of South Dakota. The mountain into which the monument is carved was known to the Lakota Sioux as Six Grandfathers but was later renamed for Charles Rushmore, a prominent New York lawyer who visited the spot in 1885. Joining Rushmore on the expedition was David Swanzey, whose wife, Carrie, was the younger sister of author Laura Ingalls Wilder.

In 1923, an American historian proposed the idea for a massive sculpture that would bring tourists to South Dakota, and in 1927 sculptor Gutzon Borglum began work. Borglum was born the son of Danish immigrants in Idaho, where his father worked as a woodcarver. As a young man, Borglum studied art in Paris where he became friends with the great French sculptor Auguste Rodin, who carved *The Thinker*.

Borglum was fascinated with the idea of making art on a gigantic scale that would stir the heart and portray themes of heroic patriotism. Upon seeing the Mount Rushmore site for the first time, he declared, "America will march along that skyline." Between 1927 and 1941, Borglum and 400 workers sculpted sixty-foot carvings of the nation's greatest leaders—George Washington, Thomas Jefferson, Abraham Lincoln, and Theodore Roosevelt—to represent the birth, growth, development, and preservation of the United States.

Borglum died before the colossal project could be completed, but his son Lincoln Borglum continued the work. Originally, it was planned that the figures would be carved from head to waist, but insufficient funding forced the younger Borglum to abandon the project once the heads were completed. In the decades since, the monument has grown in fame as a symbol of America. Today, nearly three million people from around the world visit Mount Rushmore each year.

IMAGINE THAT

We usually think of the imagination as an amazing place where fire-breathing dragons stand guard over sleeping princesses and giants eat meatballs the size of houses. But the imagination is much more than simple make-believe. It's a place of boundless creativity, a place where dreams come true. People's imaginations have given the world the Eiffel Tower, Van Gogh's "Starry Night," *The Wizard of Oz*, and "America the Beautiful." And the wondrous thing about imagination is that everyone has one! You use your imagination every time you sit down to draw a picture, write a letter, or solve a puzzle.

The Eiffel Tower. Photo: Tognopop.

The poet Carl Sandburg said, "Nothing happens unless first we dream," and he was right. The truth is, you cannot accomplish *anything* without first imagining it, whether it's climbing a tree or winning an Olympic medal. Think about it. For the briefest of moments before you make yourself a sandwich, you imagine yourself reaching for the peanut butter and jelly and bread. You imagine yourself wearing the blue or the green shirt, and then you get dressed for the day. You imagine the words you might say to a friend, and then in the next instant you say them. (And you can never call the words back, so think carefully before opening your mouth to speak.)

Television advertisers are quite clever in appealing to the imagination. A recent car commercial shows a man getting ready to cross the street when a great-looking new automobile passes in front of him and he's startled to see himself behind the wheel. Advertisers know that if they can get viewers to imagine themselves driving a new car, it won't be long before they begin thinking they need that car.

In our story "The Wooden Bird," Ivan was jealous of Sasha's gift for woodcarving. Ivan spent his time thinking about what he *didn't* have—his father's praise, Sasha's talent—so instead of being thankful and kind and working hard to develop his own skill, Ivan bullied the kids at school and stole Sasha's carving. You see, Ivan's trouble did not begin when he lied to his father about who carved the bird; the problem started when he imagined what life would be like if the bird were his.

You might ask why God should care about our thoughts and actions that don't harm other people. After all, no one was hurt when Ivan took the bird, right? But someone *was* injured. Remember how Ivan lay awake worrying and feeling guilty after he lied to his father? Think of how sad Mr. Kerensky must have felt when he discovered that Ivan had taken something from his store without asking. And how will Ivan's parents feel when they learn what he has done? The truth is, our actions *do* affect other people, and the things we choose to think about determine our actions.

How Are You Feeding Your Mind?

"Garbage in, garbage out" is a computer programming term meaning if you input faulty data, your results will also be faulty. Even the most powerful computer can only work with the information it's been given, so if the information it receives is wrong—if, for example, the programmer tells the computer that 1 + 1 = 3—the computer will be incapable of correctly doing even the simplest math. The term has also been used to describe the consequences of unhealthy eating habits: If you eat a lot of junk food ("garbage in") then you will experience low energy and poor health ("garbage out").

Photo: Daniel Martini.

You are wired very much like a highly complex and sophisticated computer. Your mind is the hard drive where you store the information you gather each day through your experiences, your emotions, and your physical senses. And like a computer, what you put into your mind is what you will get out of it. If you study the dictionary eight hours a day, chances are you'll become a top-notch speller and develop a tremendous vocabulary. If you provide your mind with a steady supply of God's Word, then you will know the truth, you will recognize truth when you hear it, and you will speak truth to others. However, if you feed your mind with a steady stream of "junk food"—TV shows, movies, books, blogs, magazines, music, and video games that glorify unbiblical attitudes while telling half-truths or outright lies—then your mind will soon become a lazy jumble of confused thoughts and conflicting emotions. Eventually, those same unbiblical attitudes and half-truths will find their way into your own words and actions.

The things you choose to watch, read, listen to, and think about will definitely influence your behavior and the kind of character you exhibit to others. Remember, everything you do or say, good or bad, great or small, begins in your thoughts. Jesus made it perfectly clear that sin begins in our hearts and minds:

"All these evil things begin inside a person, in his mind: evil thoughts, sexual sins, stealing, murder, adultery, selfishness, doing bad things to other people, lying, doing sinful things, jealousy, saying bad things about people, pride, and foolish living" (Mark 7:21–22, ICB).

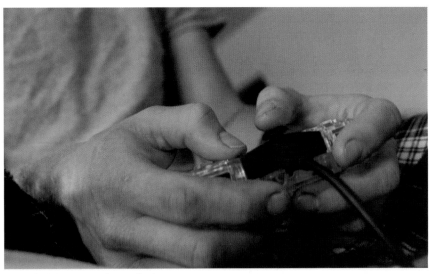

Photo: flickr.com user RebeccaPollard.

If we fill our minds with words and images of fear, envy, greed, hate, anger, violence, or foolishness, then our thoughts will return to these things time and again until we become fearful, envious, greedy, hateful, angry, violent, or foolish people. "For out of the overflow of the heart the mouth speaks," Jesus said. "The good man brings good things out of the good stored up in him, and the evil man brings evil things out of the evil stored up in him" (Matthew 12:34–35). Unhealthy input will corrupt anyone's mind.

Perhaps you remember a song from Sunday school that goes, "Oh, be careful, little eyes, what you see." Other verses begin, "Be careful, little ears, what you hear" and "Be careful, little feet, where you go." It's a simple song with a very big message: Be careful what you allow to enter your mind, and therefore your heart, because evil leads to more evil and the wages of sin is death (Romans 6:23). Proverbs 4:23 says, "Above all else, guard your heart, for it is the wellspring of life." Another translation reads, "Be careful what you think, because your thoughts run your life" (NCV).

So what shows do *you* like to watch? What kinds of games do you play? Which sites do you visit on the Internet? What books do you read? What do you talk about with your friends? What are your friends watching and listening to? As you know, your enemy the devil prowls around like a roaring lion looking for someone to devour (1 Peter 5:8), and he will use anything he can—including friends—to make an evil thought seem harmless or even good.

MAKE A NOTE OF IT

Think of a time recently when you saw a movie (or read a book or heard a song) that made you feel uncomfortable. What was it that bothered you about it? Did the program (or book or song) use inappropriate language or imagery? Did the writer express some truths that made you uncomfortable? Or did the writer present ideas that you knew were not true according to God's Word? Are you more likely to seek out or avoid other works by the same artist?

THE SCREWTAPE LETTERS

Have you ever wondered what the devil thinks about you? *The Screwtape Letters* by C. S. Lewis is a fictional story told through a series of letters from a senior demon, Screwtape, to his nephew, an inexperienced tempter named Wormwood. The younger demon has been assigned to a man they call "the Patient" who has just become a Christian. Through his letters, Screwtape teaches Wormwood how to lead the Patient astray with confusing thoughts, with the goals of weakening the man's faith and encouraging him to sin.

Sometimes we think of the devil as going about trying to trick us into committing huge and terrible sins. Yet Screwtape teaches his nephew that "the safest path to hell is the gradual one." For example, when the Patient is tempted to forgive someone who has hurt him, Wormwood is instructed to point out to the man how the other person is dressed or how he speaks, so that the Patient instead becomes distracted thinking how different and strange that person is.

By describing everyday life, with all its simple temptations and human mistakes, through the eyes of a demon, C. S. Lewis exposes the schemes of the devil and shows us how we can easily become angry or frustrated and fall into sin when we don't stop to think about everything we see or say or do in the light of God's truth.

Statue of C.S. Lewis in Belfast, Ireland.
Photo: flickr.com user Genvessel.

Though Lewis said it was a distasteful book to write, *The Screwtape Letters* became one of his most popular books and a classic of Christian literature. Lewis dedicated the book to his good friend J. R. R. Tolkein, a fellow teacher at Oxford University in England and author of *The Lord of the Rings*.

SIX THINGS TO THINK ABOUT EVERY DAY

The apostle Paul said, "Don't copy the behavior and customs of this world, but let God transform you into a new person by changing the way you think" (Romans 12:2, NLT). The New King James Version reads, "Be transformed by the renewing of your mind." To be **transformed** is to be changed completely. Transformed people live differently, talk differently, and spend their time doing different things. Most importantly, they *think* differently.

The Bible says that when we become followers of Christ, we are transformed into something entirely new (2 Corinthians 5:17). We no longer carry the burdens of sin and worry that infect the world around us. We are brand-new creations, and we must leave behind our old ways of doing things. We must allow God to **renew** our minds by changing the way we think, as well as changing the things we think about.

In his letter to the church in Philippi, Paul identified six things Christians should spend their time thinking about: "Finally, brothers, whatever is true, whatever is noble, whatever is right, whatever is pure, whatever is lovely, whatever is admirable—if anything is excellent or praiseworthy—think about such things" (Philippians 4:8). Let's take a brief look at each of these.

THINK ABOUT WHATEVER IS TRUE

We are to spend our time thinking about what is true—that is, ideas that are factual, real, and reliable. One way we can learn and think about what is true is by reading and listening to others who claim to know the truth. Parents, pastors, teachers, doctors, scientists, authors, poets, philosophers, and others tell us many things that are true. But we must be careful. We must not be deceived by sheer size or scope—a well-written four-panel comic strip can offer the kind of insight and wisdom found in the average 900-page novel. And remember, not everything you read or hear will be true.

So how can you know for sure whether something is true? Go straight to the source of *all* truth. God is our Rock, and everything He says is absolutely true (Psalm 119:160). Compare everything you see and hear to the truth found in God's Word. Read your Bible every day, and you will be prepared to separate the truth from the lies and half-truths. Commit yourself to memorizing Bible passages. Store them away in your mind and heart, and His Word will keep you from sin (Psalm 119:11), protect you from false teaching (2 Timothy 3:13–15), fill your heart with joy (Jeremiah 15:16) and peace (Psalm 85:8), provide you power in prayer (John 15:7), and prepare you to do good (2 Timothy 3:16–17). When you spend your time taking "righteousness in," your life and character will produce "righteousness out."

THINK ABOUT WHATEVER IS NOBLE

Sir Thomas Malory was a knight and a member of the English parliament. Shortly before his death in 1471, Malory wrote *Le Morte d'Arthur* ("The Death of Arthur"), a collection of English and French stories about the legendary King Arthur and his Knights of the Round Table.

King Arthur and the Knights of the Round Table.

Published in 1485, *Le Morte d'Arthur* would become an enduring classic and help define the ideals of chivalry, the code of behavior of the medieval knight. Malory's book also gave rise to the popular perception of the knight as a noble warrior sworn to uphold the values of faith, loyalty, courage, and honor.

Something that is noble displays outstanding character, high ideals, or godly behavior and is worthy of respect. Remember, the way you think will determine your character and behavior. The Bible says, "For as [a person] thinks in his heart, so is he"(Proverbs 23:7, NKJV). If you want to become a person of excellent character, someone who is faithful and courageous and honorable, then you should seek out people and books and art that reflect God's moral standards and truths and think about these things.

A role model is a person who sets an example of behavior that is imitated by others. A wide range of media role models has impacted young people in our society. Some have set an example that is noble, good, and helpful; others have behaved in ways that are immoral, dangerous, and harmful. The Bible tells us that "bad company corrupts good character" (1 Corinthians 15:33), yet sometimes we're not careful about whom we "hang" with or follow. "Walk with the wise and become wise; associate with fools and get in trouble" (Proverbs 13:20, NLT).

Whom do you look up to? Whose behavior will you choose to imitate? When seeking an appropriate role model, the best place to start is in your own family and among people in your church. Watch for people whom others turn to for advice and spiritual guidance. Does this person live to serve others? Is he or she regularly leading people to faith in Jesus? Look for men and women who are Christlike in their attitudes and actions and do as they do.

THINK ABOUT WHATEVER IS RIGHT

The book of Judges speaks of a time, before there was a king in Israel, when "everyone did what was right in his own eyes" (Judges 17:6, NKJV). But when Paul told us to think about whatever is right, he did not mean whatever is right in our own eyes or what the world thinks is right. He was telling us to focus on what is right in the eyes of God.

We live in a world that suffers still from the effects of the Fall, when Adam and Eve chose to do what was right in their own eyes. Sin has ravaged our planet, and we see the wreckage everywhere we look—yes, in war-torn lands and quake-damaged cities, but also in broken homes and broken lives. And yet, as we sort through the rubble, as we open our hearts to those who are hurting and show them the compassion of Christ, as we do what is right in God's eyes, we will find treasures of truth and beauty and faith and courage in unexpected places. For although it is fallen, this is still our Father's world.

San Francisco after the 1906 earthquake.

THINK ABOUT WHATEVER IS PURE

The word *pure* refers to something clean, chaste, and holy. Our thoughts are to dwell on what is pure and not defiled by sin and corruption. In fact, our lives are to contain "not even a hint" of impurity (Ephesians 5:3). If you have become a follower of Christ, you are a new person (2 Corinthians 5:17) and the Holy Spirit lives inside you; therefore, you must leave behind your old sinful nature and selfish desires and turn your thoughts toward the things of God:

> *Those who are dominated by the sinful nature think about sinful things, but those who are controlled by the Holy Spirit think about things that please the Spirit.* (Romans 8:5, NLT)

Paul goes on to say in this passage, "Those who are still under the control of their sinful nature can never please God" (v. 8). It's difficult in this life to completely avoid unclean ideas and images. A change of the channel, a new song on the radio, or the turning of a page in a magazine can bring us face to face with a violent or suggestive image or lyric. When this happens, do you immediately turn away? Or do you linger there and allow yourself to wonder what you're missing? You may have heard someone say, "Get your mind out of the gutter." If you linger in the gutter, don't be surprised when your mind is

> *One should, each day, try to hear a little song, read a good poem, see a fine picture, and if it is possible, speak a few reasonable words.*
> **Johann Wolfgang von Goethe**
> 1748–1832

covered with filth and slime.

What happens if you do have a sinful thought? Don't let it run wild. Confess it to the Lord. "Capture" it and "make it give up and obey Christ" (2 Corinthians 10:5, NCV). If you hold on to an ugly or unhealthy thought, if you allow it to hang around in a dark corner of your mind, sooner or later it will cause you to sin.

The Inspiration of Saint Matthew by Caravaggio.

THINK ABOUT WHATEVER IS LOVELY

Something that is lovely may be physically attractive, or it may be beautiful in spirit or deed. We are talking about something that delights the senses or engages the mind or gratifies the heart while pleasing the spirit. A painting by Caravaggio or an oratorio by Handel can be lovely, as can a breathtaking sunset or a refreshing sea breeze. A mother's touch, a friend's smile, a kind gesture—these can be lovely too.

Loveliness suggests an endearing quality, one that you will recall fondly in the days to come. And when you spend your time thinking about loveable and attractive things, others will begin to think of you as loveable and attractive as well. People who set their minds on what is beautiful tend to say and do beautiful things, and they make the world a more beautiful place.

THINK ABOUT WHATEVER IS ADMIRABLE

In Philippians 4:8, the apostle Paul defines "whatever is admirable" as something that displays excellence or is worthy of praise. When you go to the library, do you seek out great stories and novels that have stood the test of time, or do you check out the latest teen vampire romance? Do you enjoy classic films with award-winning performances and witty dialogue, or do you prefer modern special-effects extravaganzas with crude language and little or no thought given to story or characterization?

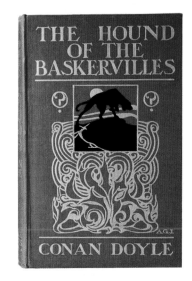

Before you sit down to read a book, watch a television show, or listen to a CD, think about whether it is going to be worth your time and contemplation. Will this music build your mind and lift your spirit? Does the show's content reflect godly virtues and biblical truths? Have people you know and trust recommended this book to you? Have godly reviewers given the movie high marks? Don't settle for the world's cheap imitations of creative excellence. Hold yourself, your time, and your entertainment to a higher standard.

DON'T DWELL ON THE NEGATIVE

Proverbs 16:24 (NCV) says, "Pleasant words are like a honeycomb, making people happy and healthy." Have you ever noticed how much fun it is to be around people who keep a naturally positive attitude? They always seem genuinely pleased to see you. A negative or faithless word never crosses their lips. And no matter how bad the weather, no matter how difficult their circumstances, they are happy, content in the knowledge that they are children of the Most High God.

Jesus once said, "The mouth speaks the things that are in the heart" (Matthew 12:34, ICB). Have you ever stopped to listen to yourself? Would your family and friends say you're usually pleasant to be around? Do you like to talk about the good things that happened during your day, or do you focus on the bad things that happened? Do you look for the good in others, or do you tend to point out their mistakes and weaknesses? You probably spend more time focusing on the negative than you'd care to admit. Why is that?

Do you spend hours on the phone, listening to your friends complain about their parents or gossiping about other friends? So many young Christians fall into the trap of thinking they can lift up a friend who spends much of his or her time wallowing in a pit of despair. All too often they instead end up being dragged down by the friend's negative outlook or disrespectful attitudes.

Do you spend your time looking at magazines or watching TV shows that make you feel as though you should be something you're not—thinner? prettier? smarter? taller? stronger? wealthier? more popular? It's easy to become dissatisfied with yourself and your circumstances when you constantly compare yourself to others.

When it's time to do your math homework or clean your room, do you start by thinking negatively? *I can't do this. It's too hard.* Henry Ford, the great inventor and automobile pioneer, said, "If you think you can do a thing, or think you *can't* do a thing, you're right."

Someone once said, "Every thought is a seed. If you plant crab apples, don't count on harvesting Golden Delicious." If you think you cannot, you probably will not. If you expect defeat, you will likely lose. If you focus on how you are misunderstood, you will soon become angry and bitter. If you think angry thoughts, angry words are sure to follow. And unpleasant words will only lead to more unhealthy thoughts. Remember, what you put into your mind must eventually come out. Sooner or later, what you choose to think about is what you will become.

Photo: Bresson Thomas.

WHAT IS BIBLICAL MEDITATION?

Let's look one more time at Philippians 4:8. Paul says, "Finally, brothers, whatever is true, whatever is noble, whatever is right, whatever is pure, whatever is lovely, whatever is admirable—if anything is excellent or praiseworthy—think about such things." Where can you

find each of these things in abundance? In God's Word, of course! If you want God's best for your life, then start with good thoughts—God's thoughts, to be exact. And God's thoughts are found in the Bible.

After God gave His commandments to His people, He said, "Do not let this Book of the Law depart from your mouth; meditate on it day and night, so that you may be careful to do everything written in it. Then you will be prosperous and successful" (Joshua 1:8). Psalm 119:147–148 says, "I have put my hope in your word. My eyes stay open through the watches of the night, that I may meditate on your promises." When Paul gives instruction to Timothy, he writes, "Meditate on these things" (1 Timothy 4:15, NKJV).

Today, when we hear the word "meditation," we tend to think of a long-haired guru or a bald monk sitting in the lotus position, with his legs folded like a pretzel, touching his thumbs and forefingers together and chanting, "Ommmmmmmmmmm." But that's not what the Bible is talking about when it says, "May the words of my mouth and the meditation of my heart be pleasing in your sight, O Lord, my Rock and my Redeemer" (Psalm 19:14).

Biblical **meditation** is simply a mental exercise in which you focus your thoughts on a passage from God's Word. Meditating involves quietly pondering, or thinking deeply about, the passage to better understand its meaning and how it applies to your life. In Eastern religions, such as Buddhism and Hinduism, meditation is about emptying the mind of all thoughts; but biblical mediation is about emptying your mind of selfish and sinful thoughts in order to *fill* your mind with what is right and true according to God's Word.

Oswald Chambers said, "To think is an effort; to think rightly is a great effort; and to think as a Christian ought to think is the greatest effort of a human soul." He was right. If you're going to learn to think in a way that pleases the Holy Spirit, if you're going to keep your mind clean by stomping out the world's lies and negative messages, that's going to require some effort on your part.

First of all, you need to eliminate distractions. You need to eat properly and get a good night's sleep so that your body isn't nagging at you. Then you need to turn off your TV, computer, radio, cell phone, and anything else that cries out for your attention. Go someplace quiet where you will not be disturbed—your bedroom, a closet, a tree, an open field. Take only your Bible and a notebook or journal for writing down any helpful insights you may receive. You may also want to take a dictionary to look up the meaning of any words you're unsure of.

There is no one right way to meditate on God's Word. The important thing to remember is to slow down, focus, and listen carefully. The Bible has something important to tell

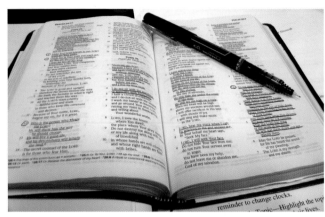

you, if you will have the wisdom to hear it. Select one or two verses—the book of Psalms is a great place to start. Pray and thank God for His Word. Ask Him to show you His thoughts in a new way, then let His words speak to you as if you had never read them before. Be still, be patient, and listen. Imagine yourself sitting with the earthly writer of those words and having him speak them to you personally. What is God saying about Himself in this passage? What is He saying about you? Is God showing you something you need to do, or something you ought to stop doing?

Photo: DrGBB.

How long should you meditate? A good rule of thumb is to start by meditating one minute for every year of your age. As you get more practice, you will find yourself able—and wanting—to spend a longer time thinking deeply about the Word.

Afterward, in your notebook, write out the passage you've meditated on. Now write it again, this time using your own words. Then write down anything you heard God saying to your heart during your meditation and believe it. Pray and talk with God about what you learned. Then, if He has shown you something you need to do, do not put it off. Go and do it. After all, it's no use spending time with God's Word if all you do is then go away and forget about it (James 1:22–25).

At bedtime, just before you go to sleep, take a few moments to think again about the passage you meditated on earlier. This is an excellent way to end each day, because God's Word will watch over you and guard your heart even in your sleep (Proverbs 6:22).

> *God speaks in the silence of the heart.*
> **Mother Teresa**
> 1910–1997

WHAT SHOULD I DO?

Just before the verse in which Paul lists the things Christians should think about, he gives us a command and a promise:

> *Do not worry about anything, but pray and ask God for everything you need, always giving thanks. And God's peace, which is so great we cannot understand it, will keep your hearts and minds in Christ Jesus.* (Philippians 4:6–7, NCV)

Mamertine prison in Rome. According to tradition, Paul and Peter were both held here before being executed. Paul's words in Philippians 4:6–7 should be a powerful encouragement to us when we consider the circumstances in which he often found himself. Photo: Chris 73.

If you fill your head with thoughts of fear and worry and anger, you will live in constant turmoil, with an anxious mind and a troubled heart. But if you pray and ask God for all you need, He will provide. And if you keep your heart full of joy and gratitude, always giving thanks for everything you receive, you will walk in the peace of Jesus Christ Himself (John 14:27).

A PRAYER

Dear God, thank you for making me in your image. Thank you for giving me a mind so I can know your beautiful words and precious thoughts. Renew my mind by changing the way I think. Help me to think only about things that are true, noble, right, pure, lovely, and admirable. Help me to hide your Word in my heart and meditate on it day and night. Help me to be anxious for nothing and give me your peace. I ask this in the name of Jesus. Amen.

Photo: NASA.

WORLDVIEWS IN FOCUS
MEET KIET

Kiet is a twelve-year-old boy who lives in Thailand. Kiet (pronounced KYET) lives with his father and mother, his younger sister Mali, and his grandmother in the city of Chiang Mai, in the mountains of northern Thailand. Kiet's real name is Khemkhaeng, which means "strength," but his parents and friends all call him Kiet. In Thailand almost everyone has a nickname.

Kiet's mother and her family have lived in Chiang Mai (pronounced CHYENG-MY) all their lives and are descended from the hill tribes that come from this area. Kiet's father came here from Bangkok, the capital of Thailand, to find work after his term of service in the Thai army. Now he holds a government job helping to oversee the affairs of the Chiang Mai province. He is very busy, leaving before sunrise each morning and getting back after dark.

Kiet wakes up around six o'clock each morning and washes last night's dishes in the sink while his mother makes a quick breakfast. Kiet likes omelets best, but this morning his mother is warming up rice porridge left over from yesterday. She has to hurry off to her job at a local factory, so she dishes up some porridge for herself and Kiet, then leaves the rest to keep warm on the stove. When three-year-old Mali wakes up in a few hours, Kiet's grandmother will feed her.

Kiet likes having his grandmother live with them. Because of his mother's job, Kiet often sees more of his grandmother than he does his mother. He appreciates, though, that his mother works so hard for all of them. Kiet's father also works hard and is very stern, and sometimes Kiet doesn't know whether his father is proud of him. However, Kiet tries to make decisions that will make his father proud, because in Thailand, respect for elders is very important. Young people are expected to show honor to

their parents and grandparents. One of the ways Kiet shows respect is the *wai*, or greeting. When he first sees his mother or grandmother in the morning, or when his father comes home at night, Kiet will bow, pressing his hands together as if for prayer. Kiet also tries to do his chores well to honor his parents for all their hard work providing for him.

After breakfast and chores, Kiet gets dressed in his school uniform. He

Buddhist amulets called *phras*. Photo: Mattes.

is especially careful to wear the amulet, or protective charm, his grandfather gave him. The amulet shows a picture of Buddha, a man seated cross-legged, and hangs from a cord Kiet wears around his neck. Before he puts it on, he folds the amulet in his hands and bows to show honor to Buddha. Kiet believes that wearing the amulet will protect him from harm. In Thailand, about ninety-five percent of the people are Buddhists, which means they follow the teachings of the man they call Buddha.

Kiet has heard stories about Buddha all of his life. Buddha's real name was Siddhartha Gautama, and he lived about 2,500 years ago in the country of India. According to legend, his father was a wealthy ruler, and Siddhartha grew up in a sheltered environment of wealth and comfort. When he was twenty-nine years old, he left his family and went in search of

the meaning of life. He believed he could find truth by denying himself all the comforts he once enjoyed as a prince. At the age of thirty-five, Siddhartha ended his wanderings. Physically weak from a long fast, he ate a bowl of rice and sat down beneath a fig tree to meditate until he either found the truth about life or died of starvation. Buddhist tradition says that during these hours of intense meditation Siddhartha finally became *enlightened* about the

A mural from a Buddhist temple showing the Buddha just before attaining enlightenment.

true nature of the universe. From this time on, he was called Buddha, which means "awakened one" or "enlightened one."

After this experience, Buddha began to gather followers and taught them the Four Noble Truths, his philosophy of the meaning of life. The first truth Buddha taught was that to live is to suffer. Second, he said that people's suffering is caused by "craving," or being attached to worldly things. Third, he said that to stop suffering, people have to stop desiring worldly things. Finally, he said that the best way for people to stop this craving is to follow a special set of rules, which he called the Eightfold Path.

Buddha's rules for living include such things as do not tell lies or gossip; act only in ways that will not harm other living things, even insects; avoid all evil thoughts, words, and deeds; and meditate in order to fully understand the nature and meaning of life. For Buddhists, meditation involves sitting quietly, usually in a cross-legged posture called the lotus, and focusing on breathing while emptying their thoughts. Although his school sets aside a time each day for meditation, Kiet still has trouble concentrating and tends to let his mind wander.

Kiet's father believes very strongly in Buddha's teachings. He says that if he had not been conscripted into the army, he would have become a monk and spent his life studying Buddha's teachings. Kiet's mother prefers the practical side of Buddhism to the intellectual side. She keeps a statue of Buddha in a small living room shrine. She prays to it twice a day, lighting incense and candles and leaving offerings of fresh fruit, rice, and flowers. Buddhists believe that statues of Buddha are

Home shrine. Photo: Shelley Mannion.

spiritually connected to him and so have supernatural qualities.

Dressed in his school uniform of white shirt and khaki shorts, amulet around his neck, Kiet gathers his books and leaves for class. Although motorbikes are the preferred form of transportation in Chiang Mai, Kiet rides to school each day on a *songthaew*, a small two-row bus made out of a pickup truck. The bus is usually crowded, but Kiet likes to stand on the back platform and hang on tightly as it zips in and out of traffic.

School starts exactly at eight o'clock, and everyone must be present for the national anthem and the raising of the Thai flag. Like all students, Kiet removes his shoes before entering

The inside of a songthaew. Photo: Henry Flower.

the school building. In addition to science, math, and the Thai language, Kiet also takes a class in English. Many residents of Chiang Mai have learned to speak English, in part because tourism is very important to the local economy. Kiet is also expected to participate in Boy Scouts at school so he can learn how to be a good citizen, and he wears his scouting uniform to school once a week. After classes end at 3:15, Kiet remains at school for a required "home-work" session. Afterward, he goes to basketball practice, then takes the bus home.

Today is Friday, and although Kiet must return to school tomorrow morning to take a computer class, he doesn't mind. He loves working with computers. He still has Saturday afternoon and all day Sunday for his favorite activities. Because Buddhists worship every day at their home shrines or in temples, they don't gather together for worship on a certain day of the week like many other religions do. Sometimes Kiet just stays home and watches TV or reads comic books. Other times he will go out with his mother and sister to fly kites or walk around town with friends.

However, his happiest times are when his father works with him on his Muay Thai boxing skills. Muay Thai is the national sport of Thailand, and Kiet loves training and learning new moves. His father learned the martial arts technique when he was in the army. Although Muay Thai requires self-discipline and control, Kiet and his father always look forward to this special time together on the weekends.

Muay Thai. Photo: flickr.com user Willy_G91.

Kiet likes living in the city because there is always something happening there. Chiang Mai is the second-largest city in Thailand, so there are always many tourists visiting from around the world. Although there are many modern shopping centers in Chiang Mai, the city

Chiang Mai. Photo: Thaimissions2006.

is famous for its Night Bazaar. The bazaar covers several city blocks, with stalls set up to sell everything from clothing and jewelry to televisions, CDs, and DVDs. Kiet's favorite part of the bazaar is bargaining for a good price. Sellers *expect* buyers to argue about prices, and Kiet has become a master haggler from watching his grandmother at the market! Many vendors are superstitious and believe it is bad luck not to complete a sale, so Kiet has learned that if he simply walks away from a negotiation, the seller will often chase him down and agree to his offered price.

Chiang Mai also has open-air markets where delicious food is sold by street vendors. On weekends, Kiet's mother rarely cooks. Instead, the family buys their meals from the street vendors that seem to pop up wherever there is a crowd. Sometimes they buy fresh chopped fruit, kept cool in the hot Thailand sun by big blocks of ice. Other times they decide on steaming, grilled sausages or a spicy Thai salad made with papaya, shrimp, green beans, and peanuts, tossed together in a lime-and-chili sauce. Soft drinks are sold by the bottle, each one paired with its own bag of crushed ice to keep it cold. Kiet's favorite is Coke.

Chiang Mai is also home to one of the grandest temples in all of Thailand. A very beautiful golden statue of Buddha is kept there, and soon, during the *Songkran* festival, the statue will be paraded through the streets of

Wat Phra Singh in Chiang Mai. Photo: CenkX.

Chiang Mai. Songkran, or Thai New Year, is Kiet's favorite holiday. For three days during the hottest part of the year (April), the Thai people relax, visit relatives, eat good food, and honor

People celebrating Songkran. Photo: Love Krittaya.

their ancestors. It is a time to wash everything and everyone clean—literally! For a week before the festival, Kiet's mother cleans the house from top to bottom. In the city, people stand on street corners with hoses, buckets of water, and even squirt guns and do their best to get passersby wet. No other city in the world celebrates Songkran quite like Chiang Mai!

During the festival, Kiet and his family make sure to visit the temple. Each person brings a handful of sand to the temple grounds to replace the dirt they have carried away on their feet the rest of the year. The family also brings food to give to the Buddhist monks who live on the temple grounds. They believe this act of kindness will earn the family merit and bring them extra blessings in the coming year.

The Thai form of Buddhism teaches that everything in the universe is connected, so everything a person does, good or bad, has natural consequences, like ripples when a stone is tossed into a pond. This is called the law of *karma*. In each life, a person is punished or rewarded based on his past actions during this life as well as earlier lives. Buddhists believe that after death they are reincarnated, or reborn, again and again. Each person is said to be reborn as someone else of greater or lower birth, based on the good things or bad things done in a previous life. If a person does not do enough good things in this present life, he or she may even be reincarnated as an animal! Buddha said that the only way to escape from this cycle of a life of suffering is to follow his rules, being kind to all living things and not wanting or desiring anything. Once a person has finally reached the place where all desires, needs, and ignorance are extinguished—like blowing out a candle—this is called *nirvana*. Nirvana is very difficult to reach, and Kiet's father worries that he hasn't done

enough good things or gained enough merit to achieve nirvana and escape from the cycle of rebirth, especially since he has never served as a monk.

Last week, Kiet saw his cousin Yai became a monk. Yai is almost twenty, the ideal age for ordination. Most young Thai men serve as monks for a period of time before they begin a career and get married. Yai decided to follow tradition and become a monk so that he could earn merit for himself and his parents. Having a son or brother who is a monk gives a person a great deal of merit.

The first part of Yai's ordination ceremony was held at the local temple. Yai and his parents lit incense to honor their ancestors and to tell them that Yai was going to become a monk. Then Yai carefully washed the feet of all his elders as a sign of respect and to beg forgiveness for any bad things he had done to them. Then it was time for his head and eyebrows to be shaved. Kiet got to hold the lotus leaf that collected all the hair. He tried not to laugh at the sight of Yai's bald head! After all, this was a very serious occasion. After Yai had been shaved and washed clean, he put on white robes and rode through the city to show the spirits that he was becoming a monk.

The second part of the ceremony took place the following day. Yai's friends and family made up a large procession, complete with dancers and a band, that followed Yai as he walked to the Buddhist temple. After circling the shrine three times, Yai knelt and prayed. Then he threw a handful of coins over his shoulder to show that he was giving up worldly possessions. These coins are considered very lucky, and Kiet was able to grab one! Kiet hopes that he won't be away too long, as Yai is his favorite cousin.

Although Kiet follows the Buddhist traditions, he doesn't worry too much about the future—except when it includes a math test or English essay! He doesn't spend a lot of time thinking about personal enlightenment or nirvana. Yet he tries every day to gain a little wisdom and earn merit. He figures one day he will probably become a monk himself and then learn the real importance of the Four Noble Truths and Buddha's Eightfold Path. For now, Kiet just likes playing basketball with his friends, helping his grandmother around the house, and learning Muay Thai with his father.

Buddhist monk at a temple. Photo: Tevaprapas Makklay.

WHAT'S THE DIFFERENCE?

- How is the way Kiet lives different from the way you live? How are your lives similar?

- Kiet wears an amulet which he believes protects him from harm. As Christians, what do we believe protects us from harm?

- How is Buddhist meditation different from the kind of meditation the Bible teaches?

- Why do you think Kiet's family is so careful to follow Buddhist traditions? What does the Bible teach about "earning" your way to heaven?

- How is the Buddhist concept of reincarnation different from what the Bible teaches about life and death?

- The Buddhist religion is unusual in that Buddhists do not worship a god as most other religions do. How does this differ from the biblical Christian view of God?

CAN YOU TRUST YOUR FEELINGS?

> WHY ARE YOU DOWNCAST, O MY SOUL? WHY SO DISTURBED WITHIN ME? PUT YOUR HOPE IN GOD, FOR I WILL YET PRAISE HIM, MY SAVIOR AND MY GOD.

PSALM 43:5

THE BIG IDEA

On March 2, 1933, when the movies were still young, producer Merian C. Cooper unleashed a beast upon New York City. That day, audiences at the Radio City Music Hall caught their first glimpse of *King Kong*. Inspired by the African explorers he read about as a boy and his own adult experiences as a maker of wildlife documentaries, Cooper had enlisted special effects wizard Willis O'Brien to bring to life the giant ape Kong, the Eighth Wonder of the World.

The story begins with a larger-than-life filmmaker leading a ship and its crew to an uncharted island in the Indian Ocean. Spurred by rumors of a giant gorilla worshiped by natives, the filmmaker is determined to capture footage of the mythic beast for his new movie. But disaster strikes when the natives kidnap his lead actress and offer her as a sacrifice to Kong. The monster appears and carries the young woman to his mountainside lair where, to her surprise, he protects her from attack by dinosaurs and other giant creatures. One of the ship's crew manages to rescue the girl, and an enraged Kong pursues them through the jungle. Kong destroys the native village before the resourceful filmmaker subdues the giant ape using gas bombs.

Kong is taken to New York and put on exhibition, but he breaks his chains, retakes the young actress, and goes on a destructive rampage through the city. In a memorable climax, Kong climbs to the top of the Empire State Building while carrying the girl. A squadron of military airplanes is called in, and Kong is badly injured in a hail of machine-gun fire. Rejected by the frightened girl and mortally wounded, his grasp slips and Kong falls to his death in the street below.

Of course, the movie's special effects seem primitive by today's standards. But the film remains powerful because of the character at its emotional center: not the filmmaker, not the girl, but the giant ape himself. Kong is not merely a monster, but is a highly emotional creature who displays anger, jealousy, pride, affection, curiosity, tenderness, melancholy, rage, and the pain of rejection. *King Kong* is a cautionary tale about what can happen if we remove our emotions from their proper place and let them run wild. The potential for chaos and destruction (and an unhappy ending) is tremendous.

You and I were made to experience many different emotions, and we feel them at varying levels of intensity at different times. Sometimes our feelings are rather mild and barely noticeable, while other times they come on so strong that they threaten to overpower us. And because our emotions change so quickly and with such force, even the most pleasant emotions can leave us feeling upset and uncertain.

However, this does not mean we need to become unfeeling robots. Nor does it mean we are to lock our feelings away, hidden from the rest of the world. The truth is that our feelings are a wonderful part of being human! They add laughter and delight and richness to life. The Bible clearly tells us that God has emotions, and the capacity to feel and express emotion is an important part of what it means to be made in His image.

Your emotions are a gift from God. It's just that some days this gift can be a real challenge to deal with. Perhaps you were feeling crabby this morning because you didn't sleep well. Then, as you brushed your hair, you became frustrated by your hair's refusal to cooperate. Over breakfast your sister complimented you on your new shirt, and though you pretended to be annoyed with her, you were also secretly pleased. Later you were excited to receive a birthday card and ten dollars in the mail from your grandmother. Then you were really embarrassed when you spilled your milk at lunch. That's a lot to feel in one morning, and you haven't yet discovered that your baby brother has torn several pages from your favorite book!

We tend to think of some emotions as "good feelings," while others, such as hatred and jealousy, we consider "bad." Yet, as we will see, feelings are neither good nor bad in the way that sharing is good or stealing is bad. Solomon wrote that there is "a time to weep and a time

to laugh, a time to mourn and a time to dance" (Ecclesiastes 3:4). Some emotions are obviously unpleasant to feel, but that doesn't make them bad. What tends to be good or bad about your feelings is how you choose to express them. If, in a moment of anger, you lash out and hit your brother or insult a friend, then you have made a poor decision. (It's amazing the damage one emotional outburst can do to a friendship.)

Psalm 4:4 (NCV) says, "When you are angry, do not sin." The New Living Translation reads, "Don't sin by letting anger control you." Notice it does not say that being angry is a sin. You can't always help how you feel, but you can learn to control how you respond to your feelings. The important thing is to not allow yourself to be controlled by your emotions. Maybe you don't think of yourself as an "emotional person," but if you're not careful your feelings can still boss you around. And they don't always tell you the truth. Emotions can color your perspective, impairing your ability to see things the way they really are. Meanwhile, your feelings often insist on having their say RIGHT NOW, before all the facts are in.

However, you must choose to live by truth and wisdom, not simply act on what your feelings are telling you. When Jesus died on the cross as payment for your sins, He made it possible for you to live in harmony with yourself. To help you, God has given you His Word and His Spirit. In His Word, you learn how Jesus dealt with His emotions without ever sinning. And if you are a follower of Jesus Christ, God the Holy Spirit lives inside you to guide you and give you peace, if you will let Him. Remember, "letting your sinful nature control your mind leads to death. But letting the Spirit control your mind leads to life and peace" (Romans 8:6, NLT).

WHAT YOU WILL DO

» You will understand the importance of controlling your emotions instead of letting your emotions control you.
» You will examine how Jesus expressed His emotions without ever sinning by always acting in wisdom.
» You will develop skills for managing your unpleasant emotions.

THE LAST SUPPER

The Last Supper by Leonardo da Vinci is one of the most recognizable and imitated artworks in the world. Da Vinci completed the work in 1498, just a few years after Columbus discovered the New World. The original mural is twenty-nine feet long and fifteen feet tall and was painted on the wall of a church in Milan, Italy.

The subject of the painting is taken from the thirteenth chapter of the Gospel of John, in which Jesus and his disciples have gathered for the Passover meal. There, Jesus washes his friends' feet and tells them He will be betrayed that very night. His disciples stare at one another, at a loss to know which of them He means. This is the moment captured in da Vinci's painting.

The disciples are shown reacting to the Lord's announcement with confusion, shock, and anger. The three on the far left of the painting are Bartholomew; James, son of Alphaeus; and Andrew. Then come Judas Iscariot, Peter, and John. Judas is leaning away from Jesus and holding a small bag, perhaps containing the silver he's received for betraying the Lord, while Peter is holding a knife and appears angry. To the right of Jesus are Thomas; James, son of Zebedee, with his hands in the air; and Philip, who seems to be asking a question. On the far right are Matthew and Thaddeus, who are talking with Simon the Zealot.

In 2003, a best-selling novel by Dan Brown called *The Da Vinci Code* caused a stir by proposing that the person just to the left of Jesus in the painting is not John, but Mary Magdalene, whose presence in the painting was a coded message from da Vinci to his followers. However, a notebook kept by Leonardo da Vinci and discovered in the nineteenth century clearly indicates that the person seated next to Jesus is the apostle John.

Sadly, da Vinci's painting of *The Last Supper* has not withstood the ravages of time very well. Within a few years of completion, the mural had already begun showing signs of deterioration, and by 1652 the mural was so damaged that it could barely be seen, and a doorway was cut through a portion of the priceless work! Several attempts to restore the painting have taken place, including the most recent effort, which took more than twenty years.

THE ALTAR

"Please, Mr. Kerensky. Please don't make me tell my father."

"Your father must know," Mr. Kerensky said firmly but with understanding. "Neither Sasha nor I can lie to him and tell him the bird is your carving. Nor should you."

"But you don't know how angry he will be," Ivan pleaded. "He won't let me work here anymore. And he'll punish me very harshly."

"If you would like me to, I will go home with you after school today, and you can tell him while I am there. I have something else I'd like to discuss with him anyway."

Hoping that perhaps his punishment—and his father's anger—would be less severe if Mr. Kerensky was with him, Ivan readily agreed to the old woodcarver's offer.

"Can you meet me by the post office after school?" Mr. Kerensky asked.

"Yes, sir. And thank you for coming with me and for not being angry about what I did."

"Anger does not help the heart," Mr. Kerensky said. "I shall see you at 3:30. Now hurry along, or you'll be late for school."

In spite of Mr. Kerensky's offer to go with him, Ivan deeply feared what his father would do and say. He wasn't at all certain that he wanted Mr. Kerensky to witness it either.

"I'm home, Father," Ivan announced in a small voice as he opened the door. "And Mr. Kerensky is here to visit with you."

"Why, do come in!" Mr. Yushenko seemed pleased to receive a visit from Mr. Kerensky. He stood and shook the woodcarver's rough hand. "What brings you to our home?"

"Ivan has something he needs to share with you," Mr. Kerensky replied. "And since it

113

relates to something that happened in my shop, I thought I should be here with him."

"What is it, boy?" Mr. Yushenko snapped, his pleasantness abruptly draining away as he stepped toward his son. "Have you damaged one of Mr. Kerensky's carving tools? Speak up."

Ivan could not even look at his father.

After a long silence, Mr. Kerensky spoke. "Ivan, share with your father what happened. Just tell him. Or if you wish, I will tell him."

After another long silence, Ivan looked up at his father and said in a trembling voice, "The carved bird that I showed you last night. I, uh . . . I—"

"You what?" Mr. Yushenko demanded.

"I didn't really carve it," Ivan blurted. "It was Sasha's. I took it from the shop after my lesson. I wanted you to think I made it."

"Why, you're a thief! And a liar too," his father shouted, "I have a mind to—"

"Please, Mr. Yushenko, wait a moment," Mr. Kerensky said as he stepped between Ivan and his father. "I think we all need to sit down. I have a few things to share that may be helpful to both of you. First of all, Ivan knows that what he did was wrong. We've already had a long discussion about that in my shop this morning. I'm quite sure Ivan is sorry for what he did and that it won't happen again. More importantly, I think Ivan sees that some things in his heart need to change."

"His mother and I have always taught Ivan that stealing and lying are wrong," Mr. Yushenko said, his anger cooling. "I can't believe he'd do something like this."

"I've seen more good things than bad happening in the boy's life since he began working in my shop," Mr. Kerensky assured him. "I would like you to allow Ivan to continue working for me this summer."

Ivan's father looked at Ivan and asked, "Do you want to continue at the shop? Do you think you can stay out of trouble? Seems to me that you're always in some kind of trouble."

Ivan looked back at the floor and said quietly, "I do want to continue, Father."

"All right," his father answered gruffly. "But if you cause any trouble again for me or Mr. Kerensky or anyone at school, you'll answer to me. And I won't come to your rescue like Mr. Kerensky has this afternoon. Do you understand?"

"Yes, Father."

As Mr. Kerensky saw and heard for himself the anger and ill will Mr. Yushenko directed toward his son, he made up his mind that he needed to spend as much time with Ivan as possible in the months ahead.

"Mr. Yushenko, I have one more idea I would like you to consider—and you, too, Ivan," Mr. Kerensky said with enthusiasm.

"And what's that?" Ivan's father asked.

"A new church is being built in the village of Bovitsa, up near the mountains. It's about six hours from here by wagon. I've been asked to build the altar and the communion table. I think I could use Ivan's help for a couple of months this summer if you would agree to it. I'm also going to ask Mr. Petrov if Sasha can join me. There's a small parsonage near the church where we can stay. And if the boys were to get homesick, I think we could arrange a visit or two to Dmitrov over the summer."

Ivan's face lit up. "May I, Father? Oh, please, may I? I'll work hard, very hard, and I've never been to the mountains. Please, Father."

Mr. Yushenko seemed surprised by the extraordinary offer but, after further discussion, agreed that the work and the experience would be good for Ivan. In doing so, he tried to mask his feelings of relief that Ivan would be gone for two months and that the money he would earn would benefit the family.

Russian village in the Ural mountains. Photo: Ondřej Žváček.

When the school year ended in early June, Mr. Kerensky, Ivan, and Sasha loaded a wagon with supplies, said their good-byes, and departed for Bovitsa. They arrived at the outskirts of the small village late that afternoon. Mr. Kerensky stopped the wagon, and the three travelers could see the steeple of the nearly completed church building rising over the village. In the distance, beyond the town, were the beautiful Ural Mountains, whose highest peaks were still dressed with winter snow.

"May we work for your glory, Father," Mr. Kerensky prayed quietly as he drove the wagon into town. "And may Ivan and Sasha be blessed by their work here this summer."

Mr. Kerensky guided the horses into the churchyard, and the boys climbed down from the wagon to stretch their stiff muscles. As they breathed in the cool mountain air, a man walked out of the church and greeted them. "Welcome, my friends," he said. "I am Father Yuri. I was checking the day's progress, and you're just in time. I think we're ready for you to begin your part of the work. But excuse me. I'm getting ahead of myself. You must be very tired from your journey. Let me help you unload your supplies. My house is just behind the church, and my wife has prepared dinner for you. You do like *pelmeni*, I hope."

Ivan and Sasha looked at each other with hungry smiles. "Pelmeni!" they both exclaimed. "We love pelmeni."

After introductions, a delicious meal, and a discussion about the details of the work they would be doing, Mr. Kerensky sent the boys off to bed.

"They're good boys," he said to Father Yuri. "Sasha has had some difficulty learning to cope with his disability. But just last year, I think he came to understand a bit more about who he is as one of God's children. He's a good Christian boy from a good family, and I think this summer he'll grow even more in his relationship with God."

"And what about Ivan?" the priest asked. "He seems like a strong, healthy boy."

"Oh, he's strong and healthy," Mr. Kerensky agreed. "But he struggles with a difficult relationship with his father, who seems unable to show him much love. In fact, Ivan doesn't have many friends other than Sasha. I'm hoping that this summer God will heal his heart and he will come to know Jesus as his Savior."

"We'll certainly be praying for both boys," Father Yuri's wife, Julia, promised.

The first week of work passed quickly. While Mr. Kerensky carefully carved pieces for the altar, Ivan and Sasha helped other workers paint the walls and install the doors and windows.

One Friday evening, after supper, as Mr. Kerensky sat on the front porch of Father Yuri's house carving a small piece of wood, he asked Ivan and Sasha, "Would you boys like to do

a little fishing tomorrow? I think some relaxation and fun might be good for the three of us. There's a beautiful river just up the valley."

Without hesitating, Ivan and Sasha agreed.

"Then off to bed, both of you. And don't forget to say your prayers."

The hike to the river the next morning was more challenging than the old woodcarver had anticipated. He paused often to catch his breath. "I guess I'm not as young as I thought I was," he laughed. "And you, Sasha, how are you doing? Are we going too fast?"

"I'm okay," Sasha assured him. In spite of his limp, he had managed to keep pace with Ivan and Mr. Kerensky.

Mr. Kerensky slowed his pace for all their sakes. Before too long, they reached the banks of the river. They drank in the sight of the crystal-clear water twinkling in the summer sunshine and felt refreshed.

While Ivan watched, Mr. Kerensky and Sasha quickly baited their fishing lines and cast them into the river.

"I've never been fishing before," Ivan admitted after watching them for several minutes.

"Is that right?" Mr. Kerensky asked without showing his surprise.

"My father never took me or showed me how," Ivan said with a tinge of bitterness. "He's never showed me how to do anything."

"I understand." Mr. Kerensky handed Ivan his pole, keeping his eyes on the fishing line.

"No, you don't understand," Ivan said. "Nobody does." Then he caught himself and apologized. "I'm sorry for saying that, Mr. Kerensky. But I don't think anyone knows what it's like to be me."

Sasha could not help overhearing but realized this was not his conversation. He moved a little farther down the river and cast his line in another spot.

"Ivan, I do understand," Mr. Kerensky said, "more than you know."

"But how could you? I'm the school bully. Everyone is frightened of me, but I can't seem to help myself. I feel terrible about the things I've done to the other kids. I'm angry and lonely and scared all at the same time. How can you know what that feels like? And I'll bet you never had a father like mine."

"I never had a father at all," the woodcarver said. "Oh, I had a father, like all children do, but I never knew him. In fact, I never knew my mother either."

"Why not?" Ivan asked, suddenly more interested in Mr. Kerensky than himself.

The old woodcarver glanced at Ivan and said, "For reasons I was never told, I was taken to an orphanage outside Moscow shortly after I was born. I spent my entire childhood there. And when I was old enough to leave . . . well, I just left and began living on my own."

"Is that when you became a woodcarver?"

"Oh no, my boy." Mr. Kerensky took a deep breath and sat down on a large tree stump near the water's edge. "You see, Ivan, when I was a boy, I was much like you are now. I didn't have many friends. I was angry most of the time, and yes, I was known as the school bully. In fact, I was the *village* bully."

"Not you, Mr. Kerensky!" Ivan protested with a puzzled look. "Why, I think you're the kindest person I've ever known."

"Well, I appreciate the compliment, Ivan, but it's only by God's wonderful love and mercy that I'm the person I am today. You see, I spent several years of my life in prison. Oh, that was many years ago, but in some ways it seems like only yesterday."

Ivan didn't know what to say. Instead of looking at Mr. Kerensky, he just stared at the rapidly flowing river. Finally, he asked timidly, "But why did you have to go to prison?"

"That's not really important," Mr. Kerensky said sadly. "I was guilty of a crime, and prison was what I deserved. But what I didn't deserve was for God to reach down and mend my broken life."

Ivan's mind raced with questions. It didn't seem possible that the man he admired more than his own father could ever have been in prison. "So when did you learn to carve wood? When did you get out of prison? How did God change you?"

"Whoa!" Mr. Kerensky laughed, grateful for the chance to lighten the mood. "One question at a time. I learned to carve wood while I was in prison. Carving gave me something to do and helped me stay out of trouble. I was released from prison almost thirty years ago. That's when I moved to Dmitrov. I had a friend there who helped me to open a wood shop. Soon after, I met Father Yakov."

"Is that when God changed you?"

"Not immediately. My heart was still quite hard and rough—a little like that block of wood you're still carving back in the shop. But Father Yakov was kind to me—not like some other people who still thought of me as a criminal. One day he asked if I'd be willing to build the altar for the new church in Dmitrov."

"Did you do it?" Ivan asked with increasing interest.

"I did," replied the old woodcarver. "But only because I needed the work, not because I was interested in the church. But during those weeks I was working on the altar, I met many fine people who called themselves Christians. And most importantly, I met God. On the day we dedicated the new church building, I asked Jesus to be my Lord and Savior. That was the day I became a new person."

"And is that when you became a nicer person—like you are today?"

"Oh my, young man! You do have questions, don't you." Mr. Kerensky laughed. "I wouldn't say I'm such a nice person, Ivan. But I can say I'm a *new* person—a new creation. On that day God began to shape my new heart, and He's been working on it ever since. He's sanded off many of the rough parts of my life, but He's not finished yet. He's the Master Craftsman, you know. You see, I can't do it myself. I cannot make my heart new. But He can. And He is, day by day."

Ivan didn't ask any more questions that day. But the story Mr. Kerensky shared with him by the river was never far from his thoughts.

Summer in Bovitsa passed quickly. Ivan and Sasha kept busy helping the other workers while Mr. Kerensky carefully designed and carved the panels for the communion table.

"What are you carving now?" Ivan asked, not recognizing the scene Mr. Kerensky was creating on a panel of wood.

"Why, it's the Last Supper," Sasha said. "Don't you know about the Last Supper?"

"Not really," Ivan admitted. "We don't go to church except for Christmas."

Mr. Kerensky paused in his work and told Ivan the story. "Well, on the night before Jesus was crucified on the cross, He ate the Passover meal with His disciples in Jerusalem. The Jews celebrated the Passover as a reminder of the night God set their ancestors free from slavery in Egypt many, many years earlier. On that night, God told the Israelites to sacrifice a lamb and put some of its blood on the doorframes of their houses. He was going to send an angel to punish the wicked Egyptians by killing the firstborn child in every family. But when the angel saw the blood on the doorframes of the Israelites' houses, he knew to pass over them. In this way, not one of the firstborn Israelite children was killed. That very night, the king of Egypt freed the Israelites from slavery."

Photo: Wolfgang Sauber.

Mr. Kerensky made a few more cuts on his carving as Ivan and Sasha looked on. "Ivan, Jesus is our Passover Lamb. He gave His life for us. He shed His blood and died for us. Do you know why?"

"I'm not really sure."

"He died for us to set us free from our sins, just like the Israelites were set free from their slavery to the Egyptians. When we believe that Jesus is God's Son and our Savior, we become His children." The old woodcarver blew some of the sawdust away from his carving. "Well, I think that just about does it. What do you boys think?"

"It's beautiful," Sasha said quietly.

"Yes, it's beautiful," Ivan said. "But aren't you going to keep sanding it until it's smooth? It still looks a little rough."

"No, I think it's finished. I'm not going to make it any smoother."

"Why not?" Ivan asked.

"I want it to remind people that the work God begins in our hearts will never be finished until the day Jesus returns to earth and takes us to heaven," Mr. Kerensky explained. "We're all like rough blocks of wood, still being shaped by the Master, being made into something beautiful."

Ivan smiled, putting together the pieces of all Mr. Kerensky had shared with him since the day in the wood shop when he was caught with Sasha's carving.

"Now, boys, help me mount this carving to the front of the communion table. I think everything else at the altar is finished and ready for Sunday," Mr. Kerensky said with a smile of satisfaction.

It seemed as if everyone in Bovitsa was crowded into the new church building that Sunday. Father Yuri dedicated the building to the service of God and for His glory. Then he thanked all who had helped with the construction of the new building.

"I want to especially thank our three visitors from Dmitrov who are responsible for this beautiful altar and communion table," Father Yuri announced. "Mr. Kerensky, Ivan, and Sasha, please stand so we may all thank you."

Hesitantly, Mr. Kerensky stood between the two boys with his head slightly bowed, not wanting any special attention or thanks. Then as Ivan and Sasha stood with him, he reached for their hands and held them in his. With humility, the woodcarver thanked the congregation for inviting them to help build the new church. Then he looked at Ivan and Sasha, and simply said, "Thank you, boys, for your help. Thank you very much."

Ivan looked at Mr. Kerensky's rough, leathery hands. Then he looked at the carving of the Last Supper. Through the old woodcarver's hands, he had seen love expressed not only toward him but also toward God. In the carving he saw an expression of an even greater love— the love God had for Mr. Kerensky, for Sasha, and yes, even for him, Ivan Yushenko.

After everyone had left the church, the woodcarver and his two young helpers stood quietly in front of the altar. It seemed a special, even sacred, moment for the three of them.

Finally, Ivan spoke. "On our fishing trip, you told me about the Sunday you asked Jesus to be your Savior. You know, when the people in

Dmitrov dedicated their new church building with the altar you built."

"I'll never forget that day, Ivan," Mr. Kerensky answered quietly.

"Well, I was wondering," Ivan said, "do you think I could ask Jesus to be my Savior, right now, right here at the altar in this new church?"

Mr. Kerensky smiled through the tears that began to fill his eyes. He put his arm around Ivan and asked, "Do you really want a new heart, Ivan? Do you really want God to carve and sand and shape your heart to become like His?"

"I do, Mr. Kerensky. I know I do," Ivan said without hesitation.

"Well, I can think of no better place or time than here and now at this new altar in this new church."

Then, just as the woodcarver had knelt at a new altar thirty years before, Ivan knelt and prayed and asked Jesus to be his Savior. And he, too, became a new person.

THINK ABOUT IT

» What kinds of feelings does Ivan have trouble controlling? How has this contributed to his becoming a bully?
» Think about the relationship between Mr. Yushenko and his son, Ivan. Do you think Mr. Yushenko loves his son? If Mr. Yushenko loves Ivan, why is he "relieved" when Ivan is invited to go away for the summer?
» Why do you think Mr. Kerensky takes such a personal interest in helping Ivan?
» What do you think Ivan's life will be like when he returns home after being with Sasha and Mr. Kerensky all summer? Why?

WORDS YOU NEED TO KNOW

» **Impulse:** A sudden or spontaneous urge to do something you hadn't planned to do
» **Wisdom:** Knowing, loving, and obeying God's Word and applying that knowledge to make good decisions

HIDE IT IN YOUR HEART

Patience is better than strength. Controlling your temper is better than capturing a city. (Proverbs 16:32, NCV)

Be joyful always; pray continually; give thanks in all circumstances, for this is God's will for you in Christ Jesus. (1 Thessalonians 5:16–18)

A FISH STORY

Have you ever gone fishing with your father, a grandfather, or an uncle? For many people, fishing is a fun and relaxing hobby. People who fish for fun often talk about how wonderful it is to sit on a bank

Ancient *Ichthus* graffiti at Ephesus. Photo: Mufunyo.

or in a boat, holding a fishing pole and just being quiet. Being still as you wait for a fish to nibble at your line is a great time to pray or meditate on the Word while you exercise your patience.

Jesus spent much of his time preaching near the Sea of Galilee, and many of His first apostles were fishermen, including Peter, James, and John. But these fishermen didn't go out with a pole, fishing in a stream or lake for fun—fishing was the way they earned their living and put food on the table. Jesus told these rugged laborers He would make them "fishers of men" and called them to leave their fishing nets behind and follow Him.

Have you seen the "Christian fish" symbol displayed on T-shirts, car bumpers, and business logos? The Greek word for *fish* is spelled ΙΧΘΥΣ. These letters spell out an acronym used by early Christians—*Iesous Christos Theou Uios Soter*—which means "Jesus Christ, Son of God, Savior." The Greek word for *fish* is pronounced ICK-thess, which is why the fish symbol is called an *Ichthus*.

As for fishing, Huckleberry Finn had it right: You don't need a fancy rod and tackle. You can make your own fishing pole by following these simple instructions. All you need are some fishing line, a bamboo pole or trimmed tree branch eight to ten feet in length and an inch or two in diameter, a #10 snelled hook, and a plastic bobber or cork.

Cut a length of fishing line as long as your pole and tie one end tightly to the pole's tip, cutting a notch if needed to prevent the line from slipping. Tie the hook to the other end of the line. Then attach the bobber two or three feet up from the hook. Adjust the bobber so your hook stays off the bottom of the lake or river. Drop the bobber and baited hook into the water and lift up when you see the bobber dip beneath the surface.

WHY DID GOD GIVE US FEELINGS?

People have struggled with their feelings since Adam and Eve ate the fruit from the forbidden tree. Yet we were made to live in perfect harmony, to be at peace with our God, with ourselves, and with each other. However, when sin entered creation, that peace was destroyed and sin caused people's emotional lives to become marked by disharmony, turmoil, and frustration. So why did God give us feelings to begin with?

We experience emotions because God has emotions. He is not a cold, distant, unfeeling deity who created the universe on a whim and left it to its own devices. God is passionate about His work, and He made people in His image to be the crown jewels of His creation. He made us to be in relationship with Him, and although His love and care for us remains constant, throughout the Bible we see Him express a wide range of emotions toward mankind, including joy (Isaiah 62:5), anger (1 Kings 11:9), pleasure (1 Kings 3:10), jealousy (Exodus 34:14), compassion (Judges 2:18), hate (Proverbs 6:16), delight (Zephaniah 3:17), and grief (Genesis 6:5–6). Yet He loves us so much that He gave His only begotten Son to pay the price for our sins (John 3:16).

Your emotions are a gift from God. They make you feel alive and unique. You can be excited, disappointed, thrilled, and terrified. You can be moved to both tears and laughter. You can be pleased, perturbed, and perplexed. And that's all in just one afternoon at Disneyland!

To be human is to have feelings and passions. But what if we didn't experience emotions? Wouldn't life be dull if there were never any joy or sorrow, only endless days of robotically doing our schoolwork, chores, and jobs? There would be no romance and no heartbreak. There would be no music, poetry, movies, or stories of any kind. There would be no flags or national anthems. No one would be driven to accomplish or invent anything. Imagine winning an Olympic gold medal and simply walking away without any fanfare and feeling no happiness or relief or pride in your achievement.

Among the things that make life special are our feelings about the people, places, and events in our lives. Feelings enable us to express our love to God and to enjoy His many gifts to us. Our emotions can move us to run laughing through an open field or enjoy a beautiful sunset or whisper a prayer for a friend in need. Even feelings like sadness, loneliness, and grief contribute to the quality and richness of our lives. Both pleasant and unpleasant emotions play a part in how we experience the wonders of life—as long as we keep them in their proper perspective.

The Bible teaches that we are not to let our feelings get the best of us. Here are just a few examples of emotions we are instructed to keep under control:

Patience is better than strength. Controlling your temper is better than capturing a city. (Proverbs 16:32, NCV)

Do not be anxious about anything, but in everything, by prayer and petition, with thanksgiving, present your requests to God. (Philippians 4:6)

So we say with confidence, "The Lord is my helper; I will not be afraid. What can man do to me?" (Hebrews 13:6)

Keep in mind that emotions themselves are not sinful. However, we often express our feelings sinfully. Only God expresses His emotions with complete righteousness. But we allow them to sway our thoughts and spur us to unwise action. In the heat of the moment, we tend to be rash, quick to do and say things we later regret.

However, God did not give us feelings to be an excuse for sin. He gave us emotions so that we would be sensitive to the feelings and needs of others. As children of God, we are not to be ruled by our feelings, but we are to be moved to show compassion and understanding to those who are hurting or in need. The Bible says, "He comforts us in all our troubles so that we can comfort others" (2 Corinthians 1:4, NLT). Whenever you become angry or sad, remember that other people feel the same way sometimes. Think of what you could say or do to comfort them. Follow God's example and be "gracious and compassionate, slow to anger and rich in love" (Psalm 145:8).

WHEN YOU LET YOUR FEELINGS DO THE DRIVING

Someday, in the not-too-distant future, you will learn to drive a car. Once you have earned your license and purchased insurance and have access to an automobile, you will be able to drive yourself to church or a job, run errands, and attend your choice of various leisure activities. Until then you must rely on a parent, an older sibling, or a friend's parent to get you where you want to go. When you climb into the car and buckle your seatbelt, you trust the driver to take you to your planned destination. If your mom says she is taking you to Little League practice, you can be pretty certain you're going to end up at the ball field.

Emotions, on the other hand, are notoriously unreliable drivers. You never know where they might take you. Depending on your circumstances—whether your dad got the job he was hoping for, whether you found the watch you thought you'd lost, whether you had scrambled eggs or donuts for breakfast—you might find yourself flying down the highway of good cheer or circling the cul-de-sac of fear. Your emotions change from day to day, from hour to hour, even moment to moment, often without warning. They also have a tendency to lie to you. Jeremiah 17:9 (NKJV) says, "The heart is deceitful above all things, and desperately wicked."

Nevertheless, countless movies, books, poems, and pop songs urge young people to follow their hearts. This sentiment sometimes makes for good entertainment, but it's a poor strategy for living. When we let our emotions lead the way, we inevitably wind up feeling lost, hopeless, and out of control. If we should find ourselves in a difficult situation, a wave of emotions sweeps over us, and we feel powerless to do anything about it. But just because your feelings seem overwhelming at times does not mean you have to let them run your life. God does not want you to be ruled by your emotions. He wants you to experience the peace and joy that come with knowing how to control your emotions.

Emotions can be like playground bullies: If you let them, they will push you around, making life difficult for you and everyone around you. But just because you feel emotions does not mean you have to act on them. Doing so can lead to tragic mistakes. Proverbs 28:26 (NKJV) says, "He who trusts in his own heart is a fool." Yet many people are determined to do whatever they feel like doing at any given moment. Their motto is "If it feels good, do it." Likewise, there is no shortage of people who refuse to believe something they read in the Bible because it doesn't "feel right" or it goes against some tradition they were brought up to believe in.

You need to make decisions based on what is *true* rather than on what you *feel*. Remember, what you are feeling may not line up with the facts. There may be times when you *feel* like God doesn't care about you, and yet He loves you more than you can possibly grasp. You may *feel* like your parents don't understand you, but they understand much more than you think. You may *feel* unappreciated by a friend, but a smile or kind word from you today may make all the difference to that friend.

Trust and obey God's Word, not your feelings.

LET WISDOM BE YOUR GUIDE

An **impulse** is a sudden or spontaneous urge to do something you hadn't planned on doing. We all have impulses from time to time, but impulsive people tend to act on their feelings rather than giving careful thought to the consequences of their actions. For example, your mom sends you to the grocery store just to buy some milk for breakfast, but waiting for you at the checkout counter is a mouth-watering display of candy, gum, and chocolate. Suddenly, you have a powerful craving for something sweet. If you stop to think about it, you will remember you're saving your allowance to buy a new tennis racket. Also, you had two cavities when you visited the dentist last week, and dinner will be ready in an hour . . . but you just *love* the way M&Ms melt in your mouth. So instead of doing the wise thing, you act on your impulse and buy the M&Ms.

Acting on our impulses can get us into all kinds of trouble. That's because we're making decisions based on feelings rather than truth. We've already seen that feelings are unreliable, and as any military officer will tell you, it's not a good idea to make decisions based on unreliable information.

The Bible tells us to get wisdom instead:

Wisdom is the most important thing; so get wisdom. If it costs everything you have, get understanding. (Proverbs 4:7, NCV)

Wisdom is knowing, loving, and obeying God's Word and applying that knowledge to make good decisions.

How can you tell the difference between wisdom and what "feels" like the right thing to do? When confronted with a difficult situation, wisdom will tell you to be patient and take your time making a decision, while your emotions will demand that you take action immediately. Wise people weigh the consequences and make decisions today they will be pleased with tomorrow, whereas people ruled by their emotions are only concerned with what's happening to them right now at this moment.

James 1:5 says, "If any of you lacks wisdom, he should ask God, who gives generously to all without finding fault, and it will be given to him." Pray and ask God for wisdom. Then keep your eyes on the Word of God and do what it says, not what you feel like doing. The Bible will show you the way (Psalm 119:105). Before you decide on a course of action, check God's Word to see if it's the wise thing to do. Then choose to follow the truth instead of your feelings.

> *Hear God's Word often. Do not go to bed, do not get up, without having spoken a beautiful passage— two, three, or four of them—to your heart.*
> **Martin Luther**
> 1483–1546

WHAT DID JESUS DO?

We sometimes forget that Jesus faced the same challenges you and I come up against every day. The devil's tactics don't change much. Oh, he recycles them, dresses them up a bit, and gives them new names and catchy slogans; but he's been pulling the same old tricks since the garden of Eden, and Jesus had to deal with them just like we do today. Hebrews 4:15 says, "For we do not have a high priest who is unable to sympathize with our weaknesses, but we have one who has been tempted in every way, just as we are—yet was without sin."

Jesus knows what it's like to be human. He knows our feelings, He shares our feelings, and He can be trusted with our feelings. He had the same feelings you and I do, yet He never sinned because of them. So what better way to learn how to control our emotions than to look at how Jesus handled His?

On the night before His crucifixion, after the events of the Last Supper, Jesus walked with His disciples to the foot of the Mount of Olives. They had met often there in a place called Gethsemane. But on this night, as they entered the olive grove, Jesus told His friends, "Sit here while I go and pray." He took only His closest companions— Peter, James, and John—and went deeper into the garden. There Jesus became "deeply troubled and

The olive grove in the Garden of Gethsemane as it appears today.
Photo: ©2009 Deror Avi.

distressed," and He said to them, "My soul is crushed with grief to the point of death" (Mark 14:32–34, NLT). Then He walked a short distance away and fell to His knees.

Can you imagine how He must have felt? What thoughts and emotions must have been running though His mind? Jesus knew what lay ahead for Him over the next several hours—interrogation, humiliation, torture, and death. He had just said good-bye to friends He had known and loved and trusted for three years. And one of them, Judas, was on his way at that very moment to betray Him to the authorities. Worst of all, Jesus would soon endure the whole of God's wrath by taking upon Himself the sins of the world. The emotional pain was so great, so agonizing, that His "sweat fell to the ground like great drops of blood" (Luke 22:44, NLT).

So what did He do? He talked to His Father:

He prayed that, if it were possible, the awful hour awaiting him might pass him by. "Abba, Father," he cried out, "everything is possible for you. Please take this cup of suffering away from me. Yet I want your will to be done, not mine." (Mark 14:35–36, NLT)

Jesus was horrified by the knowledge of what was to come. Understandably, He wanted the pain to go away. So did He get up, brush Himself off, and prepare an ambush for the temple guard that was coming to arrest Him? Did He call down legions of angels to smite those who were determined to kill Him? Or did He decide it wasn't worth all this trouble, pack it up, and go back to the carpentry business in Nazareth? No, no, and no. He chose to go through with God's plan.

The Taking of Christ by Caravaggio.

Yes, Jesus did not feel like going to the cross, but He refused to be led by His feelings. He would not allow His emotions to stand in the way of God's will. He resisted the temptation to do what He felt like doing and chose instead to obey His Father. He felt the fear and went to the cross anyway.

How was Jesus able to overcome His emotions? First of all, He knew the Word of God. The Bible says that, as a child, Jesus "grew and became strong in spirit, filled with wisdom" (Luke 2:40, NKJV). He did this by studying the Scriptures. When tempted by Satan in the wilderness, Jesus answered him by quoting from the Word. When He was crushed with grief in the garden, He remembered the many prophecies from Scripture concerning His destiny and knew what He must do. It's difficult to resist temptation and say no to your feelings if you do not know your Bible and carry its words in your heart and mind.

Because He knew God's Word, Jesus was not moved by so many of the things that move us. His own neighbors once tried to push Him off a cliff, and He simply turned and walked right past them (Luke 4:28–30). He was able to do this because He knew that no one could do anything to Him if the Father didn't allow it. Jesus rested in the knowledge that He was safe in God's hands. He understood that God had a plan and a purpose for His life and, until these were fulfilled, He had nothing to fear. He was able to speak peace to the raging storm (Mark 4:35–40) because He never allowed His emotions to become a raging storm inside Him.

Also, Jesus knew who He was. He knew the God of the universe was His Father and would provide for all His Son's needs. You and I need to understand that we too are children of God, and we must place all our confidence in Him. We do not have to live on an emotional roller coaster, where our feelings go up and down from one day to the next. Instead, we can live as Christ lived, with an unwavering sense of peace and security that comes from knowing who we are and to Whom we belong.

MAKE A NOTE OF IT

Read John 2:13–17. This is the story of how Jesus cleared the moneychangers from the temple. What emotion did He express during this incident? Jesus fashioned a whip of cords and drove the men and their animals out of the temple, overturning the moneychangers' tables and dumping their money all over the floor. Why do you think He took such dramatic action instead of simply teaching against the practice of buying and selling in the temple? Do you think Jesus sinned that day? Why not?

HOW TO DEAL WITH UNPLEASANT FEELINGS

When you get sick or injured, your body tells you something is physically wrong. Aches, pain, fever, coughing, fatigue—these are just a few of the ways your body lets you know that you need rest, recuperation, maybe even medical attention. Likewise, unpleasant emotions are your heart and mind's way of letting you know that they need some attention. For example, feelings of anger or hatred may be telling you that you need to sit down and calmly work things out with another person. Boredom may be alerting you that you need physical or mental exercise. Fear may be warning you to be careful or even stop what you are doing. Guilty feelings may be telling you that something is wrong with your behavior, while encouraging you to do the right thing.

Although you don't want to be ruled by your emotions, you should not ignore or deny the way you feel. Feelings are a vital part of being human and are not meant to be pushed down or locked away. If we don't express them—if we bury them and pretend they don't exist—unpleasant emotions will eventually make us ill physically, emotionally,

THE FINAL FRONTIER

In 1966, a new kind of television series was beamed into American homes. Combining the popular western and science fiction genres, with a bit of Jonathan Swift's *Gulliver's Travels* thrown in for good measure, *Star Trek* went where no TV show had gone before. Each week, as Captain Kirk and the crew of the Starship *Enterprise* explored strange new worlds, they also examined many issues that concerned our earthbound culture, including racism, human rights, and the role of technology in society.

The Vulcan salute.

Interestingly, the most popular character on the original *Star Trek* series was the one that had worried NBC network executives: Spock, the Vulcan first officer of the *Enterprise*. With his trademark pointy ears and slanted eyebrows, Spock bore a passing resemblance to how the devil was depicted in art since the sixth century. But what was most unusual about this alien character, what set him apart from his shipmates, was the fact that he did not express emotions.

Spock was born on the planet Vulcan where inhabitants were taught from an early age to suppress all emotions and live lives of rigid self-control, mental discipline, and pure logic. This does not mean Vulcans have no emotions. Indeed, Vulcans are depicted in the Star Trek universe as an extremely emotional people capable of great passion—and great violence. However, they long ago developed extraordinary mental techniques to suppress their feelings precisely *because of* the damage emotions could cause if left unchecked.

Back on Planet Earth, human beings were created to feel and express emotion. God does not want us to suppress or ignore our feelings but instead choose our words and actions wisely. If we are to live truly healthy lives, we must learn to communicate our feelings in constructive ways. It's the only logical thing to do!

and spiritually. Remember, the idea is not to be free from emotions; the idea is to be free from their control.

We can choose to express our feelings in healthy or unhealthy ways, in constructive or destructive ways. No matter how you look at it, both pleasant and unpleasant feelings need to be released, and it will be easier on you and everyone around you if you choose to express them in a constructive way. So we are going to look at a few skills to help you express some of your more unpleasant feelings in healthy ways. As we do, remember: Nobody's perfect. You are going to blow it occasionally and say or do something you later regret. The good news is that God is a loving God who will never leave you or forsake you. So when you do blow it, turn to Him for forgiveness and ask Him for the strength to do better next time.

ANGER

Everybody gets angry now and then, and that's okay. But it's never okay to express your anger by intentionally hurting another person, either physically or emotionally or by damaging that person's property.

When you feel you're about to lose your temper, take a deep breath and slowly count to five. This will give you a moment to calm down so you don't do something you'll feel sorry for later. It's also a good idea to step away from a heated conversation and give your anger time to cool before you try to work things out. In the meantime, try one of these ideas for releasing and resolving your anger in a healthy manner:

- Go for a long walk, run through the park, shoot some hoops—any physical activity (preferably outdoors) that will allow you to "blow off steam" and help you focus on something else for a while.

- Write a letter to the person you're angry with. Be honest about how you feel. Don't hold anything back. Then rip up the letter and throw it away. This way you can express your feelings without hurting anyone.

- Investigate what the Bible says about how to deal with your anger. Read and meditate on these verses: Psalm 37:8; Proverbs 15:1, 18; Luke 6:28; and Colossians 3:13.

MAKE A NOTE OF IT

Imagine that you and a friend have had a huge fight that has left you feeling angry and frustrated. Be specific as to what you're fighting about. Then sit down and make a detailed list of possible actions you can take in response. Get creative and write your list in the style of a restaurant menu. Include both negative, destructive reactions and positive, constructive options you can choose from. Be sure to include little things you can do to help you cool down or just feel a little better. Now examine what the Bible teaches about dealing with anger and add these commands to your menu. When you are finished, look over the menu and choose a "healthy meal" of five or six items that will help you deal with your anger and resolve the problem in a positive, healthy way.

FEAR

Faith is believing that God will always hear your prayers and respond in wisdom and love. *Fear* is believing He won't. Put your trust in God, for He is "our refuge and strength" and "an ever-present help" in times of trouble (Psalm 46:1). Remember that He has not given you a spirit of fear, but He has given you power, love, and self-control (2 Timothy 1:7). These are your most important tools for controlling the emotions of fear and worry.

To help you face your fears, try writing down in great detail what you are afraid of, then think about what you've written. What's the worst thing that could possibly happen to you? What's the likelihood of it happening? And would it really be so terrible if it did? Once you determine that what you're afraid of is unrealistic, give your fears the boot.

SADNESS

Sadness is one of those feelings we experience with different levels of intensity at different times in life. If you're feeling overwhelmed by sadness, be sure to ask your parents for help. Most of the time the blues can easily be treated by getting exercise, spending time outdoors, eating better, not sleeping in, avoiding negative people, and writing or drawing in a journal.

However, one tool stands above the rest: When you're feeling down, praise God. If possible, get together with family or friends or church members and worship the Lord. Put on "a garment of praise instead of a spirit of despair" (Isaiah 61:3). Listen to uplifting music, meditate on the Word, and seek out good biblical teaching.

When David wrote Psalm 43, he was struggling with discouragement and sadness, perhaps even depression. Ungodly people had been telling lies and making unfair accusations against him. David felt lost and rejected by God, yet he knew this was not really the truth. He asked himself, "Why am I discouraged? Why is my heart so sad?" Then he hit on the solution to his problem: "I will put my hope in God! I will praise him again—my Savior and my God!" (Psalm 43:5, NLT).

We need to do the same. When we're feeling low, we need to lift our voices in praise and thanksgiving to the Lord. You may not feel like singing, but if you will do it in obedience to His Word, God promises to lift you up from the depths of sadness and discouragement and set you in the high places (Habakkuk 3:18–19).

GRIEF

Grief is a deep sorrow usually brought on by the loss of a friend or loved one or even a beloved pet. This loss may be caused by a long-distance move, the break-up of a close friendship, or death due to tragedy or illness. Perhaps the most important thing to understand about grief is that it's okay to cry. In John 11, when Jesus saw Mary and Martha anguished over the death of their brother Lazarus, He wept with them. He knew He was about to raise Lazarus from the dead, yet He allowed Himself to feel and openly express sorrow.

One way to deal with grief is to honor the one you've lost by creating a scrapbook with photos, small mementos, and thoughts about your time together. It's also healthy to reminisce with other people who knew your loved one and share your favorite memories.

It's important to keep in mind that even the worst feelings will eventually pass. Sometimes when we're sad or lonely, we don't think our feelings are ever going to change, but they will. When we're really hurting, perhaps when a dear friend moves away, it may seem like the pain will never leave, but it will. Psalm 30:5 (NLT) says, "Weeping may last through the night, but joy comes with the morning." Just as the seasons come and go, feelings will inevitably change. During a long, cold winter, it sometimes seems that spring will never come, but it always does, bringing with it warmth, life, and growth. Likewise, you can be sure that painful feelings will give way to a springtime of pleasant, life-giving feelings and emotional growth.

> *If one is joyful, it means that one is faithfully living for God, and nothing else counts; if one gives joy to others, one is doing God's work.*
> **Janet Erskine Stuart**
> 1857–1914

WHAT SHOULD I DO?

The Bible tells us, "Be joyful always; pray continually; give thanks in all circumstances, for this is God's will for you in Christ Jesus" (1 Thessalonians 5:16–18). This does not mean we're supposed to walk around happy all the time. And it doesn't mean we're supposed to put on a smile and *pretend* to be happy. God doesn't want us to be phonies.

Joy is a deeper pleasure, a constant delight that does not depend on your circumstances. True joy comes from being a child of God and living daily in fellowship with Him. Whatever you are doing, whatever is happening around you, you can have confidence that God loves you and His power is at work in your life.

Nehemiah 8:10 (NLT) says, "Don't be dejected and sad, for the joy of the LORD is your strength!" When you make the choice to rejoice, you will find the strength needed to control your emotions. Remember, your feelings will eventually change, so why not choose joy today?

A PRAYER

Dear God, thank you for making me in your image and giving me emotions. I am so glad you understand the way I feel and that you don't hold my feelings against me. Help me to control my emotions and not let my emotions control me. Help me to be quick to forgive those who have wronged me. And help me choose to live joyfully every day. In Jesus' name. Amen.

Photo: NASA.

Can You Trust Your Feelings?

WORLDVIEWS IN FOCUS

MEET ELLIE

Ellie is a twelve-year-old girl who lives in Salt Lake City, Utah. Ellie and her family are Mormons. She has two older brothers, Mason and Elijah; a younger brother, Bridger; and the twins, Levi and Leah. Today her three-year-old sister, Leah, has a bad cold, so Ellie sits with her to keep her out from underfoot and coaxes her to eat something. After helping her mother clear the breakfast dishes, Ellie and her brothers grab their books and lunches and pile into the car. Because they have only one car, Ellie's mother drives them all to school, then takes Ellie's father to work at the manufacturing plant.

Ellie attends public school, where many of the children, though not all, are from Mormon families. Ellie can always tell which kids are Mormon because of the way they dress. The boys wear slacks instead of jeans, and the girls mostly wear knee-length skirts, except when in PE class. Ellie studies all the usual subjects in school, such as math, grammar, and science, but her favorite subject is history. She loves hearing stories about the pioneers who came by covered wagon and settled the American West. Ellie is proud of the fact that her family is descended from the original pioneers who came to Utah with Brigham Young, one of the early leaders of the Mormon Church. Ellie's mother has encouraged her in the study of her family history, which is called *genealogy*.

When Ellie gets home from school this day, she can see that her mother has been busy sewing. Ellie wears mostly skirts and dresses that her mother makes. This helps her parents to save money and

133

ensures that Ellie's clothes are always modest. As a Mormon girl, she knows that she should always be neat, clean, and modest. Today Ellie's mom has finished sewing a cornflower-blue skirt for Ellie and started a new Sunday dress for herself. Once that is finished, she is going to make new shirts for the boys; it is her responsibility to make sure the whole family looks immaculate.

On Sundays, Ellie and her family attend services at their local meetinghouse. Meetinghouses are different from Mormon temples. Most church services and social activities take place in meetinghouses, which are open to the public. Temples, however, are private. Only special services, like weddings and baptisms, are held at temples. People need a special pass, called a "temple recommend," to enter a Mormon temple. To keep their temple recommend, members must be interviewed every other year by a church official, called a bishop, to make sure they are living correctly and are tithing to the church. Ellie's parents are careful to keep their temple recommend up to date.

A Mormon church service has three parts. First, families sit together in the chapel, sing hymns, and listen to short talks given by members of the church. The most important part of the service, though, is the passing of the sacrament: Everyone eats a piece of bread, drinks a small cup of water, and meditates on Jesus' death and resurrection and how to be a good Mormon. Afterward, families split up and go to Sunday school. There Ellie learns about the basic beliefs of the Mormon Church. For the final part of the Sunday service, men and women go to separate meetings: Ellie's father and older brothers go to Priesthood, while Ellie's mother goes to Relief Society. There she listens to the bishop's wife and other important women talk about how to be a good Mormon woman.

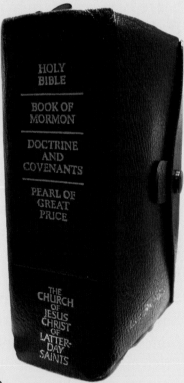

This month in Sunday school, Ellie and her class are reading from the *Book of Mormon*, the most important book of scriptures in the Mormon Church. Mormons believe that there are four sacred books, known as the standard works. These include the *Book of Mormon*, the *Doctrines and Covenants*, the *Pearl of Great Price*, and the *King James Bible*. Ellie's Sunday school teacher says that although the Bible contains trustworthy messages from God, people have corrupted it over time. That is why the *Book of Mormon* was given to Joseph Smith—to correct errors that had crept into translations of the Bible.

Mormon scriptures. Photo: Ricardo630.

The Mormon Church was founded in western New York in 1830, when a man named Joseph Smith said that an angel named Moroni appeared to him in a dream. Joseph Smith said that the angel told him where to find and how to translate a book that he called the *Book of Mormon*. From this book, Joseph Smith started what is known today as the Church of Jesus

Salt Lake Temple in Salt Lake City, Utah. Photo: Diliff.

Christ of Latter-day Saints, or the LDS Church. When Joseph Smith died a few years later in Illinois, his friend Brigham Young took over leadership of the church and led a large group of Mormons west to settle in Utah. Ellie's teacher says that today nearly two-thirds of the people living in Utah are Mormons, but that most Mormons live outside the United States, in countries like Brazil, Australia, and the United Kingdom.

Ellie's teacher says that Mormons consider themselves to be Christians and that the rest of the world's Christians are following wrong beliefs. Only the Mormon Church has received the truth, and therefore only Mormons can go to heaven. She says that this is why the Mormon Church emphasizes missionary work. It is also why people who leave the Mormon Church are treated harshly. Mormons believe that anyone who stops following Mormon practices has been led away from the true faith. Such people are *excommunicated*, or asked to leave the church. Since no one wants to go through this kind of humiliation, devout Mormons do everything they can to stay true to their faith.

Ellie has learned that the most important part of being a Mormon is having a strong faith. Her teacher says that Satan has set many traps to lure the faithful away from Mormonism, and so it is very important to obey the church leaders, who have a special gift for discerning truth. A person who has doubts about the church or the *Book of Mormon* needs to grow stronger in his faith. Ellie's teacher warns that curses wait for those who stumble or doubt, but that many blessings are in store for those who believe and obey.

Although Ellie loves seeing and talking with her friends, Sundays always make her feel a bit uncomfortable. There are many rules a Mormon must follow. For example, Mormons aren't allowed to drink alcohol or anything with caffeine in it, like tea, coffee, or Coke. They also aren't allowed to use tobacco or watch R-rated movies. The church teaches that these things distract from the path of faithfulness. Ellie sometimes wonders if she will ever be good enough to get to heaven.

To help Mormon families avoid worldly things that may distract them, the church provides lots of activities to fill their time. In addition to church services, Ellie has just started going to Young Women organization meetings once a week while her brothers attend a Boy Scouts meeting. Her father is also careful to oversee her personal study time and to lead the family in prayer and scripture study every day. This is difficult for him, since he works such long hours, so sometimes Ellie's mother will follow the lesson he has outlined and teach in his place. On Monday evenings, the family gathers together and reads from a lesson given to them by the church.

Because Ellie's family has a larger house than some other families in their district, they often host traveling speakers, bishops, and other church officials visiting their area. These visits always make Ellie's mother nervous. She spends hours cleaning the house, preparing meals, and making sure that Ellie and her siblings are perfectly dressed. Ellie's mother worries that if the officials see anything less than a spotless house, they will give a bad report to the local bishop, who could choose not to renew the family's temple recommend.

Because Ellie is the oldest girl, she is responsible for helping her mother with the majority of the chores. She likes being her mother's main helper. After spending a few hours on her homework, Ellie goes downstairs to help her mother cook dinner and set the table. They eat dinner later than most other families so that Ellie's father and Mason, who picks him up at the plant after work, can join them. After dinner and family study time, Ellie clears the table, puts away the food, and washes the dishes. Her mother is usually very tired after such a long day, so Ellie is glad to help—most of the time. She tries to remind herself that someday she will be raising a family of her own and needs to learn how to cook and clean and take care of children more than she needs to play or study.

Although sometimes the noise and confusion make her want to lock herself in the bathroom, Ellie likes living in a big family. There is always someone to play with or help her with her homework. Elijah is especially good at math. Many Mormon families have several children. Ellie's father says that this is because of the Mormon doctrine of preexistence. This teaching states that peoples' souls have existed forever with God before coming to earth. But unless they live human lives, they cannot be saved and go to heaven. This means that human parents need to provide bodies for these souls by having children. Ellie's father says that refusing to have children decreases the amount of blessing a husband and wife will experience. Ellie hopes her parents will consider themselves blessed enough with the children they have—she's not sure her mother could manage any more babies.

Ellie's mother and father were married by a justice of the peace to satisfy the laws of the United States. Afterward, they went to a temple and were sealed. Ellie's mother said that sealing ensures that she and Ellie's father will be together for all eternity after they die. This is called *celestial marriage*. Mormons believe that being sealed into a celestial marriage will help them reach the highest level of heaven. Ellie's mother said that since she and Ellie's father were sealed before they had children, Ellie and her brothers and sister are automatically sealed with them. Ellie's mother finds comfort in the thought that her family will always be together, even after death.

By living righteously and performing all the right ceremonies, her parents hope to earn *exaltation*. This Mormon teaching states that the very best people can one day enter the highest of three heavens and become gods, equal with Jesus Christ. Practices like baptism, the sacrament, celestial marriage, and a lifestyle of obedience to the church are required in order to be exalted in heaven and live eternally with God.

Ellie often wonders what non-Mormons think about her family and her faith. In Utah, most people are used to the Mormon beliefs and lifestyle. But Ellie is curious to know what Mormons look like to people who are unfamiliar with them. Once she asked a friend at school what she thought of Mormons before her family moved to Utah. With a shrug, her friend Ashley said that many people think that being Mormon means having more than one wife and lots of children. Confused by this, Ellie later asked her mother why any man would want more than one wife. Her mother said that some early Mormons be-

Joseph Smith, Jr, the nephew of the founder of Mormonism, with his wives and children circa 1900.

lieved that marrying many women, a practice called *polygamy*, would bring them more blessings. Some of Ellie's own ancestors practiced polygamy, but since this practice was against the law, the church eventually stopped promoting it. Ellie's mother said that today many outsiders associate Mormonism with polygamy because it is still practiced by a few fundamentalist groups that have broken away from the true Mormon faith.

Ellie's father jokes about polygamy and says he couldn't *afford* another wife. All Mormons are expected to give the church ten percent of their income each year. This is called *tithing*. There is also a monthly *fast offering*, given to support the church's welfare work, which families are supposed to pay for by skipping two meals per month. For Ellie's family, with so many mouths to feed, obeying these principles is sometimes difficult. Ellie's father sometimes worries how he is going to provide for all the things the family needs and still pay his tithe to the church.

Ellie's parents are trying to save up enough money so that her oldest brother Mason can go on his missionary trip. Every Mormon young man is expected to spend two years after high school graduation living as a Mormon missionary in another part of the world. Mason is working after school to help save the money he will need to support himself for two years. After his application has been accepted, he will go to the Missionary Training Center in Provo, about an hour away from home. Mason is hoping to be assigned to South America, but he won't find out where he is to be sent until he arrives at the training center. After spending a few months learning the skills he will need as a missionary, Mason and his assigned partner will be sent out to try to persuade people to join the Mormon Church. Ellie will miss him a lot when he goes.

Most days Ellie likes being a Mormon girl. She enjoys living in a big family and likes having family roots that stretch all the way back to pioneer times. But some days she worries that she doesn't have enough faith. She is afraid of making mistakes that might cause her to lose her salvation or be asked to leave the church. She also has some questions about God that she is hesitant to ask her Sunday school teacher or parents—she doesn't want anyone to think she isn't a good Mormon.

But these thoughts don't usually last for long. Ellie keeps busy cleaning up after dinner or chasing the twins around the house to give them their bedtime bath. At the end of a long day, she climbs into bed, says her prayers, and falls asleep, knowing that tomorrow is a fresh start.

WHAT'S THE DIFFERENCE?

- How is the way Ellie lives different from the way you live? How are your lives similar?
- Why do you think Ellie's family is so careful to follow Mormon teachings?
- What do you think visiting a Mormon meetinghouse or temple might be like? What would Ellie think of your church if she visited it?
- The Mormon Church teaches that by living righteously, believers may one day become gods themselves, like Jesus Christ. How does this differ from the biblical Christian view of God and heaven?
- Quoting from Genesis, Jesus said, "A man will leave his father and mother and be united to his wife, and the two will become one flesh" (Matthew 19:5). Not three or four or more, but *two* people, man and wife. Yet Jacob, David, and Solomon all took more than one wife, and each time it led to grief. Why do you think the early Mormons believed in polygamy? What do you think it would be like to have several mothers?
- How are Mormon missionaries different from most Christian missionaries? Who are the missionary families your church supports?

THE HOUSE OF TRUTH: THE SEVENTH PILLAR

You have learned that people were created in God's image to rule over creation with glory and honor. We were made to live in perfect harmony, not only with our God, but also with ourselves and with each other. But when sin entered creation, harmony was destroyed and these relationships became broken. Sin has caused people's emotional lives to be marked by disharmony, turmoil, and frustration. In this lesson, you erected the third pillar in your Image-Bearing Wall:

BIBLICAL TRUTH 11

SIN CAUSES DISHARMONY WITHIN ME.

Biblical Truth 9
God created me in His image

Biblical Truth 10
God has crowned me with honor and glory

Biblical Truth 11
Sin causes disharmony within me

IMAGE-BEARING WALL
My relationship with myself as I become more like Jesus

Biblical Truth 2
God is the only true and almighty God

FOUNDATION OF WISDOM
Knowing, loving, and obeying God my Rock

THE ROCK
God and His Word

139

WILL YOU CHOOSE WISELY?

> TRUST IN THE LORD WITH ALL YOUR HEART AND LEAN NOT ON YOUR OWN UNDERSTANDING; IN ALL YOUR WAYS ACKNOWLEDGE HIM, AND HE WILL MAKE YOUR PATHS STRAIGHT.

PROVERBS 3:5-6

THE BIG IDEA

In Lewis Carroll's classic children's tale *Alice's Adventures in Wonderland*, young Alice is wandering through the forest when she comes across the Cheshire Cat and asks for directions. "Would you tell me, please, which way I ought to go from here?" she asks the grinning feline.

"That depends a good deal on where you want to get to," the Cat replies.

"I don't much care where—" Alice says.

"Then it doesn't matter which way you go," says the Cat.

Decisions, decisions. We all make dozens of decisions every day. *Which socks should I wear? Which cereal shall I have for breakfast? Which friend will I call? Which movie should I go see? Should I stop and talk with the homeless man who's asking me for money?* Some of these decisions have little or no lasting impact on how we live. Many of the decisions we make seem harmless and insignificant at the time, but they later turn out to be very important indeed. Other decisions that seem monumental or overwhelming when we make them in fact turn out to be of little consequence down the road. Does it matter then which choices we make or how we go about making them? Absolutely!

God never intended for us to wander through life aimlessly, making reckless, arbitrary decisions about where we go, what we do, what we watch, and how we spend our time. God is never reckless or arbitrary, nor does He expect His children—who are made in His image—to live this way. In fact, God gave us an entire book, the Bible, as a guide for how we are to

conduct our lives and make choices. He gave us His only Son, Jesus, to model good decision-making for us. And to those who choose to follow His Son, God gives the Holy Spirit to counsel them and encourage them toward wisdom. He also surrounds us with knowledgeable people who can provide us with godly wisdom and help us find the answers we're looking for.

Many of the poor choices we make are the result of rushing hastily into a decision. As we've discussed, it's not a good idea to take action based solely on how you feel, because emotions can be unreliable indicators of truth. When you base your decisions on bad information, you often get bad decisions. That doesn't mean you need to consult three translations of the Bible before choosing what to eat for breakfast—God's Word doesn't contain specific direction concerning corn flakes. However, the Bible does have a great deal to say about food, nutrition, and the Bread of Life (John 6:35). If you make reading your Bible a daily priority, if you choose to pursue truth and wisdom in all things, you will soon begin to make better mealtime decisions and develop better eating habits.

As you grow up, you will be asked to make more complicated, more difficult choices involving relationships, college, and a career. Some decisions—such as whom you choose to marry—will change your life forever. Although the decisions you make now, when you're young, will probably not have such long-term consequences, you can give yourself a big head start in life by developing good decision-making habits now.

Begin by talking with God throughout the day; put Him first in everything you do and everything you think about. Read from the Bible every day; meditate often on the nuggets of wisdom you find in the book of Proverbs, and you will soon find yourself living truth and making better choices. Recognize that you don't always know what's best; talk to adults you trust about the decisions you're making and ask for their advice. Finally, learn from the mistakes you make; admit when you were wrong and determine to do better next time.

WHAT YOU WILL DO
» You will recognize that we choose God because He first chose us.
» You will practice seeking and applying God's wisdom when making decisions.
» You will examine how respecting God will help you make wise choices.

KNIGHTS IN THE MIDDLE AGES

Lancelot. Ivanhoe. Galahad. Lochinvar. Gawain. Noble knights are among the most famous characters in all literature. Although the romantic notions of knighthood were first popularized in books and songs and poetry, the "gentleman soldiers" of the Middle Ages were very real. Knights were elite warriors who were expected to be good men in addition to being good fighters. They swore to fight for justice and order, to protect those who couldn't defend themselves, and to remain loyal to their king or lord.

Knights were considered more important than regular foot soldiers, in part because they had better training and equipment. Most knights came from upper-class families who could afford to purchase expensive armor, weapons, and war horses. Knights had a reputation as excellent riders, and their horses needed to be strong, agile, and unafraid amid the noise and confusion of battle. In addition to his trademark armor, every knight was equipped with a sword and other durable weapons, such as lances for jousting and daggers for close combat.

To become a knight, a boy was sent around the age of seven to be trained as a page in a knight's household. Pages carried messages, ran errands, cleaned the castle, helped care for the horses, and started learning how to fight and joust. After seven years, a page could become a squire. A squire was a knight's personal attendant, carrying his shield or banner into battle, keeping his armor polished, and looking after his horse. After seven more years, a squire could be dubbed as a knight. If he demonstrated particular courage on the field of battle, a squire might be promoted on the spot. He would then swear loyalty to a king or nobleman and join his army of knights.

Around the fifteenth century, guns and rockets were introduced to the battlefield and began to render knights in armor obsolete. Yet many of the medieval orders of knighthood continue to exist in several countries, including the Order of the Garter in Great Britain. Today, the knights of old serve as an example of how to live with honor, upholding the cause of righteousness and sacrificing oneself to protect and care for others.

THE FEAST

The trumpets sounded a great fanfare, and the herald stepped forth to make his proclamation. "My lords and ladies, noble knights, good people of Cambridge—it is my unspeakable honor and deepest privilege to present to you a knight who truly needs no introduction. His valor is legendary, his stature extraordinary, his skill with sword and lance unsurpassed. His mighty deeds are known throughout the realm and all of Europe. In the courts of France and Spain, warriors and princes quake at the very mention of his name. His armor shines as the morning sun, and his shield lights the way for the armies of the king. I give to you your undefeated champion: the dauntless, the magnificent, the humble Sir Brandon of—"

"Put some elbow grease into it, varlet! I want to see my reflection in that floor before the feast!"

Young Brandon was startled from his daydream.

Quentin, the eldest page, nearly two years Brandon's senior, scowled down at him. Quentin was a full head taller anyway, so that he now towered over the younger boy, who was on his knees and supposed to be scrubbing the floor of the great hall.

Photo: Misterzee.

"The floor is made of wood, not glass," Brandon protested. "Besides, it's going to be covered by a carpet."

"That's beside the point, commoner. Do it right, or I'll have you scrubbing pots and pans for the cooks all night." This was no idle threat. There was a pecking order among the pages that was determined by age. Quentin was nearing fourteen, at which point he would ascend to the position of squire and train to become a knight. In the meantime, he could make life miserable for Brandon, so long as his orders did not contradict those of a knight or the baron.

The younger page sighed and returned to his work.

Quentin continued to glower at him for a moment, then kicked over the wash bucket, turned on his heel, and marched out of the hall.

Brandon now knelt in a pool of suds and brown water, his breeches soaked. He caught his reflection in the puddle and stared at the dirty face and the brown, matted hair he saw there. *Who am I kidding?* he thought. *I'll never make squire, let alone become a knight. I have no connections, no family. I have a better chance of sprouting wings and flying.*

He gathered up his empty bucket and trudged outside to the courtyard to refill the bucket at the castle well. A family of ducks scurried out of his path, kicking up dust and down that stuck to Brandon's wet breeches.

"Pardon me, kind sir. Will you yield to a lady?" His friend Gwyneth came up from behind him with an empty bucket of her own.

"A lady?" Brandon snorted. "Who said you were a lady?"

"Oh my. What's got you in a snit?"

Brandon stopped frowning and allowed himself a smile. "I'm sorry, Gwyneth. It's been a difficult day. The Baron de Lisle is returning unexpectedly from Calais, and everyone is rushing about and working hard to prepare the great hall for a feast."

"Well, that explains why Lady Isabel is all in a lather. William must be accompanying the baron. She's spent the whole day deciding what to wear."

"As a matter of fact, I've heard that the feast is to be held in William's honor."

"Whatever for?" Gwyneth asked as she drew her water from the well. "I mean, William is wonderful and all, but he's only a squire."

"I don't know. But it will be good to see William again. He's the only one around here who treats me like a real person."

Gwyneth tried to look indignant. "Well, thank you very much, Master Brandon!"

"What I meant to say was, he's the only one whose opinion counts who—"

"I beg your pardon!"

"No, that's not what I meant—" Brandon stammered. "That is to say, I—"

"I know what you mean." Gwyneth smiled mischievously. "You're talking of men and their silly squabbles over rank and titles. Well, I'll have you know that I *do* count." She held up her chin. "After all, I am the daughter of a king."

"A *king*? Don't be ridiculous. Everyone knows your father is the Earl of Warwick. That doesn't make you a princess. You're only an attendant to Isabel, who is herself a lady-in-waiting to the Lady de Lisle." Brandon took his turn lowering the well bucket into the gloom until a splash echoed from below.

"Oh, but I *am* a princess. I learned all about it this morning in my lessons. I have been adopted into the family of God. My earthly father may possess lands and a manor, but my heavenly Father rules over all creation!"

Brandon turned the hand crank to lift the full bucket. "It must be nice having two fathers," he said. "I don't even have the one."

"I almost forgot you were a foundling. Now it's my turn to be sorry, Brandon. I didn't mean to hurt your feelings."

"That's all right, Gwyneth. It's just that I have no idea who my parents are. Probably some poor peasants who couldn't afford another mouth to feed. They abandoned me at the gates of a nobleman who couldn't be bothered with me either, and so I ended up here at Cambridge Castle doing menial labor for the lady of the house." They both picked up their buckets and began moving slowly into the castle interior.

"But you are a page! Not just anyone is allowed to be a page. And one day you will be a squire, then eventually a knight!"

"If I were born of noble blood, sure! Then my father would arrange to pay my room and board and training fees with the expectation that I would one day earn a knighthood. But I don't even know who is paying for my upkeep, or whether he will continue paying for it, or if he even remembers that I'm here. Quentin and the others never let me forget this. They call me 'varlet' and 'commoner' and lord it over me all day long. I have no earthly reason to expect I shall ever become a knight."

Gwyneth set her bucket down, put her hands on Brandon's upper arms, and held his gaze steady. "Now you listen to me, Master Brandon. You *will* be a knight—one of the greatest ever. William believes in you. I believe in you. Even Lady Isabel believes in you. Now *you* must believe. If you continue to think of yourself as a lowly page with no prospects for advancement, surely that is all you will ever be." She smiled. "But who knows? Maybe a position will open up in the castle for a tinker. Or town crier. Or maybe even court jester!"

Brandon laughed aloud at this, and his mood began to lift. He said, "Without family or connections, court jester may be the highest post I can aspire to. Perhaps I should learn to juggle. Say, what do you call an unemployed jester?"

"I give up. What *do* you call an unemployed jester?"

"Nobody's fool."

Gwyneth and Brandon laughed heartily for some time before Gwyneth turned serious once more. "Do not carry this burden alone, Brandon. Seek the Lord in prayer, and He will guide you and protect you."

"But I have an awful time memorizing the prayers the vicar gives me. For one thing, they're all in Latin, so I don't even know what I'm saying."

"Then talk to God like you're talking to William. God is so much more than a king—He is your friend. You can talk with him about anything. Be open and honest. Tell Him your fears and concerns. Ask Him for whatever it is you need."

Brandon looked puzzled by this. "But He is God. Doesn't He already know what I need?"

"Of course! But He wants you to ask because He wants you to depend on Him for everything. He is our rock, our strength, and an ever-present help to even the greatest of the king's knights."

This certainly gave Brandon plenty to think about as he returned to the great hall to scrub floors.

That afternoon, as Brandon was mucking the stables, a commotion arose outside. Boys were shouting and cheering, and above all the noise Brandon heard a familiar voice. *William.* He dropped his pitchfork and ran outside to see William ride into the yard astride his horse, Maximilian, surrounded by pages and squires. They greeted him with questions and shouts of congratulations. William was wearing an oversized knee-length shirt of chainmail and a tunic in the baron's colors. He spotted Brandon and waved to him, then dismounted.

Brandon stood outside the melee as the older squires pushed forward past the smaller pages. William was all smiles as his friends slapped him on the back in greeting and shook his hand, though he said little. The questions kept coming, one on top of another, until he laughed and held up a hand. "Hold! Hold!" he called. "I will tell you all everything over evening meal. For now, I have duties of my own to attend to."

"And a lady to see," someone shouted from the crowd.

Everyone laughed heartily as William blushed. Then the crowd began to disperse, and the boys went back to their chores.

William walked his horse over to where Brandon stood, but before handing the reins to the page, William offered his right hand. Brandon smiled and shook his hand vigorously. Then he took the reins and led the horse to the stables as William walked alongside him.

"How fare you, Master Brandon?"

"I'm fine, Will, but what about you? And what's with the hauberk? Chainmail is not exactly standard dress for a squire."

"That's true. But then, I am no longer a squire."

Brandon stopped. "What?"

"You are now addressing a knight of the realm. Sir William, at your service." He gave a small bow.

Brandon gasped, then grinned broadly. "But how? You're only just nineteen and will not be of age for two full years."

William began walking again, and Brandon followed, Maximilian in tow. "I received a field promotion. We left Calais one morning on a standard patrol of the area. The baron was leading our small company through a grove of trees when we were ambushed by a French raiding party. Before we knew what was happening, the baron had been wounded by a lancer and thrown from his horse. Without thinking, I took up the baron's sword and slew the enemy lancer, then disarmed another and wounded him. Although we were outnumbered, the knights of our company easily dispatched several of the enemy, and the rest turned tail and fled on foot. Baron de Lisle had been pierced in the shoulder, though it turned out to be only a flesh wound. He knighted me then and there in the forest, and he gave me his own chainmail to wear. As you can see from the ill fit, the baron is broader of shoulder than I, but he promised to have it resized for me once we returned to Cambridge. And here we are."

"Congratulations, Wi— I mean, Sir William."

William laughed. "We are friends, you and I. When we're alone, please call me Will."

"Yes, Sir Wi— I mean, Will. But what about the ceremony? I was really hoping to see you knighted when the time came."

"And so you shall. The baron is making an announcement this evening: The king himself will be arriving in a fortnight to perform the ceremony and induct me into the Order of the Garter."

"That's wonderful! I'm as proud as if you were my own brother."

As Brandon led the horse into its stall and settled him in, William turned thoughtful and serious. "I need your advice, Brandon."

Brandon snorted. "What could *I* possibly say that would be of any use to you?"

"I must choose a squire to attend me. Whom do you suggest?"

"Well . . . the baron has many good squires with years of training in arms and horsemanship and—"

"Yes, they're all fine lads, but I am barely older than most of them. No, I have set my mind toward selecting a squire from among the pages—someone I can teach, someone I can trust, someone I can instruct in the faith and in the ways of chivalry."

"I see what you mean. Well, Quentin is the oldest of the pages and next in line to make squire. He's tall and strong and comes from a wealthy family, and he—"

"And he makes life difficult for you, does he not?"

Brandon grinned. "I cannot honestly say I'll be sorry to see him go, should the two of you return to Calais."

"I'm sure Quentin will make a fine knight one day, once he learns some humility. Arrogance is a dangerous quality to carry onto the battlefield. No, I was thinking of someone with a more teachable spirit."

"What about Gregory? He's good with—"

"I was thinking of you, Brandon."

"Me? But I'm not worthy to— I'm not of noble birth. I don't even know who my parents are. I— I'm nobody, Will!"

"On the contrary. You are a child of the One True God, the King of all creation, made in His image and crowned with glory and honor. That makes you someone very special."

"No," Brandon protested, "I am only twelve. I have no skills, no training, no education. I am little more than a servant."

"Is that so?" William replied. "You know, Christ came to us as a servant. His mother was young and of lowly birth, from a village of no importance. He held no titles or rank. He was the only begotten Son of God, yet He came to serve, not to be served. Do you believe that He died to pay for your sins, and that He rose again on the third day and now sits at the right hand of the Father?"

"Yes, of course."

"Good. The Scriptures say that because you choose to believe, you have been given the right to be called a child of God. In his epistle to the Romans, the apostle Paul says that, as His child, you are a co-heir with Christ. If you share in His sufferings, you will share in His glory."

"Does it really say that?" Brandon asked.

"It does. I see you have much to learn about who you are in Christ. Brandon, our Father in heaven has a plan for your life. It's a plan only you can fulfill, and its completion will bring Him glory. No one else possesses the unique combination of talents and gifts required to see this plan through. But you must *choose* to do God's will; He will not force Himself upon you."

"What should I do?"

"God has chosen you to follow Him. I have chosen you to stand at my side as my squire. Do you still insist you are unworthy to carry my sword?"

Brandon was silent for a moment. Then he got down on one knee and said, "Sir William, I do have much to learn. But I would be honored if you would take me as your squire and teach me all I need to know to serve you and bring glory to my Father in heaven."

"Excellent!" William clapped his hands and rubbed them together. "As for your age, I will take it up with the baron. In the meantime, we have much to do before the ceremony in two weeks." He pulled Brandon to his feet. "My first command to you is to help me remove this awful hauberk. I do believe this chainmail weighs as much as you!"

That evening, at the feast held in William's honor, the Baron John de Lisle stood and toasted his newest knight, who was seated at his side on the raised dais. The baron recounted for all the tale of the skirmish in the forest and of William's courage. "In the moment after I had fallen," he said, "William had a choice to make. He could see we were outnumbered and his commander was down. He was unarmed, aside from a small dagger, and could not be expected to hold his own against seasoned soldiers. He could have believed his eyes, seen that he was helpless, and chosen to run and hide. Instead, William saw the situation through the eyes of faith. He knew himself to be more than a squire, that he was a child of the living God, and he was certain that God had a great plan for his life. And he knew that so long as that plan remained unfulfilled, he would not taste death. So William took up my sword and, without hesitating, saved my life."

The great hall erupted in applause. Gwyneth, who stood at the side of the Lady Isabel, jumped up and down, clapping.

The baron motioned for silence and continued. "As you know, William was knighted on the field of honor, but an important step remains. A fortnight from now, the king himself will grace our presence here at Cambridge Castle, and he will induct Sir William into the illustrious Order of the Garter."

The applause turned to cheers, and the air was suddenly filled with hats tossed by their owners. Brandon, grinning from ear to ear, caught William's eye. William smiled and nodded to him. Tomorrow, his training would begin.

THINK ABOUT IT

» Brandon's story takes place in the year 1354, during what we call the Middle Ages, or medieval times. How did daily life during the Middle Ages differ from the way you live today?

» Baron John de Lisle was a real person. He fought in the Hundred Years' War and was one of the founding members of the Order of the Garter. Cambridge Castle was also a real place. Find the city of Cambridge on a map of England. Do you know what the city is most famous for today? If not, look it up online or at your local library.

» Brandon dreams of becoming a great knight in the king's service, yet when William asks him to be his squire—the next step toward becoming a knight—Brandon feels undeserving of the honor. Why does he feel this way? Who has told him he is unworthy of becoming a knight?

HEAVY METAL

Chainmail, or *chainmaille*, is a flexible armor made of many small metal rings linked together to form a tight mesh. Forged from brass, iron, or steel, chainmail was the first word in protective wear for knights of the Middle Ages, before the development of full plate armor.

Shirts of chainmail weighed up to fifty-five pounds, depending on their size and length, and could be difficult to move about in. However, the mesh was effective at stopping an enemy's sword or lance or the sharp edge of an axe. Although mail did not protect the knight from heavy blows from a blunt weapon, it generally prevented the skin from being pierced, thus limiting the potential for fatal infections which often followed such injuries in medieval times.

Each garment of chainmail was fashioned specifically for the part of the body it was intended to protect. Differences in size were easy to accommodate, simply by adding or removing rings from the garment. Gauntlets called *mitons* were worn as gloves. Mail shirts came in knee-length tunics called *hauberks*, mid-thigh-length tunics called *haubergeons*, and waist-length tunics called *byrnies*. If the knight's tunic had a hood, or *coif*, attached, he'd have to almost stand on his head to remove it because the tunic could have no fasteners, which would leave the wearer's neck and shoulders vulnerable to attack.

Today, chainmail still has its uses. For example, it is often worn by butchers who work with meat-cutting machines. Scuba divers sometimes wear it as protection against sharks, and animal-control officers use it to protect themselves from animal bites. Chainmail is also popular for its decorative uses, especially on military uniforms or as jewelry.

151

WORDS YOU NEED TO KNOW

» **God's will:** God's plans and purposes for everything He created

» **Fear of the Lord:** An attitude of reverence toward God in which I recognize His right to rule over every area of my life

HIDE IT IN YOUR HEART

Even before he made the world, God loved us and chose us in Christ to be holy and without fault in his eyes. (Ephesians 1:4, NLT)

The fear of the LORD is the beginning of wisdom, and knowledge of the Holy One is understanding. (Proverbs 9:10)

GOD WANTS YOU!

In 1916, *Leslie's Weekly* magazine commissioned artist James Montgomery Flagg to paint a portrait of the fictional character Uncle Sam for the cover of its July 6 issue. Pressure was mounting on the United States to enter the Great War taking place in Europe, and the magazine was calling on readers to begin doing their part immediately to prepare for the coming war effort. Less than a year later, the U.S. officially entered the war, and Flagg's painting was used to create what he later called "the most famous poster in the world." Four million copies were printed of the poster depicting a stern Uncle Sam pointing his finger at viewers and declaring, "I Want YOU."

Flagg's poster was a recruiting tool for the U.S. Army, a way to encourage young men to volunteer to fight for their country. Today, the Lord God is looking for a few good men and women to follow Jesus, serve one another, and carry the good news of salvation to every corner of the world. Many will hear the call of God—Romans 1:18–23 tells us that the truth about God has been made obvious to everyone, and therefore

Painting: James Montgomery Flagg.

no one has an excuse for not following Him—but sadly, few among us will truly listen and respond to God's call (Matthew 22:14).

Have you answered God's call? Have you chosen to accept His free gift of salvation? If you believe Jesus is the Son of God and that He died for your sins and was raised from the dead, if you call Him Lord and have chosen to follow Him, you are a bona fide child of God. You are royalty! John 1:12–13 says you have been born again into the family of the King of kings, the Most High God. You know what's really amazing? This was no accident. God *chose* you:

Even before he made the world, God loved us and chose us in Christ to be holy and without fault in his eyes. (Ephesians 1:4, NLT)

Brothers, the Lord loves you. God chose you from the beginning to be saved. (2 Thessalonians 2:13, ICB)

If you have chosen God, it's because God first chose you. Let that sink in for a moment. God chose you! He chose you before He created the world so that you would choose Him and want to live your life for Him.

Why you? Good question. Perhaps you feel unworthy to be called a child of God. Maybe you have a shortcoming you think disqualifies you from serving in His kingdom. If so, you're in good company. Moses stuttered, and Jacob was a liar. Abraham and Sarah were too old, and David was too young. Miriam was a gossip, and Hosea's wife was a prostitute. Elijah was burned out, and Lazarus was dead. Gideon had doubts, and so did Thomas. Peter was afraid, and Jonah ran from God. Noah got drunk, and Paul was a murderer. Yet God used every one of these people for His glory.

You see, God is not interested in your report card or your résumé. He

The Tomb of Lazarus as it appeared in 1893.
God chose to use Lazarus even though he had died!

doesn't care how much money your parents make, how many friends you have, what kind of car your family drives, or whether you graduate from an Ivy League school. It doesn't matter to Him what you look like or how well you speak. He's not worried about the mistakes you've made or the mistakes you *will* make. He doesn't require you to take a test or interview for a place in His kingdom. If you have chosen to follow God, your position is secure: You are a chosen one.

Again, you may ask, "Why me?"

Ephesians 1:5 says that God chose you *just because He wanted to.*

And every choice God makes is absolutely perfect.

GOD WANTS YOU TO CHOOSE WISELY

Every kid feels powerless now and then. After all, so many decisions that affect you each day are made by someone else. Somebody else tells you where you're going to live, what you will have for dinner, what time to get up in the morning, which songs to sing in church, and which subjects to study for school. Sometimes it seems as though every important decision in life is beyond your control.

It's true that God, in His great wisdom, places children in families and gives them parents and other adults to guide them, teach them, and make many critical decisions for their benefit. That's because children do not yet have the knowledge, experience, or maturity to make wise decisions about such things as meeting the family's housing and nutritional needs or making a household budget.

Someday you will be required to make these kinds of choices for yourself and *your* family. Until then, you must learn and practice good decision-making skills by choosing to live each day in a way that is pleasing to God. Now, many of the decisions you will be asked to make as a child may seem small and insignificant. But the Bible teaches that we "should not think that small beginnings are unimportant" (Zechariah 4:10, NCV). Jesus said, "If you are faithful in little things, you will be faithful in large ones" (Luke 16:10, NLT).

Jesus showed us the right way to make decisions. As we have seen, He had the same feelings and passions we have. He had friends who trusted Him to make good decisions and who counted on Him to lead them. And He had enemies who insisted that He change His way of doing things. Jesus had to make some tough choices. Yet He always knew the right thing to do because He kept His focus on God the Father: "For I have come down from heaven not to do my will but to do the will of him who sent me" (John 6:38).

The truth is, even as a child you are not powerless. You, too, have decisions to make. Although God has a plan for your life, you have a responsibility to choose wisely. Every day, every hour, every minute, you must choose to do what is right or to do what is wrong. You must choose between actions and words that are wise and those that are unwise. You can choose to do what you want to do or what God wants you to do. How will you choose?

MAKE A NOTE OF IT
List five decisions you've made today. Now write a brief paragraph about each of these decisions: What were your options? Why did you choose the way you did? What were the consequences of your decision? For example: Let's say you decided what to eat for breakfast this morning. What were your possible choices? Did you make your choice based on flavors, nutritional content, the color of the box it came in, your energy needs for the day, or a combination of factors? How did your decision work out for you? Did you have good energy all morning? Or did you get hungry again an hour before lunchtime?

WHY DO PEOPLE MAKE UNWISE CHOICES?

Knowing the wise thing to do in most situations is really not all that difficult. We have defined wisdom as knowing, loving, and obeying God's Word and applying that knowledge to make good decisions. If you and I will read and study the Bible and carry its words in our hearts and minds, we should be able to make the wise choice every time.

So why don't we? The Bible says that even those people who choose not to read God's Word know about God and His holiness (Romans 1:18–20). And we were all created with the ability to think and reason and understand the difference between right and wrong. So why do people make so many unwise decisions?

We often make poor decisions in part because "the heart is deceitful above all things" (Jeremiah 17:9, NKJV). We can talk ourselves into doing just about anything. We can find any number of "good reasons" for doing things we really know are wrong: *My friends are all doing it. I'm not hurting anyone, and there's no law against it. Besides, nobody's going to find out.* So often people make choices based not on what is wise but on what they think they can get away with. And so to justify their poor choices, they must lie to themselves.

Why do you suppose so many people make unhealthy choices when it comes to what they eat? It's not because they lack information about what's in the food. It's no secret that a McDonald's Big Mac sandwich contains 560 calories and 30 grams of fat. (That's before you add fries and a soda!) And you don't have to look far to learn that Taco Bell's Burrito Supreme has 440 calories and 18 grams of fat. If you're an eleven-year-old girl, you probably need about 2,200 calories per day, depending on your activity level. As for the prepackaged food we buy at the supermarket, nearly every item these days is labeled with nutritional facts. These facts include the number of calories per serving and a complete list of ingredients. Look closely and you will see that many of America's favorite foods contain chemicals and coloring agents that are known to be potentially harmful to humans. So why do we continue to consume foods we know may be hazardous to our health?

Much of the reason is that we simply refuse to acknowledge the truth of what the foods we eat are doing to our bodies. We lie to ourselves. We like the way it tastes, so we ignore the labels and eat it anyway. No one is saying these foods aren't delicious or fun to eat, but are a few moments of fun worth the long-term consequences that can lead to obesity, illness, or even death?

Likewise, when making decisions people tend to ignore the flashing warning signs. We conveniently "forget" the wisdom and truth of God's Word. We see something that looks good, smells delicious, or sounds fun, and we want it. So we tell ourselves, *It's okay, it's just this once*, and we dive in without giving any real thought to the consequences of our actions. But poor choices—like sins—have a way of multiplying. You may quickly find yourself making more poor choices to cover up the mistakes you've already made, until a pattern of poor decision-making is established.

How can you break this pattern and begin making wise decisions? First you must face the facts. You must acknowledge the truth and stop lying to yourself. If you want to make good choices, if you ever hope to be healthy both physically and spiritually, you must be honest with yourself and admit that you already know in your heart what God would have you do. Know the truth, choose the truth, and the truth will set you free (John 8:32).

MAKE A NOTE OF IT

Go to your cupboard or kitchen pantry and find a box of breakfast cereal. If you don't eat cereal, any packaged food product will do. Write down the complete list of ingredients listed on the side of the box. Now, with the help of a parent, go to the Internet or your library and look up each one of the ingredients. Find out what it is and what it does. Are there any health warnings or advisories connected with this ingredient? If so, talk with your parents about replacing the cereal with a healthier alternative.

HOW TO MAKE A WISE DECISION

Knowing the wise thing to do is not always as simple as reading the Surgeon General's warning on a package of cigarettes. We cannot always be sure of the consequences that may result from choosing between two seemingly good options. For example, should you join the church choir or help care for the babies in the nursery? Should you take piano lessons or learn to play the guitar? There's not always a right or wrong choice, but there are some important strategies for making good decisions. Let's look at a few.

ASK GOD FIRST

No decision is wise if you make it without first talking to God. After all, He knows everything there is to know—past, present, and future. "To God belong wisdom and power; counsel and understanding are his" (Job 12:13). He knows the consequences, large and small, of every decision you make. And like all good fathers, He wants only the best for you, His child.

When Jesus needed to choose twelve apostles from among His many followers, He could have simply selected the twelve handsomest or the twelve best public speakers or the twelve who had displayed the greatest measure of faith. Instead, Jesus went off to a mountain and spent the entire night in prayer, asking God whom He should choose (Luke 6:12–15). King Saul, on the other hand, did not wait for an answer from God. Confronted by an advancing army of angry Philistines, Saul was afraid. So he went to a medium, a psychic, and asked *her* advice (1 Samuel 28). For this, the Lord put Saul to death and gave the kingdom of Israel to David (1 Chronicles 10:13–14).

This does not mean you must wait for an angelic visitation before deciding to go camping. God speaks to His children in many ways—in His Word, by the Holy Spirit, through the advice of godly counselors, and through our past experiences. Your heavenly Father cares about every detail of your daily life, and He will never leave you to face your dilemmas alone. When you have a difficult decision to make, pray about it. Spend time reading the Bible and meditating on its words. Then listen for God to answer.

Keep in mind that God will never contradict Himself. If you think something you saw on TV or heard in a sermon is God's way of trying to tell you something, compare it to what you find in the Bible. You can always trust what you read in God's Word.

In His will is our peace.
Dante Alighieri
1265–1321

LISTEN TO THE HOLY SPIRIT

One of the ways God speaks to us is through the Holy Spirit. The Holy Spirit is God's special gift to every person who chooses to follow Christ. The Holy Spirit is called the Counselor or Helper, and He lives inside every believer. Jesus said, "He will teach you everything and will remind you of everything I have told you" (John 14:26, NLT). In fact, the Bible says, "He will guide you into all truth" (John 16:13). And when you are facing a difficult decision or temptation and don't know what to pray for, the Holy Spirit will even pray *for* you (Romans 8:26–27)!

Remember, the Holy Spirit is God, and He lives in perfect unity and harmony with God the Father and God the Son, so He will never contradict God's Word. He will never lead you to lie, steal, or gossip, for the Bible has already told us these things are not godly. But if you will allow the Holy Spirit to guide your life and control your thoughts, then you will not give in to temptation and choose what your sinful nature wants (Galatians 5:16; Romans 8:5–6).

SEEK WISE COUNSEL

Not long after Solomon was crowned king of Israel, he found himself a bit overwhelmed by his new responsibilities. Then one night, the Lord appeared to Solomon in a dream and made him an offer: "What do you want? Ask, and I will give it to you!" (1 Kings 3:5, NLT). Imagine God appearing to a young man nowadays and offering to give him anything he wanted. What would most people ask for? What would *you* ask for? Good looks? A great singing voice? Chicken pox for the neighborhood bully? A horse of your own to ride in the Kentucky Derby?

Judgement of Solomon.

Here's what Solomon asked for:

"O LORD my God, you have made me king . . . but I am like a little child who doesn't know his way around. . . . Give me an understanding heart so that I can govern your people well and know the difference between right and wrong." (1 Kings 3:7–9, NLT)

Solomon made the smart choice: He asked for wisdom. The Lord was so pleased the young man had asked for understanding instead of riches or fame that He made Solomon the wealthiest, most famous person in all the world *and* gave him wisdom beyond that of any man or woman who ever lived (1 Kings 3:10–13). Solomon later became an architect, poet, philosopher, scientist, and scholar—a truly remarkable person. Yet he would write often about the importance of asking for and listening to good advice:

> *A wise man will hear and increase in learning, and a man of understanding will acquire wise counsel.* (Proverbs 1:5, NASB)

> *The way of a fool seems right to him, but a wise man listens to advice.* (Proverbs 12:15)

> *Without wise leadership, a nation falls; there is safety in having many advisers.* (Proverbs 11:14 NLT)

Why did the smartest man in the world make such a big deal out of seeking counsel and advice from others? *Because* he was the smartest man in the world! Even after God granted Solomon extraordinary wisdom, he continued to surround himself with trusted advisors. Wise people know when they don't know something, and they're not afraid to ask those who *do* know. Only fools believe they have all the answers.

Proverbs 1:5 (ESV) says, "Let the wise hear and increase in learning, and the one who understands obtain guidance." No matter how successful you may become, no matter how many college degrees you may earn, no matter how many young people you may teach one day, you will never outgrow your need for good advice. So begin to develop good decision-making habits now by asking for help from trusted adults. When you're having trouble making a decision, talk to your mom and dad, your Sunday school teacher, or your pastor. Ask what they would do in your situation. Ask them to pray with you about the issue and help you find answers in the Bible. Ask them to recommend a good book that might help you evaluate your choices.

I know it's hard to believe, but the adults in your life were once your age. And they probably had to deal with the same kinds of problems you're facing now. In October 1962, the youngest man ever elected president of the United States was confronted with a grave decision of his own. The Soviet Union had delivered nuclear missiles to the island nation of Cuba, just ninety miles off the coast of Florida. President John F. Kennedy demanded the missiles' immediate removal. Tensions were high and people were scared, as the U.S. and Soviet Union stood on the brink of a deadly war. Instead of rushing into action, President Kennedy picked up the telephone and called three men who had served as president before him—Herbert Hoover, Harry S. Truman, and Dwight D. Eisenhower. Kennedy asked for their advice, and each man had valuable insights to offer. After discussing the options with his

President Kennedy receiving advice from advisors on his executive committee during the Cuban Missile Crisis in 1962. Photo: Cecil Stoughton.

LINCOLN'S CABINET

The President's Cabinet is the name given to a select group of high-ranking officials in the American government. These people are chosen by the U.S. president to advise him or her on how to run the country and execute our nation's laws. The president relies on these men and women to provide him with good information and good ideas to help him make decisions that will benefit the whole country.

First Reading of the Emancipation Proclamation by Francis Bicknell Carpenter.

Every person who serves on the Cabinet is appointed by the president but first must be approved by the U.S. Senate. Currently there are fifteen Cabinet members and each is in charge of a different government department—state, treasury, defense, justice, interior, agriculture, commerce, labor, health and human services, housing and urban development, transportation, energy, education, veterans affairs, and homeland security. The first president, George Washington, appointed a Cabinet that had only four members.

Proverbs 15:22 says, "Plans fail for lack of counsel, but with many advisors they succeed." When Abraham Lincoln was elected president, he knew he was going to need a lot of help. The nation was divided, and a bloody civil war was inevitable. Lincoln wanted to get the opinions of the smartest people of his day on how to see the country through this crisis, even if those people didn't always see eye to eye with him. So instead of choosing men for his Cabinet who would agree to his proposals without question, he chose to appoint his political rivals, men who had run against him in the race for president.

A less confident man might have surrounded himself with personal supporters, but President Lincoln said, "These were the very strongest men. I had no right to deprive the country of their service." This decision, along with a great deal of prayer, helped Abraham Lincoln bring the United States through the Civil War and secured his place as one of the most respected presidents in American history.

closest advisors, including his brother Robert, President Kennedy chose a course of action that reduced the tension between the two countries while causing the Soviet leaders to rethink their position. War was prevented.

James 1:5 says, "If any of you lacks wisdom, he should ask God, who gives generously to all without finding fault, and it will be given to him." One of the ways God will provide you with the wisdom you need is through the counsel of others. But like Solomon, you must first understand that you don't know everything and then ask God for wisdom. Then talk with godly men and women you know and listen to what they have to say.

CHOOSE CHRIST

The Gospel of Luke tells the story of sisters Mary and Martha and how Jesus visited them one afternoon in the village of Bethany. Martha welcomed Jesus to their home and then immediately set about preparing dinner. She was determined to honor their guest with a clean home and a sumptuous meal. Meanwhile, Mary sat down at the feet of Jesus and listened to Him talk about the kingdom of heaven. Martha needed her sister's help getting dinner ready and probably let her know exactly how she felt long before she said anything. There was probably some glaring, a few pointed remarks, and a lot of banging of pots and pans to remind her sister there was still work to be done. But Mary barely noticed and never moved from her spot.

Martha and Mary by Tintoretto.

Martha's frustration mounted until finally she had had enough. "Lord," she said, "doesn't it bother you that my sister has left me to do all the work by myself? Tell her to come and help me!"

Jesus simply smiled and said, "Martha, Martha, you are worried and upset about so many things, but only one thing is necessary. Mary has chosen what is best, and it will not be taken away from her" (Luke 10:38–42, CEV).

Notice that Jesus did not criticize Martha or say, "Why can't you be more like your sister Mary?" He did not say that old-fashioned hard work is unnecessary or that being a good servant is not important. Scripture clearly states that we are to do our chores to the best of our ability as though we are "working for the Lord" (Colossians 3:23).

But Martha and Mary both had a choice to make. Jesus Christ was in town and coming to *their* house! The sisters could choose to hang out at the village well and spread the news of their good fortune. (Talk about having friends in high places!) Or they could choose to rush about cleaning house and preparing the finest gourmet meal anyone in Bethany had ever seen. Or they could choose to take the opportunity of a lifetime to worship and learn at the feet of the Master.

Martha made a good choice. But Mary made the *best* choice.

Put Jesus first in everything you do and everything you say. Spend time with Him every day by reading His Word. Obey His commands. Remember what He has done for you. Allow the Holy Spirit to guide your thoughts and actions, and He will help you become more and more like Jesus. Worship Christ for He is King!

WHAT SHOULD I DO?

When Solomon wrote, "The fear of the LORD is the beginning of wisdom" (Proverbs 9:10), did he mean we are supposed to be afraid of our heavenly Father? No. Solomon was talking about keeping a healthy respect for God and choosing to obey His commands. We must remember who God really is—the all-knowing, all-powerful, ever-present Creator of all things. When we consider the awesome grandeur of God, if we truly understand how amazing He is and the incredible depth of His love for us, the only appropriate way for our hearts to respond is to show reverence for Him. Deuteronomy 13:4 says, "It is the LORD your God you must follow, and him you must revere."

We demonstrate reverence for God by worshiping Him through prayer and praise, adoring His perfection, and giving Him first place in every area of our lives. We need to acknowledge His right to rule over everything He has created and surrender to His will for us. As we surrender our lives to Him, He will reveal more of Himself and His wisdom to us. And the more we understand of God's character and wisdom, the greater will be our ability to make good decisions.

A PRAYER

Dear God, thank you for choosing me to be your child. Thank you for creating me and for giving me the ability and freedom to make choices. Please give me the wisdom to make good choices and help me to remain in your will. Guide me and teach me through your Holy Spirit. Help me to always remember and obey your commands. Thank you for sending godly people into my life to teach me about you. Thank you especially for sending your Son, Jesus, to save me from the punishment I deserve for my sins. Help me to always choose Him. In Jesus' name. Amen.

Photo: NASA.

WORLDVIEWS IN FOCUS

MEET DEV

Dev is an eleven-year-old boy who lives in New York City. He lives with his father and mother, his older sister Chandra, his younger brother Rajani, his baby sister Bina, and his grandmother Nani. Dev's father emigrated from India when he was a young man. Although it meant leaving his parents, siblings, and extended family, Dev's father believed that there were many more opportunities for wealth and advancement in America.

Even though Dev and his family live far away from India, Hindu religion and practices are still a large part of their lives. In the morning, Dev wakes up early, bathes, and gets dressed. Then he goes downstairs to meet with his family for morning worship. They have a special prayer room in their house, and every day Dev and his family gather there to kneel and pray to their gods.

Hindus believe that everything that exists is part of a god they call Brahman. Brahman is not a person; it is everything. They believe that Brahman manifests itself as different, personal gods and that they can choose which one to worship. Dev's father prays to Rama, a god whose name means "lord of virtue." Rama is described as having blue skin, which is a sign of deity. By devoting himself to Rama and following his example, Dev's father hopes to live a perfect life.

Although Dev's mother worships Rama along with her husband, she has taken the goddess Sita, Rama's wife, as her example and guide. The love story of Rama and Sita is one of her favorite tales. Long ago in India, Princess Sita married the Lord Rama. When Rama was exiled from his kingdom, Sita volunteered to join him. Then she was kidnapped by an enemy of Rama. Through many hardships, she remained faithful to Rama and was eventually rescued by him. For Dev's mother, the story of Rama and Sita is the perfect picture of loyalty and virtue between husband and wife. She wants to be as faithful to her husband as Sita was to Rama.

The prayer room in Dev's house contains colorful statues of both Rama and Sita. Dev's father and mother recite *mantras*, or chants, to honor the gods. They meditate to clear their minds of distracting thoughts and attitudes. Sometimes they use yoga to help them focus. Afterward, Dev's mother lays an offering of fresh fruit and flowers in front of the gods and asks them to watch over her family.

After morning prayers, Dev and his family eat breakfast together, sitting on cushions around a low table, before they leave for their day. Dev's father works as a sales representative, while Dev's mother works several afternoons a week as a hostess in a nearby restaurant. Because her job helps bring in money to feed her family, Dev's mother doesn't feel that working outside the home goes against her responsibility to care for her family. Many middle-class Indian women work part time, and Dev's mother is grateful that there are so many opportunities open to her in America.

Dev likes living in New York City. Although it is not as colorful as some of the cities he has visited in India, Dev prefers the bustling excitement of New York, where there is always something to do or see. Often Dev's father takes the whole family to visit a famous landmark, like the Empire State Building, or to see a matinee of a play or musical. Dev's father

Times Square in New York City. Photo: Michael Danser.

says that he wouldn't want to move back to India because there are so many more opportunities, freedoms, and things to experience in the United States. For example, here Dev and his family have a home of their own, while in India they would have only a few rooms to themselves, sharing a communal kitchen with their large extended family.

Dev and his brother attend public school, where they learn subjects like math, spelling, and history. Dev's father wants him to learn about the world so that he can understand the many ways people think and believe. In addition to regular classes, Dev takes special classes at the Hindu community center a few blocks from his house. He studies Indian culture, food, and music and learns to speak Hindi, the main language of India. Dev's father wants to make sure that Dev learns all he can about India so that he understands the rich heritage of Hinduism. Dev also takes yoga classes there. The yoga teacher says that although some people just enjoy the physical benefits of yoga, its true purpose is to allow each person's spirit to get in touch with Brahman.

Dev's most important subject is Hindu religion. Dev's father volunteers as one of the religion teachers at the community center. He tells Dev and his classmates that Hinduism is the oldest living religion in the world, tracing back thousands of years. Dev's father says that he is proud to be a Hindu because it is such a welcoming religion. Hindus believe that all paths to faith eventually lead to Brahman, so no one religion is better or truer than any other.

Statue of Ganesha. Photo: Lalbal.

Dev and his family attend Hindu services at the Ganesha Temple on Sundays. Although Hindus don't have a set day of the week for worship like Dev's Muslim and Christian friends do, Hindus often meet once a week to worship together and learn more about how to be a good Hindu. When they arrive at the temple, Dev and his family take off their shoes and leave them outside. This is to show respect to the Hindu gods. Dev's father always brings a small gift for the gods, like fruit or flowers, and as they leave the temple Dev's mother always gives a little money to help the poor.

Dev likes how colorful everything is in the temple. The shape of the building reminds him of buildings in India, and the brightly colored pictures and statues representing the many Hindu gods and goddesses make the temple a cheerful place. There are many gods in Hinduism. The god Ganesha, for whom the temple is named, is one of Dev's favorites because he grew up hearing his grandmother tell many stories about him. Statues and paintings of Ganesha depict him as having four arms and the head of an elephant, and often he is shown dancing. Hindus believe that Ganesha removes obstacles in people's lives to help them become better people, so Dev honors Ganesha at the temple and at home with special chants.

The temple teacher, who is called a *guru*, explains that although Hindus worship many lesser gods such as Ganesha, the source and essence of the universe is Brahman, described as infinite consciousness and being. The guru teaches that the ultimate goal of all Hindus is to realize they are the same as Brahman and to become one with it. He explains that in order to become one with Brahman, a state the Hindus call nirvana, they must first understand that they are not really individuals with bodies, thoughts, and feelings. The guru says these are only illusions or tricks of the mind.

Next the guru explains that with careful guidance—using meditation, mantras, and other Hindu rituals—people can escape from their illusions and reach the goal of nirvana. They can, at last, experience oneness with Brahman. The guru helps Dev understand this idea by having him imagine his life as a drop of rain. One day that drop will fall into the ocean. When it does, it will lose its own identity as it becomes part of the immense ocean. In the same way, by following the right Hindu rituals and thinking, Dev will one day join the vast ocean that is Brahman and become one with it. He will have reached nirvana.

Dev knows how important it is to follow the guru's teaching because he has also been taught a frightening Hindu belief called reincarnation. According to this belief, until people reach nirvana, they will die and be reborn over and over. Dev's father says that reincarnation gives people many chances to escape the cycle of rebirth and to reach nirvana. This might sound like good news, but it also means that people fail many times in their goal of becoming one with Brahman.

Dev has learned that people are not always reborn as people, but sometimes as different kinds of animals. This happens because they did not make right choices or follow all of the Hindu teachings and rituals in their past life. As the guru explains, people earn either good or bad credits in each life, a belief called *karma*. By making right choices, they earn good credits, which give them good things in their next life. By making wrong choices or not following Hindu teachings, they earn bad credits and may be reborn as a poor person or even a rat or snake.

Because he never wants to be reincarnated as a rat, Dev works hard to be a good Hindu and make right choices, a way of life Hindus call *dharma*. Since the goal for all Hindus is to become one with Brahman, they believe that following the principle of dharma—pursuing what is righteous and avoiding what is evil—is very important. Dev's father wants very much for the whole family to live perfect lives, so he is constantly encouraging and correcting Dev.

Throughout the temple ceremony, Dev copies his father carefully as he chants mantras and prayers and bows low before the statues of the gods. He also listens as his father recites verses from the *Bhagavad Gita*, one of the holiest Hindu books. On special holidays, Dev enjoys watching dancers at the temple perform stories about the Hindu gods. He also enjoys listening to sacred songs or special readings from the *Vedas*, another set of holy books.

Dev's favorite holiday is *Diwali*, also known as the "festival of lights." For five days, Hindus celebrate the triumph of good over evil in the world and within themselves. Dev's family lights small clay lamps filled with oil, decorates their home with colorful paper lanterns, and makes bright intricate designs called *rangoli* with colored powder on the floor. Diwali comes at the end of the traditional harvest time, so it is a holiday when Hindus celebrate bounty and wealth by visiting their friends' homes for special dinners. Dev especially loves the tradition of stringing colored lights and setting off firecrackers to celebrate. The Diwali celebrations in America aren't as elaborate as in India, where Diwali is a national holiday, but that doesn't stop Dev from enjoying the traditions, excitement, and good food each year!

Although Dev enjoys going to the temple, he's always glad when it's time to go home and eat. At home, Dev's mother mixes modern American cooking with traditional Indian foods. The only thing she is careful to avoid is beef. Because Hindus believe that cows are sacred animals, they cannot eat steaks, hamburgers, tacos, or anything else containing beef. Although not all meat is forbidden for Hindus, Dev's mother prefers to make mostly vegetarian dishes. Dev loves when she fixes *curry*, an Indian dish of rice, lentils, and vegetables cooked in a spicy sauce, and serves it with fresh *naan* (flatbread). Sometimes she even lets Dev and Rajani eat traditional style—with their fingers! After dinner, Dev's mother likes to drink a cup of strong tea, while his father prefers coffee.

Even though Dev's parents agree about many things, they definitely have different opinions about other things and aren't afraid to express them. They enjoy discussing bits of news from India or arguing comfortably about American politics. But Dev can see that his father is in charge of the household and knows that his mother would never contradict him in public. Being a strong family and maintaining family honor are very important to

Hindus. Dev understands that because he is the eldest son, he will one day need to take care of his parents, so he carefully watches how his father makes decisions.

One of Dev's father's most important tasks is taking care of his mother. Hindus believe that there are four stages of life. Dev is in the first stage—student life—and is learning all he can about Hinduism and how he should live. Dev's parents are in the second stage—household life—where they are in charge of raising a family and taking care of their elders. Dev's grandmother Nani represents the third stage—retired life—and spends her time relaxing from everyday duties and passing on her wisdom to the younger generation. Eventually, she may decide to enter the fourth stage—secluded life—and renounce contact with other people in order to meditate on becoming one with Brahman. It is rare, though, for people to make this decision.

Indian wedding ceremony. Photo: Yann Forget.

Within a few days, Dev's sister Chandra is getting married and will move into the second stage of life. In Hindu families, marriage is very sacred, so most marriages are arranged. It is more important for Hindu husbands and wives to be compatible and respect each other than to be in love. This is because family is such an important part of Hindu life.

Although he is happy to be getting a new big brother, Samir, Dev is getting tired of all the wedding fuss. Almost every friend the families know is invited to the wedding, and there will be many special treats and gifts. Dev's mother and her friends have been sending invitations, gathering decorations, and preparing food for weeks. Chandra has been shopping for jewelry and a *sari* for her wedding outfit. Last night, her girlfriends painted her hands and feet with elaborate designs in the traditional fashion. The henna dye will stay on her hands for a week or so before fading away. Dev thinks it looks like she is wearing gloves and socks made of brown lace!

The actual wedding will last all day, as there are many small ceremonies and rituals that Chandra and Samir will have to perform. One of the most important rituals is the *saptapadi*, where Chandra and Samir will take seven steps around a flame, reciting to each other promises about their life together. Once the wedding ceremony is performed, with all the correct promises spoken between bride, groom, and their parents and all the correct prayers recited for a happy life together, the reception can begin! Everyone will dance and eat and have a marvelous time celebrating the start of a new family.

Upanayana, or thread ceremony. Photo: Raidurgesh.

Even though most of Dev's extended family is still back in India, they call and write often. Dev's family also visits India regularly, so that Dev and his brother and sisters can learn about the colorful culture of India, their homeland. Sometimes they also visit sacred sites and Hindu temples, leaving offerings so the gods will bless them.

This year, the trip to India will be a special one because Dev is preparing for his sacred thread ceremony, called the *upanayana*. This ceremony will mark his transition from boyhood to manhood. After bathing and putting on special clothes, Dev will receive a cord made from three threads that goes over his left shoulder, across his chest, and is tied near his waist. Then Dev will be given a special prayer and a new spiritual name in exchange for his promise to study the sacred Hindu writings. Dev's father says that the sacred thread ceremony proves Dev's commitment to Hinduism. By giving him the threads, it shows that the men in charge of his spiritual education, like his father and guru, think he is old enough to seriously study Hinduism. By accepting, Dev promises to keep his thoughts and actions pure and righteous, as every devout Hindu should. After the ceremony, Dev and his friends and family will party!

Dev will wear a thread like this for the rest of his life. When he marries or has children, he can add more threads to it, symbolizing the new responsibilities being added to his life. Once a year, he will trade the old cord for a new one. He is excited about the ceremony because it will show everyone that he is growing up. Dev's father says that after the ceremony, he will start teaching Dev important grown-up skills, like managing money.

Although Dev knows becoming a grown-up is inevitable, he still enjoys the day-to-day childhood opportunities to play with friends, go to school, the community center, and the temple, and especially to spend time with his family. He doesn't imagine his life being any more satisfying than it is right now even though he looks forward to the day he'll be a serious Hindu man like his father.

WHAT'S THE DIFFERENCE?

- How is the way Dev lives different from the way you live? How are your lives similar?

- What do you think visiting a Hindu temple might be like? What would you expect to see there? What would Dev think of your church if he visited it?

- Hindu gods and goddesses are depicted in many unusual ways in statues and paintings. Ganesha has the head of an elephant, Hanuman is a monkey, Vishnu has four arms, and Brahma (not to be confused with Brahman) has four heads—and that's after losing one! What does the Bible say about the practice of making statues of gods? According to the biblical Christian worldview, what does God the Father look like?

- Dev has been taught that people are trapped in a constant cycle of rebirth called reincarnation. What does this mean for the way Dev lives each day?

- If Dev's sister lived in India, her parents may have decided to choose a husband for her, as is the Hindu tradition. What would that be like, having such an important decision made for you? How is the Christian wedding ceremony different from a Hindu wedding?

- How is the way Dev sees himself different from the way you see yourself as a child of God?

HOW WILL YOU RUN THE RACE?

> ## I PRESS TOWARD THE GOAL FOR THE PRIZE OF THE UPWARD CALL OF GOD IN CHRIST JESUS.

PHILIPPIANS 3:14, NKJV

THE BIG IDEA

Baseball and basketball are relatively recent inventions, but sports have existed almost as long as humans. Wrestling, boxing, archery, track and field, and even polo have been around for thousands of years. Drivers have been racing against one another since vehicles were first invented to carry them. And the first Olympics took place almost 800 years before Christ was born! Athletic competition was especially popular in Ancient Greece and throughout the Roman Empire. So when the apostle Paul carried the gospel to these parts of the world, he often used sports terminology to help the people understand his message:

If anyone competes as an athlete, he does not receive the victor's crown unless he competes according to the rules. (2 Timothy 2:5)

Athletes work hard to win a crown that cannot last, but we do it for a crown that will last forever. I don't run without a goal. And I don't box by beating my fists in the air. (1 Corinthians 9:25–26, CEV)

In Paul's day, the winner of a sporting event often received a crown made of leaves from a laurel or olive plant. Today, prizes take the form of medals and trophies. Yet none of these prizes will last. Leaves wilt and die, while trophies tarnish and rust. So Paul encourages us to live our lives in pursuit of a far greater treasure:

> *I press toward the mark for the prize of the high calling of God in Christ Jesus* (Philippians 3:14, KJV).

The Christian life is like a race. Just as long-distance runners prepare themselves to compete in the Olympic games, we prepare to run the course God has set out in advance for each of us. Athletes prepare for their race by training for thousands of hours and exercising self-discipline. They run every day, eat only what is healthful for their bodies, and deny themselves any activity that might distract them from their ultimate goal. As Christians, we exercise the daily disciplines of prayer, Bible study, and worship so that we may run without giving up or losing stamina. We read, watch, and do only those things that are healthful for body, mind, and spirit. And we avoid any activity that might distract us from God's call on our lives:

> *Let us strip off every weight that slows us down, especially the sin that so easily trips us up. And let us run with endurance the race God has set before us.* (Hebrews 12:1, NLT)

So far in this study, you have been learning who you are by looking at some of the ways you reflect the image of God—you are creative, you have thoughts, you experience emotions, and you make choices. In this lesson, we will look at how you can always know the difference between the right and wrong paths as you run the race God has planned for you.

WHAT YOU WILL DO
» You will understand what it means to wear the "uniform" of Christ.
» You will identify and practice five strategies for winning the race.
» You will define and begin to exercise self-control.

ME AND MY ARROW

Bows and arrows have been in use nearly as long as people have hunted for their food. The Bible tells us Esau was "a skilled hunter" and that his father, Isaac, who "had a taste for wild game," preferred Esau over his brother, Jacob, who was more of a homebody (Genesis 25:27–28). In Genesis 27:3, an elderly Isaac instructs Esau to take his quiver and bow and bring him some of the wild game he enjoys.

For thousands of years, bows were made from a long branch or piece of wood flexible enough to store energy as the bowstring was pulled back. This energy was released when the archer let go of the string, and the arrow was propelled forward. Bowstrings were made of animal sinew or hair or plant fibers such as linen or hemp. Arrows were made with wooden shafts. The

Photo: Asadi.

arrowhead, the sharp point on the end of the arrow, was made from metal or stone. On the other end of the arrow were fletchings—feathers that helped the arrow fly straight and true. Arrows were carried in a bag called a quiver.

The strength required to draw back the bowstring and the skill necessary for aiming have always made archery a challenge. The longbow used in medieval times was six and a half feet long and was extremely difficult to aim, though a good longbowman could accurately shoot twelve arrows per minute. However, after the invention of firearms, archers became less in demand as warriors. Although a good archer could shoot faster and more accurately than a soldier with a gun, protective armor that would repel an arrow often would not stop a bullet.

In the Bible, a father's children are compared to arrows in the hands of a warrior. Psalm 127:5 says, "Blessed is the man whose quiver is full of them." Isaiah 49:2 says, "[The LORD] made me into a polished arrow and concealed me in his quiver." As arrows in the hands of our Father in heaven, how then should we live? We are to "aim for perfection" (2 Corinthians 13:11).

THE SWORD

"Take that, you villain! And that!" Brandon thrust once more with his wooden sword as he vanquished his imaginary foe.

Just then, the first evening breeze chased the autumn leaves through the clearing, and Brandon shivered. The sun was nearly down, and he was supposed to be gathering fallen branches for making a campfire. Sir William would be returning soon from his meditations, and he had promised to teach Brandon how to build a fire. The boy pulled his cloak about his shoulders and had decided he'd best return to his chore when he spotted them—a family of deer grazing amid a stand of trees not fifty paces away, just the other side of the river. Brandon froze.

"Will!" he whispered as loudly as he dared so as not to startle the beasts. *"Will, bring your bow!"* But William did not answer.

Brandon had not tasted meat in three days, and his mouth watered at the thought of a venison supper. He carefully set down his practice sword and quietly made his way to where William's longbow and quiver stood against a tree. Brandon was a fair shot himself, and he was pretty certain he could drop a deer from fifty paces.

He carried the longbow to where he had left the wooden blade and withdrew an arrow from the quiver. He nocked the arrow and was preparing to draw back the string when he felt a gentle hand at his elbow. Then he heard William quietly say, "Do not shoot, Brandon."

Brandon groaned. "Will, we've eaten nothing but nuts and berries for three days."

"Nevertheless, those are the king's deer. The baron has permission to hunt only as far north as the River Little Ouse. As you can see, those deer stand on the other side of the river."

"But the river is little more than a creek at this point," Brandon protested. "They're so close, and there's not another soul around for miles. No one will know if we take one of the smaller ones for supper."

William said, "We will know."

Brandon sighed. "You're right, of course. I'm sorry, Will."

Sir William smiled and said, "Come. It will be dark soon, and we must get that fire started."

As Brandon gathered up the quiver and bow, he heard a snuffle and a snort from behind him. A moment later, a young boar emerged from the underbrush. William too turned at the sound and said, "Ah, the Lord has provided! Looks like we'll be having meat for supper after all."

Two hours later, the pig was ready to be cooked. During this time, William had taught Brandon not only how to build a fire but also how to construct a spit for roasting the pig. Brandon was given the job of slowly turning the spit so that the meat cooked evenly.

"How much longer, Will? I'm starving!"

"Shouldn't be much longer," William replied, grinning. "Just think—this time tomorrow, we'll be

Photo: Matthias Juchem.

back at Cambridge, enjoying the finest lamb and venison in the kingdom."

Brandon stopped turning the spit and looked at his friend and master. "So we're giving up the search?"

William said, "Keep turning the spit. Yes, we're going home. The king arrives in just over a week, and our help is required at the castle."

"But what about the wolf?"

"Perhaps it's moved on to feed elsewhere. Certainly the wolf has been here. The forest is oddly quiet, and as you've noted, we've seen precious little fauna. However, we've spotted no fresh scat to indicate the wolf's current whereabouts. In any case, it's difficult to track a lone wolf over such a large area."

"I thought wolves usually hunt in packs," Brandon said.

William stoked the fire with a fallen limb to keep it roaring. "Normally, yes," he said.

"But this animal is a rogue. It obtains its food by preying on domestic sheep and cattle—in this case, the baron's livestock. The wolf we're looking for must have wandered down from the Scottish moors. Wolves have been scarce in this part of England since King Edward the First ordered their eradication more than seventy years ago."

Brandon turned thoughtful and again stopped turning the spit. "Will, I've been thinking about the deer we saw. Well, not so much about them as about me. I feel terrible about trying to shoot them. I was hungry, and I didn't stop to think about the king's law. I understand what you were saying about choosing to do the right thing even when no one is looking, but . . ."

"But why is it that sometimes the right thing is so hard to do?"

"Yes! I mean, I *want* to be good. And I do want to earn your trust. But sometimes I get distracted and don't do my chores as well as I should. Other times I just want to do what *I* want to do without worrying about what someone else thinks I should do. I love the king, and I fear God. So why isn't it always easy for me to obey them?"

Sir William smiled. "These are good questions, Brandon, and I'm glad you're asking them. By the way, your pig is starting to burn."

"Oh!" Brandon started turning the spit once more.

William asked, "Do you remember telling me how you did not feel worthy of becoming my squire?" Brandon nodded, and the knight continued. "You need to understand that each of us behaves and makes decisions according to what we believe about ourselves, the world, truth, and right and wrong. You believe that God created the world and everything in it. You believe that He made people in His image and gave us laws to live by. You know that people sinned and that God sent His only Son to die on a cross to save us from our sins. Yet you still think of yourself as a lowly page, a mere servant. You believe yourself to be an abandoned child, unloved and forgotten, without means or influence or a future beyond scrubbing the castle floors. Am I right?"

Brandon nodded again.

"Because you believe yourself to be nobody, you behave accordingly, as though no one really cares what you say or do. Brandon, you know the difference between right and wrong, but you don't always consider the consequences of your actions because you don't truly believe

they matter. You don't believe that *you* matter."

Brandon looked away, but William saw a single tear rolling down his cheek, glistening in the firelight.

William stood and put his hands on the boy's shoulders. "Brandon, I'm here to tell you that you do matter. You are a child of the Most High God, my brother in Christ. And our Father in heaven loves you more than you could possibly imagine. In fact, He has great plans for you."

"Me? Why me? I make so many mistakes. I—"

"We all make mistakes, Brandon. But God is slow to anger and quick to forgive. What is important is that we learn from our mistakes and choose to do better next time."

Brandon asked, "If God has such a great plan for my life, Will, then why am I not living it? I work all day and into the night, and I have little to show for it. I mean, if God loves me so much, it seems a little strange that I should suffer so much misery. I have no parents, no money, and few friends." Then he smiled and scratched behind his ear. "And I think I have fleas from sleeping on the ground."

William laughed. "You've got to remember, Brandon, that you also have an enemy who has sworn to defeat God's people. The devil is a thief who comes to steal, kill, and destroy, and he wants to keep you from knowing who you are in Christ. But if you understand how much God loves you, if you truly believe the promises in His Word, then you can stand firm against the devil's every scheme. Therefore, you must trust God. Lift up your eyes and head and heart toward Him. He will never let you down. Count your blessings, Brandon, and not your problems. Keep your eyes on God and the plans He has to prosper you and not to harm you, plans to give you hope and a future."

"That's from the book of Jeremiah, isn't it?"

"Very good! We'll make a scholar out of you yet! Now, it's about time we eat. What do you say?"

Brandon rubbed his stomach and shouted, "Amen!"

Later that evening, after they had cleaned up and settled in for the night, Brandon thought again about what William had said about God's plans for his life. Nearby, Will's horse, Maximilian, nickered in the moonlight as if to say, "All is well, Master Brandon." Brandon whispered, "Thanks, Max. Good night."

Photo: Andrew Dunn.

The next morning the autumn sun rose unseasonably warm, making for perfect travel conditions. The companions rode toward Cambridge in silence. They stopped about noon to water the horses and share some leftover pork, but still neither said anything. But as the day wore on, Brandon's questions piled one on top of another until, finally, he turned to William and blurted out, "But how will I know what God wants me to do? How do I get ready *now* when I don't know what He expects of me?"

William smiled but did not rein in Max's trot. "Do you know the story of King David—before he became king? David was the youngest of eight sons, and no one gave him much thought. After all, he was only a shepherd boy. His job was to tend the sheep in the fields, and he did it to the best of his ability. One day, one of David's lambs was carried off by a lion. This was unfortunate, but it was no great loss. After all, David was responsible for guarding an entire flock. No one would have thought less of him for allowing the lion to steal one little lamb. But David chased down and killed the beast and rescued the lamb because *that was his job*. He was faithful in the small things, and one day God entrusted him with an entire kingdom. Do you understand?"

"I think so," Brandon said. "You're saying that if I work hard and do my best at the small tasks I am given to do, then I can be trusted with bigger responsibilities."

"That's right."

"But how will I know when God wants me to do something 'big'?"

William said, "On the morning of his famous battle with the giant Goliath, David woke up thinking he would be doing nothing more important that day than delivering food to his older brothers. He had no idea that this day would somehow change history. Nevertheless, he was ready. You see, David knew God and trusted Him completely. He sang praises to the Lord every day, come rain or shine, no matter what his circumstances. God had saved him from the lion, and David was absolutely certain that if God were on his side, no one and no thing could hope to stand against him. So when faced with a giant challenge, he did not hesitate. And suddenly he found himself a 'stone's throw' from the throne of Israel, as God had intended."

William grew reflective, then said, "You know, Brandon, I had not planned to become a knight. Brother Dominic taught me to read when I was a young lad, and I have studied the Scriptures with him faithfully ever since in the hope that I might one day become a priest. I had

David portrayed in a psalter from the 9th century.

planned to take holy orders on my twenty-first birthday."

Brandon asked, "What happened?"

"God had other plans. When the baron was thrown from his horse that day in Calais, I knew exactly what I had to do. And I knew in that moment what I was meant to be, as sure as I've known anything in my life."

"I see, Will. I cannot know when God will call on me or what He might ask me to do, so I must be prepared." Brandon looked perplexed. "But how do I do that?"

William unsheathed his broadsword. "You've seen me practice with the sword."

"Oh, yes! You're quite good. Frankly, I don't know why you spend so much time at it. You're already the fairest swordsman I've ever seen."

"Have you ever seen me outside the castle walls *without* my sword?"

"Well, no, come to think of it. You even stand nearby when the smith sharpens your sword. Why is that?" Brandon asked.

"A knight may be called on at any moment to defend those he is sworn to protect. With their victory at the Battle of Crécy, the king and the baron made many enemies. There are even an ambitious few in the king's own court who would prefer to see the king fall—if not in battle, then by other means. Therefore, I am never without my sword. And I make a point of practicing regularly so that I am always ready to use it ably if called upon to do so."

"But, Will, I don't yet own a real sword. Nor am I likely to anytime soon."

"David had no sword and no armor. He carried nothing more than a slingshot and five smooth stones. Yet David was confident he would win the day because he was armed with something far more powerful than any spear or sword: He knew God's truth. The Bible calls God's Word the Sword of the Spirit, and it is a sword you would do well to master. 'For the Word of God is living and powerful, and sharper than any two-edged sword, piercing even to the division of soul and spirit, and of joints and marrow, and is a discerner of the thoughts and intents of the heart.' Not all enemies are visible to the eye, Brandon, and not every attack can be seen. You must learn the truths in the Word of God and carry them with you at all times. Speak them every day, in good times and bad, and practice them. Only then will you be battle-ready when the time comes."

"But I can't even read, Will. Besides, I'm no good at academics."

William sighed. "Brandon, I can teach you to read. I can teach you to ride and joust and wield a sword with the best of them. I can even teach you the proper way to court a lady. But I cannot make you love God's Word, nor can I force you to hide it in your heart. That is a commitment only you can make."

"Can't I simply ask you when I need advice?"

"What if I am away? What if I have been injured or killed? I will gladly fight with you at my side, Brandon, but I cannot promise that I will always be there to protect you. One day you will find yourself alone on the battlefield. Perhaps you will be facing a flesh-and-blood enemy, or maybe you will be sorely tempted to sin by one of Satan's minions. When the time comes, you must be armed and ready to brandish the Sword of the Spirit."

"Can you help me, Will? I *do* want to understand God's Word. Can you teach it to me?" Brandon asked eagerly.

"I will gladly do what I can. Let's start with one of my favorite passages. It's something I learned from the psalms of David." William spoke boldly, almost singing the words:

> *As for God, His way is perfect;*
> *the word of the LORD is proven;*
> *He is a shield to all who trust in Him.*
> *For who is God, except the LORD?*
> *And who is a rock, except our God?*
> *It is God who arms me with strength,*
> *And makes my way perfect.*
> *He makes my feet like the feet of deer,*
> *And sets me on my high places.*
> *He teaches my hands to make war,*
> *So that my arms can bend a bow of bronze.*
> *You have also given me the shield of Your salvation;*
> *Your right hand has held me up,*
> *Your gentleness has made me great.*

Brandon gave a low whistle. "That's wonderful, Will. Do you really think I can learn that?"

"I don't see why not."

"Then let's get started. I want to surprise Gwyneth. I can't wait to see the look on her fa—"

But William was no longer riding beside him. He had dismounted and was examining something on the ground, near the path. "Look, Brandon. Fresh tracks, no more than a day old. The wolf has returned."

HOW TO TRACK AN ANIMAL

You may have seen the footprints of birds on fresh snow or a dusting of a cat's paw prints on the hood of your family's car. Hunters, nature enthusiasts, and scientists use footprints and other signs called *spoor* to track wild animals. Spoor includes physical evidence such as tracks, scat (the animal's droppings), dropped feathers, and scratches on trees, as well as scents and sounds. These clues lead a tracker to his quarry, the animal he is pursuing.

To effectively track any animal, you need to understand something of the animal's behavior. Some animals travel in packs, while others are loners by nature. Some animals prefer wooded cover, while others tend to keep to open spaces. Knowing the animal's habits and habitat will help you know what kind of spoor to watch for. When observing spoor, a good tracker will walk alongside the trail so as not to disturb any evidence.

Tracking requires great attention to detail. You must be fully aware of your surroundings. For example, you must be careful to stay downwind from your quarry so your scent doesn't warn the animal that a human is nearby. And you must not make any quick movements or noises, as a sudden rush of birds from a tree can warn your quarry that danger is close.

Wolf tracks. Photo: U.S. Fish & Wildlife Service.

Similar tracking techniques can also be used to find people. Soldiers are trained to track enemy forces for the purpose of discerning and predicting their movements. Search-and-rescue teams also use tracking techniques to find people who are lost in unfamiliar territory.

THINK ABOUT IT

» Why did William tell Brandon not to shoot the deer? If Brandon killed one of the king's deer in the forest and no one saw him do it or ever learned of his deed, would it still be wrong? Why?

» Why do you suppose William changed his mind about becoming a priest? Can he serve God just as well by being a knight? How?

» Why does the apostle Paul call the Bible "the Sword of the Spirit" in Ephesians 6:17? How is the Bible like a sword? How can knowing the Word of God protect you?

WORDS YOU NEED TO KNOW

» **Trust:** Having complete confidence that God will always do everything He promises

» **Spiritual discipline:** An exercise that, when done regularly, helps me to grow spiritually

» **Self-control:** Doing the right thing even when I don't feel like it

HIDE IT IN YOUR HEART

But those who trust in the LORD will find new strength. They will soar high on wings like eagles. They will run and not grow weary. They will walk and not faint. (Isaiah 40:31, NLT)

Be self-controlled and alert. Your enemy the devil prowls around like a roaring lion looking for someone to devour. Resist him, standing firm in the faith. (1 Peter 5:8–9)

WHOM DO YOU REPRESENT?

Eric Liddell was born in China in 1902, the son of Scottish missionaries. When Liddell enrolled at the University of Edinburgh in 1921, he was already widely known as the fastest runner in Scotland. Wherever he went, large crowds showed up to see the famous athlete run and to hear him preach the gospel. In 1924, Liddell was selected to represent Great Britain at the Olympic Games in Paris. However, the qualifying heat for his best event, the 100 meters race, was scheduled to be run on a Sunday. Liddell firmly believed the Sabbath day was to be kept holy and set aside for the Lord, and so he withdrew from the race.

Instead, Liddell was entered in the 400 meters race. The day of the 400 meters, as Liddell went to the starting blocks, an American who had learned of the Scotsman's refusal to

Eric Liddell. Photo: Frederic Humbert.

run on the Sabbath slipped a piece of paper into Liddell's hand. On the paper was a quote from 1 Samuel 2:30, "Them that honor me I will honor." Liddell ran with the paper in his hand and won the race in world-record time. A year later, Liddell returned to China, where he served as a missionary until his death in 1945.

In many sports, athletes compete as representatives of a team or a school, often wearing a designated uniform or school colors. At the Olympics, competitors represent their home nations, and an athlete's victory is considered a win for his or her country. As a runner, Eric Liddell was known as the Flying Scotsman, after a famous locomotive of his time. At the Olympics, he wore the flag of Great Britain. Yet in some Chinese literature, he is listed as China's first Olympic champion because he was born and died in that country. So when he ran as an athlete, whom did Liddell represent? Scotland? Great Britain? China?

In the 1981 movie *Chariots of Fire*, which is based in part on Liddell's Olympic experience, Liddell is shown talking with his sister, Jenny, about whether his priorities are straight. Jenny tells Eric she worries that running has distracted him from his true purpose in life. Eric tells his sister he plans to return to his missionary work, but only after he has run in the Olympics. He says to her, "I believe God made me for a purpose. But he also made me fast. And when I run, I feel His pleasure. To give it up would be to hold Him in contempt. To win is to honor Him."

Eric Liddell knew whom he represented. Although he was a loyal Scotsman, he always gave God first place in his life. As you live and play and work each day, whom do you represent? For whose glory will you compete as you run the race of your life? Yours? Your parents'? Your hometown's? Your country's? Whose "uniform" will you wear?

Did you know that if you are a child of God you're already wearing a uniform? The Bible says that if you have accepted God's free gift of salvation, then you are now "wearing" Christ:

Eric Liddell Community Centre in Edinburgh, Scotland. Photo: Jonathan Oldenbuck.

For you are all children of God through faith in Christ Jesus. And all who have been united with Christ in baptism have put on Christ, like putting on new clothes.
(Galatians 3:26–27, NLT)

What this means is that when God looks at you now, He no longer sees your old sinful self. Nor does He see the filthy rags you wear—the righteous acts with which you clothe yourself for your friends and neighbors to *ooh* and *ahh* over (Isaiah 64:6). No, what God sees when He looks at you now is the unparalleled beauty of His Son, shining in all His glory! That is what God sees, but what about the world? What do other people see when they look at you? Do they see Jesus?

Medal ceremony for the 2008 Olympic swimming relay competition. Photo: Jmex60.

When athletes compete, they are expected to perform to the best of their ability. Their teammates, coaches, fans, and even their opponents expect them to give their best effort, be a good sport, and play by the rules. In this way, win or lose, athletes represent their team well and bring the team honor and respect. If you "wear" Christ, your words and deeds should reflect the light of God into the lives of everyone around you, just as Jesus' did. By honoring God in everything you do or say, you will cause the world to honor and respect Him and give Him glory (Matthew 5:16).

Are you living in a way that causes the world to glorify your Father in heaven? In his letter to the Colossians, the apostle Paul reminds us that if we are in Christ, we must no longer do things the way the world does them:

> *You used to do these things when your life was still part of this world. But now is the time to get rid of anger, rage, malicious behavior, slander, and dirty language. Don't lie to each other, for you have stripped off your old sinful nature and all its wicked deeds. Put on your new nature, and be renewed as you learn to know your Creator and become like him.*
> (Colossians 3:7–10, NLT)

Paul goes on to say, "In this new life, it doesn't matter if you are a Jew or a Gentile . . . slave or free. Christ is all that matters, and he lives in all [believers]" (Colossians 3:11, NLT). In other words, you may be American, Canadian, Russian, Australian, Chinese, or Welsh by birth. You may think of yourself as a Hoosier, a Hawkeye, or an Okie from Muskogee. You may be wealthy or poor, Republican or Democrat, Baptist or Presbyterian. Your skin may be white, black, yellow, or red. But in the end, all that really matters is Christ. And He is the One whom you must run for.

MAKE A NOTE OF IT

Athletes wear the colors of the teams and countries they represent. When people meet you, can they immediately identify you as a Christian? How can you wear Christ's "colors"? List as many ways as you can think of to speak, behave, and dress in a manner that clearly and accurately shows Jesus to the world.

GO FOR THE WIN!

In a scene from *Chariots of Fire*, Eric Liddell speaks to a crowd after they have just watched him win a foot race in the driving rain. He tells them, "I want you to do more than just watch a race; I want you to take part in it. I want to compare faith to running in a race. It's hard. It requires concentration of will, energy of soul." No one ever said the Christian life was going to be easy. This is a race, and not just a quick sprint—it's a race that requires endurance and commitment from all who run.

> *The ultimate measure of a man is not where he stands in moments of comfort or convenience, but where he stands at times of challenge and controversy.*
> **Martin Luther King, Jr.**
> 1929–1968

In 1 Corinthians 9:24 (NLT), Paul writes, "Don't you realize that in a race everyone runs, but only one person gets the prize? So run to win!" By comparing believers to athletes, is Paul saying that we are competing against one another, that only one of us can win? No. The apostle goes on to explain, "Everyone who competes in the games goes into strict training. They do it to get a crown that will not last; but we do it to get a crown that will last forever" (1 Corinthians 9:25).

You see, the very best athletes practice strenuously, follow a strict diet, strengthen themselves physically and mentally, and put their full effort toward winning—yet they compete for a prize that cannot last. Trophies gather dust, medals fade, and records will be broken. Few people remember who won last year or ten years ago or a hundred years ago. But if you run the race Paul speaks of, if you have chosen to follow Christ, then your name is written in the Book of Life! And if you run to win and endure to the end, your name can never be erased. When you cross the finish line, you will stand on the podium with Jesus, and He will announce your name before the Father and His angels (Revelation 3:5). And your prize? The most precious prize of all: eternal life in heaven with our loving God.

So is Paul saying you must run a great race in order to earn this prize? No! The truth is, if you are a follower of Christ, you have already won because of what Jesus accomplished on the cross. He is already preparing a place in heaven just for you (John 14:2–3). What Paul is saying is that this prize is so inconceivably wondrous—and is to be desired so greatly—you should be willing to train more faithfully and run with more determination than any athlete. You should live for Christ with more enthusiasm, greater focus, and stronger commitment than someone who is trying to win a mere Super Bowl ring or an Olympic medal.

Long-distance runners will tell you that in order to win any race you need a strategy. So let's look at some strategies for running to win.

KEEP YOUR EYES ON THE PRIZE

Wilma Rudolph was born in 1940 to a very poor African-American family in the backwoods of Tennessee. The twentieth of twenty-two children, Wilma was born prematurely and was not expected to live. The nearest hospital was segregated, and the staff there refused to treat

Wilma Rudolph, 1961. Photo: New York World-Telegram and the Sun Newspaper Photograph Collection.

her. Somehow she survived but grew into a small, sickly child whose left leg and foot were deformed and weakening. Wilma was diagnosed with polio and fitted with a leg brace. Doctors told her she would never walk again.

But her family never gave up. They believed God would heal Wilma. Her brothers and sisters took turns massaging her leg each day to keep it as healthy as possible. At the age of nine, Wilma began to learn to walk again. By the time she was thirteen, she was walking normally without the brace, amazing her doctors. But Wilma was not satisfied with walking—she wanted to run. She wanted to run fast. Faster than any woman had ever run!

Three years later, she won a bronze medal at the 1956 Olympics. But Wilma wasn't finished. In 1960, at the Olympic Games in Rome, Italy, she became the first American woman to win three gold medals—despite running with a sprained ankle! The Italian newspapers called her "*La Gazzella Nera*"—the Black Gazelle—while others called her "The Tornado." Everyone could agree that Wilma Rudolph was the fastest woman in history.

As a young girl, Wilma could have looked at her circumstances—discrimination, her illness, her family's lack of financial resources—and decided to give up on her dreams. She could have accepted the doctors' sentence and learned to live with her condition. But Wilma's mother, Blanche, was a woman of great faith. Blanche taught her children that with God all things are possible (Matthew 19:26). Later, Wilma told reporters, "My doctors told me I would never walk again. My mother told me I would. I believed my mother."

When you are running to "reach the end of the race and receive the heavenly prize for which God, through Christ Jesus, is calling" you (Philippians 3:14, NLT), you must keep your eyes on the prize. You cannot allow yourself to be distracted by what the world says about you, nor should you become discouraged because of your circumstances. Proverbs 4:25 (NLT) says, "Look straight ahead, and fix your eyes on what lies before you." Keep looking to the One who goes ahead of you—He who is far greater than any disease, unfair situation, money problem, or relationship trouble.

Everyone knows that Jesus walked on the water, but did you know that His disciple Peter did it too? Check out Matthew 14:22–31. Late one night, Jesus told the disciples to get in their boat and cross the Sea of Galilee while He went to the hills to pray. The disciples did as they were commanded, but a strong wind arose and the men found themselves fighting heavy waves. Suddenly, they spotted Jesus walking on the water toward the boat, and they were frightened at first, thinking it was a ghost. But when Jesus spoke to them, Peter called out, "Lord, if it's really you, tell me to come to you, and I will walk on the water." Jesus said, "Yes, come." So Peter climbed over the side of the boat and began walking on the water toward Jesus. But when Peter looked around him and saw the strong wind and the waves, he was terrified and began to sink. "Save me, Lord!" he shouted. Jesus immediately reached out and grabbed him, then asked, "Why did you doubt me?"

Walking on Water by Aivazovsky.

Peter was walking on water! He was experiencing the power of God firsthand, but then he took his eyes off Jesus—only for a moment—and immediately began to sink. He looked at his circumstances, and his eyes told him he should be drowning instead of walking on the waves. Paul warns us that "perilous times will come" (2 Timothy 3:1, NKJV), and it's easy to become discouraged or frightened or frustrated by your circumstances. When that happens, turn your focus once more to the Living Word and keep your eyes on Jesus. Hebrews 12:1–2 (NLT) says, "Let us run with endurance the race God has set before us . . . by keeping our eyes on Jesus, the champion who initiates and perfects our faith."

> *If you are looking for the way by which you should go, take Christ, for he is himself the way.*
> **Thomas Aquinas**
> 1225–1274

BELIEVE THAT GOD KEEPS HIS PROMISES

When George Mueller and his friend Henry Craik decided to open an orphanage for homeless children in England in the 1830s, they had no money. Nor did they intend to ask anyone for the money. They could have requested a bank loan or held a fundraiser or asked for contributions from wealthy patrons for this very worthy cause. Instead, Mueller got on his knees

George Mueller.

and prayed. He believed Jesus when He said, "But if you remain in me and my words remain in you, you may ask for anything you want, and it will be granted!" (John 15:7, NLT). He believed the Father when He said, "I am the LORD your God. . . . Open wide your mouth and I will fill it" (Psalm 81:10).

Often during the early years of the orphanage, when funds were low, Mueller had no idea where the children's next meal was coming from. Yet he always believed God would provide. Stories abound of anonymous food donations arriving at the orphanage just before the children's mealtime, or of bakers waking in the middle of the night with a sudden urge to bake bread for the orphans in time for breakfast. On one occasion, a milkman's cart broke down just outside the orphanage. The milkman knew the milk would spoil by the time the wheel was fixed, so he knocked on the door and asked Mueller if the orphanage could use some free milk.

Mueller simply smiled as the milkman brought in ten large cans of milk—just enough for 300 thirsty children.

Mueller went on to educate and care for more than 18,000 children at the orphanage. He also traveled as a missionary, sharing the gospel with more than 3 million people. In all that time, Mueller never asked anyone for a single dime. Yet his children never missed a

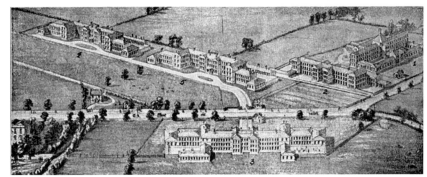

The orphanage at Ashley Down, Bristol, England, as it appeared in 1899.

meal, and his ministry never went into debt.

Running the race the way George Mueller ran—believing God will provide for your every need—takes great trust. But God is worthy of great trust. And He wants to help you. In Isaiah 41:13 (NCV), He says, "I am the LORD your God, who holds your right hand, and I tell you, 'Don't be afraid. I will help you.'" He is the One who prepared the course, and He has gifted you with the specific talents and abilities necessary to run the race. Not only has God given you a roadmap (the Bible) and a guide (the Holy Spirit), but He has promised to provide everything you will ever need.

The question is this: Will you **trust** Him? Do you believe God will do what He says

He will do, or do you just believe that He exists? Sadly, many people who say they believe in God still have difficulty believing how much He loves and cares for them. They are afraid that God does not have the time or the power to handle their personal concerns, and so they continue to struggle to solve the problems of life on their own, with their own wisdom and strength. Yet God says, "I am the LORD, the God of all mankind. Is anything too hard for me?" (Jeremiah 32:27).

God has made numerous promises throughout the Bible—big promises to you and to me. But we must believe that God will do exactly what He says. We must believe that "he rewards those who earnestly seek him" (Hebrews 11:6). Jesus said, "I tell you the truth, if you have faith as small as a mustard seed, you can say to this mountain, 'Move from here to there' and it will move. Nothing will be impossible for you" (Matthew 17:20).

Isaiah 40:31 (NLT) says, "Those who trust in the LORD will find new strength. They will soar high on wings like eagles. They will run and not grow weary. They will walk and not faint." Are you ready to believe Him?

MAKE A NOTE OF IT

Read John 14:11–13. What would the world be like if all the people in Christ's church truly believed God's promises? What kinds of things would you expect to see when you walk into a church on Sunday or any other day of the week? How might unbelievers react if they saw God's people doing "greater things" than Jesus did? How would your own home be different if you really believed God's promises?

KEEP DOING WHAT YOU KNOW TO DO

As you know, an athlete must train daily to keep in shape so that he or she can compete at the highest level. Likewise, in order to run with endurance the race set before you, you must train daily to keep your body, mind, and spirit in peak condition. This requires discipline. Discipline comes from a Latin word meaning "teaching" or "learning." It's derived from the same root as the word "disciple." A discipline is a pattern of behavior that trains and builds your body, mind, or spirit.

There are many ways to build up your body and mind—regular exercise, healthful eating habits, study, guarding your thoughts from evil—but it's also important to maintain a regimen of spiritual disciplines. These are exercises that build the spirit. A list of spiritual disciplines includes prayer, fasting, Bible study, biblical meditation, and worship, among others. We have discussed each of these disciplines in the pages of this book or in *Who Is God? (And Can I*

Really Know Him?). However, none of them will benefit you unless you do them.

Every year, on December 31, millions of well-meaning people make a list of New Year's resolutions—things they plan to accomplish or do differently in the coming year. But by February the list has been forgotten. These people started the year with the best of intentions, but they quickly grew tired or never really got started at all. (And then they wonder why things didn't work out as they had planned.) But God wants you to make good choices and then act on those choices. He wants you to follow through. He has established these spiritual disciplines to help you "work out your salvation with fear and trembling, for it is God who works in you to will and to act according to his good purpose" (Philippians 2:12–13).

Training for anything worthwhile is never easy. It's hard work. The key to seeing it through is to "be joyful always" (1 Thessalonians 5:16). As Nehemiah 8:10 says, the joy of the Lord is your strength, and you won't be able to continue long in anything without it. The athlete endures grueling workouts in order to experience the thrill of victory. Women endure the intense pain of childbirth because the joy of motherhood waits on the other side. Remember as you begin any discipline that great rewards and satisfaction await you on the other side. But for now you can find contentment and joy in simple obedience as you become a student and doer of the Word (Jeremiah 15:16; James 1:22).

LEARN FROM YOUR MISTAKES

Tom Landry was an all-pro player in the National Football League before becoming a successful defensive coach for the New York Giants in the 1950s. In 1960, he was chosen to be the first head coach of the NFL's newest team, the Dallas Cowboys. Like most brand-new teams in professional sports, the Cowboys weren't very good that first year. They made frequent mistakes and scored fewer points than any team in the league. In fact, Landry's team failed to win a single game!

But the coach refused to quit. A quiet, religious man and a tough competitor, Coach Landry once said, "I've learned that something constructive comes from every defeat." Over the next few years, his teams learned from their many losses and slowly improved. In 1966, the Dallas Cowboys played the Green Bay Packers for the NFL

Statue of Tom Landry. Photo: Jim Bowen.

THE INVENTION OF BASKETBALL

As a young man, James Naismith earned a master's degree from Presbyterian Theological College in Montreal. However, Naismith believed he could better teach principles of the Christian life through sports than from a pulpit, so in 1891, he took a job as a physical education instructor at the YMCA's International Training School for Christian Workers in Springfield, Massachusetts. His vision was "to win men for the Master through the gym."

Shortly after arriving at the YMCA, Naismith was given the task of creating an indoor game that would keep young men occupied during the harsh winter months in Massachusetts. He tried various games, including indoor versions of football, soccer, and lacrosse, but without much success. So Naismith decided to draw from all three sports to invent something no one had ever seen. This new game would involve running and passing, a round ball, and a goal at each end of the floor.

In order to reduce physical contact, and therefore injuries, Naismith placed the goals where they couldn't be easily defended—above the players' heads. For the first ever game, he nailed a peach basket at either end of the gymnasium, about ten feet off the ground. Thus, "basket ball" was born.

According to a March 18, 2010, article in *The Wall Street Journal*, basketball served as "an important evangelical tool" during the next several decades. In his book *Basketball: Its Origin and Development*, Naismith wrote, "Whenever I witness games in a church league, I feel that my vision, almost half a century ago, of the time when the Christian people would recognize the true value of athletics, has become a reality."

James Naismith never profited from the game he invented, despite the fact that today basketball is played by more than 300 million people worldwide. The Naismith Memorial Basketball Hall of Fame in Springfield, Massachusetts, is named in his honor.

Statue of James Naismith.
Photo: randomduck.

Championship. Although the Cowboys lost that game, the team went on to post twenty consecutive winning seasons, an NFL record and one of the longest such streaks in any sport. Tom Landry had taken the worst team in the league and turned the Cowboys into one of the most talented and popular teams in America.

Let's face it: Everybody makes mistakes. Even you. Sometimes you're going to blow it. You might even find yourself stuck in a losing streak to rival the 1960 Cowboys team. You might make a poor choice, give in to temptation, lie to your parents about it, fumble the excuse, then shift the blame to someone else when you get caught. Now that you're in deep trouble, do you suppose the devil will gleefully move on and find someone else to tempt? Not just yet. When you're down, Satan takes this opportunity to remind you of every crummy, rotten thing that has ever happened to you and every shameful, despicable thing you have ever done to someone else. As you hang your head in shame or regret, your heart also begins to sag. Now the devil has you where he wants you: looking at your problems instead of at the Lord.

However, after you've blown it is not the time to give up or give in to despair. Rather, it is precisely the time to turn your eyes toward heaven because God offers you the amazing gift of unconditional love. No matter what you do, no matter how poorly you follow His commands, He loves you without fail. Nothing can separate you from the love of God (Romans 8:38–39). Let Him pick you up, dust you off, and point you in the right direction. Psalm 16:11 (NKJV) says, "You will show me the path of life."

When you make a mistake, ask "Where did I go wrong?" not "Whose fault is it?" Don't play the blame game, looking for someone else you can point the finger at. Admit your mistake, accept responsibility for your actions, confess any sin, then learn from your mistake (1 John 1:8–9). God says, "I am the One who forgives all your sins. I do this to please myself (Isaiah 43:25, ICB). In the same breath He says, "I will not remember your sins," so don't brood over past mistakes. Realize you're not perfect and then move on. Continue working to become more like Christ. In Philippians 3:12–13 (CEV) Paul says, "I have not yet reached my goal, and I am not perfect. But Christ has taken hold of me. So I keep on running and struggling to take hold of the prize. . . . I forget what is behind, and I struggle for what is ahead."

When you make a mistake, learn from it and then let it go. If you have sinned, repent and accept God's grace and forgiveness. Then forget what is in the past, set your sights on Jesus, and follow His lead.

> *Winning is great, sure. But if you are really going to do something in life, the secret is learning how to lose. Nobody goes undefeated all the time. If you can pick up after a crushing defeat and go on to win again, you are going to be a champion someday.*
> **Wilma Rudolph**
> 1940–1994

STAY ON COURSE AND RUN WITH PURPOSE

In the Olympic Games, runners must obey the rules of the race if they hope to win. Although the track is at least thirty-two feet wide, each participant in a 200 meters race must stay within his or her lane, which is clearly marked by white lines set four feet apart. A runner

Photo: Petey21.

who veers off course is disqualified and cannot claim the prize. Jesus said the road that leads to destruction is wide, but narrow is the path that leads to eternal life (Matthew 7:13–14). So keep to the narrow path by following the lead of the Holy Spirit and obeying God's Word.

Deuteronomy 5:32 says, "Be careful to do what the LORD your God has commanded you; do not turn aside to the right or to the left." Proverbs 4:26–27 (NLT) says, "Don't get sidetracked; keep your feet from following evil." In other words, do not run aimlessly, as though you don't know the way. Do not allow yourself to become distracted when the world says, "I know what you need" or "Have you tried the latest thing?" or "Everybody's doing it." Keep your eyes on Jesus and stay the course (Hebrews 12:2).

Remember, the goal is to become like Christ (Romans 8:29). You have been chosen for this purpose, so run straight toward the goal "with purpose in every step" (1 Corinthians 9:26, NLT). Trust Jesus to coach you every step of the way. Get rid of everything in your life that slows you down, especially sin, which can so easily trip you up (Hebrews 12:1). And pray "that God will show you everything he wants you to do and that you may have all the wisdom and understanding that his Spirit gives. Then you will live a life that honors the Lord. . . . His glorious power will make you patient and strong enough to endure anything, and you will be truly happy" (Colossians 1:9–11, CEV).

WHAT SHOULD I DO?

Just as dedicated athletes must deny themselves junk food, tobacco products, and late-night parties if they are to be at their best to compete, so Christians must exercise **self-control** over their choices, thoughts, and emotions in order to run the race of life. Yes, self-control is a gift of the Spirit, but the exercise of that gift requires effort

on our part. We must keep ourselves from doing what we know is wrong, even when we don't feel like it. Only then can we run with purpose and stay on course.

Self-control is necessary if we are to mirror God's image and become more like Jesus. We must also exercise self-control in our lives in order to resist Satan's temptations. The apostle Peter tells us, "Be self-controlled and alert. Your enemy the devil prowls around like a roaring lion looking for someone to devour. Resist him, standing firm in the faith" (1 Peter 5:8–9). The enemy wants nothing more than to lure us off course and cause us to stumble and fall. A person who has no self-control is like a city with broken-down walls, and that person is vulnerable to constant attack and even capture by the enemy (Proverbs 25:28). Once under the enemy's control, that person will experience constant anxi-

The ruins of the city wall at Jerusalem built by King Hezekiah. Photo: Lior Golgher.

ety, despair, misery, and guilt. And he will soon lose all will to get up, brush himself off, and get back in the race.

But if you will surrender to the power of the Holy Spirit, you will enjoy victory over sin as a new creation in Christ. Self-control will be yours, as a fruit of the Spirit, enabling you to control the desires of the flesh (Romans 6:12; Galatians 5:16), the tongue (James 3:2–6), and the thoughts of your heart (Romans 12:2). As you allow the power of the Holy Spirit to help you overcome your weaknesses (Romans 8:26; 2 Corinthians 13:4), you can successfully run the great race of life, knowing that the crown of victory will be yours in Christ Jesus.

A Prayer

Dear God, thank you for choosing me to represent you to others. Thank you for clothing me in Christ so that people will see you when they look at me. Help me to run the race in a way that pleases you. Help me to keep my eyes on Jesus and not become distracted by the things of this world. Help me to truly believe all your promises. Help me practice self-control and help me learn from my mistakes. I ask this in the name of Jesus. Amen.

Photo: NASA.

WORLDVIEWS IN FOCUS

MEET SAGE

Sage is an eleven-year-old girl who lives in a small town outside Corvallis, Oregon. Her mother grew up in Eugene, where she met Sage's father at college and they got married. Sage's mother says they were too young to really know what they wanted in life. After two years, they divorced—then a few weeks later, she found out she was pregnant. Sage has never met her father, although they have talked on the phone a couple of times, and she receives a card from him every birthday.

Sage's mother owns a small health food grocery that sells mostly fruits, vegetables, and grains grown organically on local farms. She says locally grown organic foods are fresher and taste better than foods shipped from across the country and overseas. She prints flyers for the store to teach people about the benefits of healthy eating and how buying locally helps keep area farmers in business. Although Sage's mom believes in the business and the philosophy behind it, the store doesn't always bring in enough money. But Sage and her mother are determined to make it work, even if it means eating all the fruit and vegetables that are a little too old to sell.

Recently, they have branched out and begun carrying exotic herbs, soy products, vitamin supplements, and homeopathic remedies made from all-natural ingredients. They also sell candles and incense with soothing fragrances like sandalwood and jasmine. These items are popular with many in town and have started to bring more people into the store.

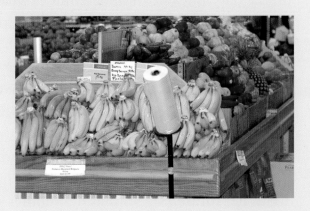

Sage and her mother are very close. They've been a team since Sage was born. Her mother has tried to teach her to work hard and be self-sufficient, especially when it comes to everyday things like laundry and meals. Sage has a few chores—including rinsing the dirty dishes and loading them into the dishwasher and sweeping up the store every night—and her mother expects her to do them without being reminded. But they also have a lot of fun together, such as snuggling up on the couch every weekend and watching "chick flicks" late into the night.

But Sage sometimes wonders if her mother is happy because she always seems to be looking for something more in life. Her mom has tried Catholicism, Kabbalah, and even Scientology but wasn't entirely comfortable with any of them. Currently, she is taking classes in yoga and does Tai Chi exercises every morning. Her best friend, Ruby, who runs a New

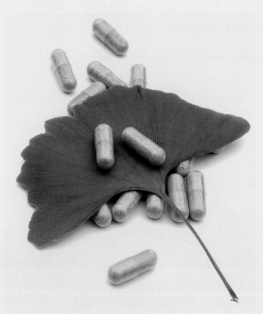

Age shop a few doors down from their grocery store, has been encouraging her to visit an acupuncturist. A few years ago, when Sage got chicken pox, Ruby and her mother spent a week trying various herbal concoctions to soothe Sage's itchy red spots. Ruby also put garnet and quartz crystals under her pillow to promote healing. Sage isn't sure the crystals were of any help, but her mother says she doesn't know what she would have done without Ruby there to help them both through it.

Sage loves Ruby and thinks she is an amazing lady. Ruby is confident and charming and always dresses in bright colors, wears lots of jewelry, and has something to say about everything and everyone. She knows a lot about using herbs and crystals to treat illnesses and has plenty of opinions about what works and what doesn't. Sage knows that Ruby has a good heart and wants to help people in any way she can. Ruby sells herbal remedies for everything from colds and headaches to depression and insomnia. She even has a few concoctions she swears help protect against cancer. Sage just likes how they make the shop smell fresh and spicy-sweet.

Ruby meditates and checks her horoscope every day. Ruby believes that astrology—studying the stars to know the future—is an accurate source of information about the world. Because everything in the universe is connected, she says, the position of the stars and planets on the day you were born determines what will happen in your life. Ruby creates personalized astrological charts for interested customers, and her services are in great demand.

Ruby also believes in reincarnation and thinks it's important to find out who you were in your previous lives. Ruby consults a psychic, or medium, who she says helped her discover that she was once a gypsy in Romania many centuries ago. Sage thinks that the whole idea of reincarnation—the idea that a person's soul goes through an endless cycle of life, death, and rebirth—is kind of creepy. Deep down, she doesn't want to learn about past lives. Her life right now is sometimes too much to handle!

Sage's mother recently visited the psychic on Ruby's recommendation, hoping to learn about her future. Sage thinks her mother seems happier since she began taking Ruby's advice. Too often her mother's smile wilts under the pressures of running her own business and being a single mom. Sage doesn't know if everything Ruby believes in works, but if there's any chance it will make her mother smile more, she is willing to give it a try.

One of her mother's latest interests is affirmations. She read a book from Ruby's shop about the power of positive thinking that says if you keep a pessimistic outlook, then life will give you only negative things. So Sage's mom has posted a list of positive statements on the refrigerator for them to read aloud every morning over breakfast. She says that these affirmations—sayings like "I am a valuable person worthy of love and respect" and "I am becoming a better person every day"—will help them both understand and unleash the mental and spiritual power that is already inside them.

After finishing breakfast and loading the dishwasher, Sage grabs her books and rides her

Bradley State Scenic Viewpoint, Oregon. Photo: Tedder.

bike to school. Living in western Oregon means getting lots of rain, so she often must wear a heavy raincoat to stay dry. But Sage doesn't mind—she loves how green everything gets in the summer because of all the moisture. She also likes the freedom of being able to ride her bike around town.

Sage enjoys school and is very good at reading, but she has a difficult time with math. Her friend Hannah teases her that she needs to take off her shoes to count, and sometimes that seems true. But Hannah is willing to help her with her math homework, especially if Sage will help Hannah with her book reports. Sage is glad to have a good friend at school, though it is awkward to talk with her about the things Ruby is teaching her mom.

After school, Sage fixes herself a healthy snack and sits down at the kitchen table to do her homework. She speeds through the history chapter and soon has a full page of notes for the test at the end of the week. She also completes her science worksheet in no time. That leaves only math. After a few minutes of struggling to understand a long-division problem, Sage gives up. She'll have to ask Hannah for help at lunch tomorrow.

When Sage has finished her homework, she grabs her umbrella and checks in at the grocery store. Usually, her mother can handle the business that comes in, so after a quick school update and kiss on the forehead, Sage heads over to Ruby's shop. She helps out around the store and watches the register when Ruby is in the back with a client. Ruby sells all kinds of things in

her shop, from tarot cards to many different kinds of crystals and semi-precious stones. Ruby says that each type of stone will help heal or strengthen a different part of the body. On Sage's birthday, Ruby gave her a necklace of lapis lazuli, a deep-blue gemstone that is supposed to help increase communication skills and protect against headaches and sore throats. Sage wears it all the time because blue is her favorite color.

Sage likes working at Ruby's shop. When people come in with questions, she often knows the answers and can help them pick out exactly what they need. People come from all over to see the wonderful new things Ruby has purchased from around the world. Ruby sells figurines and silk scarves from India, silver and spices from Thailand, masks and wooden jewelry from Africa, tea and herbs from China, and turquoise from Native American tribes in the American Southwest. Sage thinks the shop is one of the most interesting places she has ever been!

On slow days at the store, Ruby and Sage talk about life, the universe, and everything.

Ruby tells her that God is not a person like Sage or her mother, but rather, God is the universe and the universe is God. God is everywhere and lives in every rock, tree, animal, person, and star. She says it doesn't matter whether you follow the teachings of Buddha or Jesus or Muhammad or if you simply follow your own heart to find God. Since God is part of everything, Ruby says, any path that makes a person spiritually stronger is a good thing.

Ruby explains that all sorts of knowledge and power reside within every person—all people have to do is make themselves aware of it. This is called *self-realization*. In order to discover the spiritual knowledge hidden inside us, she says, we must free ourselves from negative, narrow-minded ways of thinking and create our own inner harmony. Once enough people get in touch with the God-force inside them, a New Age will begin and world peace can finally happen. Ruby tells Sage the world is a beautiful place but it will only get better if we all work together.

Because Ruby believes that everything in the universe works together, she tries to keep her life and her shop in balance with nature. One of the ways she does this is by using the Chinese art of *feng shui* (pronounced FUHNG-SHWAY) to organize her shop and her apartment. Using a compass to read the *qi* (CHEE) of the room, she has arranged her furnishings and shelves to allow positive energy to flow into the shop and to block any negative energy from entering. Sage isn't sure the room's energy has changed, but she does like how the new front window lets in so much light—it makes the shop cheerful even on gloomy days. Despite some of Ruby's odd ideas, Sage thinks she is fun to be around. When Sage grows up, she wants to be confident and dramatic like Ruby!

On the way home from the shop, Sage cuts through the back gate to check on her container gardens on the back porch. Although they don't have a lot of space outside, Sage and her mother plant a few vegetables and herbs every season. Sage can see that they're almost ready to harvest a crop of carrots and turnips to go in their favorite stew. Next spring Sage wants to plant a salsa garden—tomatoes, peppers, and cilantro—so they can have fresh salsa all summer long. She also plans to grow zucchini squash so they can make moist, yummy zucchini bread, one of her favorite foods.

Her mother says that by growing at least some of their own food, they are helping to sustain the environment and contributing less pollution and waste to the earth. She also believes that choosing nutritious fresh foods instead of processed meals helps keep their bodies strong and minds clear. A healthy body makes a healthy mind, she says. Sage and her mother are vegetarians, which means they don't eat any meat or fish. This is because Sage's mother believes that killing any living thing, even an animal, is a crime. She is a little more relaxed about using eggs, cheese, and milk because the animals weren't killed to get these things. Most of the time, Sage doesn't mind avoiding meat, but pepperoni pizza days at the school cafeteria are hard because the whole school smells so good!

Photo: Clinton & Charles Robertson.

After a meal of butternut squash soup and cheesy croutons, Sage cleans up while her mother gets out the sewing materials. For weeks they have been sewing their costumes for next weekend's Renaissance fair. Ruby goes every year to sell her herbal remedies from a booth, and this year she is taking Sage and her mother along to help out. All of them are going to dress up in medieval costumes. Sage and her mother will run the booth while Ruby plays a gypsy fortune-teller. Sage has been looking forward to this weekend all year. Her dress has a deep-blue skirt and a green bodice over a snow-white blouse, and her mother is going to look gor-geous in burgundy and cream. But Ruby's outfit is even more extravagant—a rainbow skirt with a bright yellow blouse and feathers. She will fit right in with the rest of the fairgoers, many of whom will also be in costume as knights, peasants, magicians, courtiers, and royalty.

Sage hopes to get some time away from the booth so she can see the jousting tourna-ment, but she knows how important the fair is to Ruby's business. Ruby usually makes more money this one weekend than in the rest of the winter months combined. This year, she is going to give Sage a corner of the booth to display some of the jewelry she has made. Ruby taught Sage how to design and make necklaces while she was sick with chicken pox, and it's been a hobby ever since. Sage uses all-natural materials, including semi-precious stones,

Renaissance fair in Maryland. Photo: Owenusa.

crystals, and linen or hemp fibers for the cords. For the fair, Sage has made all three of them new necklaces to match their costumes.

Her mother is also bringing some of the products her New Age customers have asked her to stock, like all-natural soaps and honey. Although the fair will be a lot of work, Sage and her mother are looking forward to it. Sage even gets to leave school early on Friday to help pack the car! If they are very fortunate, the weather will be sunny the whole weekend.

Until then, Sage needs to do her chores and homework diligently, tend her plants on the back porch, and help Ruby at the store and her mother at the grocery. Although there are many things about life she still doesn't understand, Sage is happy to be who she is, with plenty of time ahead to find answers to her questions.

WHAT'S THE DIFFERENCE?

- How is the way Sage lives different from the way you live? How are your lives similar?

- Why do you suppose Sage's mother keeps trying new beliefs and religions? What do you think she is looking for? What would Sage and her mother think if they visited your church?

- Ruby tells Sage that God is not a person but that God and the universe are the same thing. How is this different from what the Bible tells us about God?

- Ruby says people can find harmony only if they discover the part of God that lives within them. How is this different from what the Bible teaches us about how to find harmony? What does the Bible say about God living inside you?

- How is the way Ruby teaches Sage to see herself different from the way you are learning to see yourself as a child of God?

WHAT KIND OF FRUIT ARE YOU GROWING?

SINCE WE LIVE BY THE SPIRIT, LET US KEEP IN STEP WITH THE SPIRIT.

GALATIANS 5:25

THE BIG IDEA

Jesus was staying that spring in the home of His disciple Peter in the seaside community of Capernaum. On this day, the afternoon sun warmed the earth as a pleasant breeze rippled across the peaceful waters of the Sea of Galilee. The fresh air and fragrance of the season invited people to emerge from their homes, to leave behind the cares of daily life. Spring figs grew in unusual abundance this year. A pair of white-tailed eagles swooped and soared overhead in an ancient mating dance, and wild daisies and honeysuckle silently proclaimed God's glory in the fields and hills surrounding Capernaum.

Jesus gathered His disciples, and together they walked to the shore. As they made their way through town, many of the villagers fell in behind them. Soon they were joined by others from surrounding towns and neighboring regions who had come just to hear the Teacher speak. By the time Jesus reached the water's edge, a crowd had surrounded Him. The people pressed in closer, begging Him to teach. He turned and waded into the water, then climbed aboard a fishing boat anchored there. Peter and John, both experienced fishermen, maneuvered the boat a small distance from shore and dropped anchor. Now Jesus could be seen and heard by all who had gathered on the beach.

He called out, "Listen!" and a hush settled over the crowd. "A farmer went out to plant some seed," He began. "As he scattered it across his field, some of the seed fell on a footpath.

There the seed was stepped on, and the birds came and ate it. Other seed fell among rocks. The seed sprouted quickly because the soil was shallow. But the plant soon wilted under the hot sun, and because it didn't have deep roots, it died. Other seed fell among thorny weeds that grew up and choked out the tender plants. Still other seed fell on good soil and began to grow. These seeds produced fruit that was thirty, sixty, and even a hundred times as much as had been planted!"

Then He said, "Anyone with ears to hear should listen and understand."

Later, when the disciples were alone with Jesus, they asked Him what the parable meant. Jesus said to them, "If you can't understand the meaning of this parable, how will you understand all the other parables? The seed that fell on the footpath represents those who hear the teaching of God and don't understand it. Then the evil one comes and snatches away the seed that was planted in their hearts. The seed on the rocky ground represents those who hear the message and immediately receive it with joy. But since these people don't have deep roots, they believe for a while then fall away when they face temptation. The seed that fell among the thorny weeds represents those who hear God's message, but all too quickly the teaching is crowded out by the worries of this life and the lure of wealth, so these people produce no fruit. But the seed that fell on good soil represents those who hear and truly believe God's Word. They grow and produce fruit—sometimes thirty times more, sometimes sixty times more, and sometimes a hundred times more."

The Sower by Millet.

The parable of the sower (farmer) and the seed appears in chapter four of the Gospel of Mark, as well as in the Gospels of Luke and Matthew. Jesus uses this story to show how differently people will respond to the message of salvation. But look closely at this story and you will see there's more to being a Christian than simply responding to an altar call or being baptized. Now that God has saved us from our sins, He wants us to continually grow and mature and live fruitful, productive lives for Him. But to do this you must cooperate with the work of the Holy Spirit, who lives inside you for the purpose of helping you to become like Jesus.

If you've ever had a garden, you know that the work isn't finished once the seeds are planted. You must be out in the garden every day, making sure the plants have sufficient water, chasing away the rabbits, and keeping weeds from taking over. In this same way, you need to tend to your spiritual life each day. You must allow the Word of God to take root in your heart. You need to water it through worship and obedience and prayer, asking God to give you the "living water" that Jesus promises to everyone who comes to Him. And you must "weed" your life by getting rid of everything that is not pleasing to God.

If you do these things, if you allow the Holy Spirit to control your life, He will grow in you the same attitudes that characterized the life of Jesus during His time on the earth. These characteristics are called "the fruit of the Spirit," and they include "love, joy, peace, patience, kindness, goodness, faithfulness, gentleness and self-control" (Galatians 5:22–23). You can't buy this fruit on the produce aisle at the supermarket. And try as you might, you cannot consistently grow it on your own. So let's examine together what the Master Gardener has to say about how to cultivate this wonderful bounty in your life.

WHAT YOU WILL DO
» You will identify the fruit of the Holy Spirit and learn to cultivate it in your own life.
» You will learn three strategies for living a fruitful and productive Christian life.
» You will understand how keeping a pure heart will help you to grow the fruit of the Spirit.

THE CODE OF CHIVALRY

Knights of the Middle Ages followed a code of conduct called chivalry. The medieval knight was expected to work just as hard at developing his character as he did his fighting skills, thus setting an example for his fellow man by living the high ideals of gallantry, courtesy, and honor every day.

The code of chivalry was developed during medieval times and was popularized by stories of well-known historical figures like Charlemagne and Saladin and tales of the legendary King Arthur. The chivalrous knight worked to perfect his battle technique and used his prowess to serve others, not for his personal gain or glory. He was unwaveringly loyal to his lord and would never betray him or abandon him out of cowardice. In addition, the knight was to be generous and honest and always keep his word. He pledged to defend the faith, provide for the church, display godly virtues, and always protect the innocent.

According to *The Book of the Courtier*, published in 1528, the chivalrous knight was also well read and practiced in such courtly arts as singing, dancing, speaking, and writing poetry. And he was honor bound to treat every woman gently and respectfully, whether she be a queen or a dairy maid. Such ideals were thought to make the warrior a more complete person, improving him in all areas of life. A knight who followed the rules of chivalry would become noble of heart and spirit, rather than merely noble in rank.

The code of chivalry continues to influence social behavior long after most orders of knighthood have ceased to exist. Even today, most perceptions of how a "gentleman" ought to behave have descended directly from the knights' code.

THE CHALLENGE

"Ouch!" Gwyneth winced but tried to maintain a smile. Through gritted teeth, she said, "Has Sir William failed to teach you the difference between the floor and a lady's feet?"

"Watch your rhythm, gentlemen," Lady Maud said as she clapped out the time for the squires and their dance partners, the young ladies-in-waiting of the castle. "This is a dance, not a boxing match."

Brandon winced as though he was the one who had been stepped on. "Sorry, Gwyn," he whispered. "I just can't seem to get comfortable in these new shoes. I could swear they gave me two left ones."

"That's okay, Brandon. It's only your third lesson."

"Left, right, left into center, hands raised, clap three times. Left, right, left out to place, kick three times. Nice and smooth," Lady Maud intoned.

But Brandon turned right instead of left and kicked one of the older boys. "Sorry, Reginald," he said sheepishly. Turning back to Gwyneth, he complained, "Why must I take dance lessons, anyway?"

"If you are to be a knight one day," she replied, "you must be presentable at court. A gentleman knows how to dance."

Lady Maud signaled for the lyrist to stop playing. "Mistress Gwyneth," she said, "do you wish to share some morsel of terpsichorean wisdom with your fellow dancers?"

Gwyneth blushed. "I am sorry, milady. I was just encouraging Brandon."

"Yes, he does seem to be in need of some assistance." She sighed heavily. "Very well. The rest of you are dismissed. Mistress Gwyneth, you will stay behind and help Master Brandon practice his paces."

"Yes, milady."

As the other boys and girls gathered their things to leave, the Lady Maud de Lisle stepped over to where Brandon was puzzling out the turn he kept missing. "Master Brandon," she said, "I understand you are to be squire to Sir William."

"Yes, milady. That is, if the baron and the king give their approval. I am not yet of age."

"How old are you?"

"I am but twelve, milady," he replied, then added, "but I'm a hard worker, and I love Wi— I mean, Sir William. He's like a brother to me."

"Indeed? Then you will wish to do him proud, I suppose."

"Oh yes, milady!"

"But you don't see the sense of learning to dance or play music when there are swords to be polished, wolves to be hunted, and battles to be won."

"No, milady. I mean, yes, milady. I mean— well, this does all seem rather silly. How can I serve the king by tromping on Gwyn's toes?"

Gwyneth giggled, and Lady Maud said, "Brandon, I have been instructing squires in courtly etiquette for the past twenty years, and every one of them felt the same way you do—at first. Oh, prowess with a sword and horse is important, to be sure. But there is much more to becoming a noble knight. Or a good squire, for that matter."

"Yes, milady. Wi— I mean, Sir William is also teaching me to read and write. He says that a knight must be well read and well spoken."

"Sir William is teaching you well. However, as the baron's wife and the lady of this castle, I too am charged with instructing you in the ways of chivalry. You see, Master Brandon, a good knight is also skilled in speech and etiquette and has an appreciation of the arts. Such pursuits ennoble the

Portrait of a Woman by Rogier van der Weyden.

spirit, lifting man up from the dust toward the heavens. As in the tales of Saint George, an accomplished knight with a noble mind and a gentle spirit can have great influence in the lives of others. Their example inspires men and women from all walks of life toward service and virtue. When you learn to lead by example, then you will truly understand what it means to be a hero."

Brandon looked puzzled. "Gentleness, milady? But a knight is a warrior."

"A warrior who can express himself only with a sword or a spear is little more than a blunt instrument in the hands of his master. A knight must be able to make peace as well as war. The Scriptures tell us, 'A gentle answer turns away wrath, but a harsh word stirs up anger.' Yes, there are times when a knight must be fierce, but gentleness and love for one's fellow man are among the fruit of the Spirit that must be cultivated daily."

Brandon said, "I think I understand, milady. But dancing is so hard—and *my* dancing is hard on Gwyn."

Lady Maud smiled. "As a knight, you will be called upon to undertake many unpleasant, difficult, and frightening tasks. Have courage, Master Brandon. Consider this just another dragon to be slain. Now, let's begin again."

Quentin was on a rampage. Jealous of Brandon and angry with Sir William for having passed him over when selecting a personal squire, Quentin expressed his frustration by making life miserable for the younger pages. Barking his instructions, the senior page would order a boy to redo the same task over and over again until Quentin tired of the game and moved on to terrorize someone else.

Because Brandon had been busy taking lessons or doing chores for William, he had managed to avoid Quentin for the most part. But on this day, Quentin caught him off guard as Brandon was eating lunch under a tree with Gwyneth.

"Varlet! This is no time for a picnic," Quentin exclaimed as he marched up the hill to where they sat. "The king arrives tomorrow, and there's work to be done. You're not a squire yet . . . and you never will be, if I have anything to say about it."

Gwyneth shot back, "Then it's a good thing it's not your decision to make. Brandon is going to be a great knight someday."

"Don't listen to him, Gwyn," Brandon said. "He's just angry that William chose me for his squire instead of him."

"You bet I'm angry! And I have every right to be. I am the eldest of the baron's pages, and my family has money and connections at court. You just wait and see—the king is going to square this with the baron when he comes. For now, you're still taking my orders. So get back to work!" Quentin turned and stomped off.

Brandon and Gwyneth quickly gathered their things and started back toward the castle. "What a bully!" Gwyneth said.

"Quentin and I have never been what you would call friends," Brandon said, "but he's really not a bad sort. Sure, he's got a bit of a temper, and he does think an awful lot of himself. But he works hard, and he's quite good with the horses. I understand how he feels. Nevertheless, Will did choose me, and I'm not going to let him down, Gwyn."

"That's the spirit!" she said.

"However," Brandon went on, "I confess I am nervous about the king's coming. What if he doesn't approve of me? What if he finds out I'm nobody? What if I stumble when I go to kneel before him? What if during the ceremony he notices that Will's sword is dirty? What if—?"

"Brandon, you're getting yourself worked up over a lot of 'what ifs.'"

"But the king—"

"Yes, King Edward is a powerful man. But he is also known for his merciful nature as much as for his victories in battle."

"You've been to court, Gwyn. What was it like, standing in the presence of a king?"

"Oh, it was all quite wonderful! The men and women were so graceful and dressed so beautifully—they were like angels gathered about God's throne. Oh, I know that heaven will be ten thousand times more glorious, but as I stood there, I couldn't help but think of heaven and what David said about our Lord: 'In His presence is fullness of joy.'"

Brandon scoffed. "Joy? Huh. Not to hear the vicar tell it. Last week, he talked about a prophet who went to heaven. He was scared to death because he knew he was not worthy to be there. There were angels with six wings, the doors were shaking, and the place was filled with smoke. The whole thing sounded pretty scary to me."

Gwyneth said, "But then God purified Isaiah and took his sins away—just as Jesus took away your sins and mine when He gave His life on the cross. Yes, we need to remember that God is holy and almighty and revere Him for who He is. But because of what Jesus did, you and I can stand in God's presence and experience the joy of the Lord."

"Sure, someday . . ."

"No," Gwyneth said. "I mean right now! After all, there is no place we can go where God is not. All we have to do is open our eyes and our hearts to see His wonders all around us."

"I suppose that's true."

"And God has promised that if we come to Him with thankful hearts and focus our attention on Him, He will draw ever closer to us."

"I guess I never thought of God that way before. The vicar always makes it sound like God is so angry—like He's just waiting for me to make a mistake so He can strike me down with a thunderbolt."

Gwyneth sighed. "I'm afraid the vicar does tend to preach more about fire and brimstone than of God's mercy and grace."

"You know, Will has been teaching me about the Holy Ghost. It's hard to imagine God living inside me. But Will says that the Holy Ghost helps me to be good and kind to others."

"That's right! It's called the fruit of the Spirit. I learned all about it from Lady Isabel. I count myself blessed to be her companion and student."

"She's wonderful, all right. I can see why Will likes her so much."

Gwyneth stopped suddenly. "Ooh, that reminds me! I need to see to Isabel's horse! She and Will planned to go riding later."

Brandon was brushing Maximilian, and Gwyneth was helping Lady Isabel groom her horse, Charity, when Sir William appeared carrying a jousting lance and asked them to join him on the practice pitch. "A tournament is to be held after the knighting ceremony in two days," William said, "and I wouldn't want to make a poor showing in front of the king."

Brandon saddled Max and led him out to the field. Arranged about the practice field were several bales of hay, a pair of jousting targets called quintains, and a row of three tall stanchions set ten paces apart. Each of the stanchions held a six-inch ring dangling at the end of a detachable rope.

William mounted his steed at the south end of the field, and Brandon handed up the lance. Unlike William's battle lance, this one was made of soft wood, hollowed, and blunted at the tip for use at tournaments. William secured the hilt of the lance in a rest attached to the saddle. Then he lightly but swiftly applied his spurs to Max's haunches, and the horse took off, flying toward the rings at a full gallop. William lowered his lance and neatly speared each of the three rings. Gwyneth, Brandon, and Lady Isabel cheered loudly. William repeated the exercise several times over the next hour to the delight of his young supporters.

"Excellent work today, Max," William said, patting the horse's withers as he dismounted.

Lady Isabel said, "Brandon, you're doing a fine job with Maximilian. I've never seen him happier or healthier."

As they walked back to the stables, Gwyneth asked, "Sir William, I know the tournament is supposed to be a friendly

Photo: Jeff Kubina.

competition. But you ride at such frightening speeds, and people still get hurt in the joust. Aren't you afraid of being injured?"

"I certainly respect my opponents," he said, "and I understand the risks involved. However, I enjoy the challenge and the opportunity to test my skills against those of my competitors."

"I'll bet you weren't thinking of 'testing your skills' when you went to the aid of the baron at Calais," Brandon said.

"Yes, Will," Isabel said, "you could have been killed! Weren't you terrified?"

"I'll let my squire answer that one. Brandon?"

Brandon thought for a moment. "Well, the Bible says that God did not give us a spirit of fear, but He has given us a spirit of power . . . and love . . . oh, and self-control!"

William smiled. "Well said, my friend. When events conspire to destroy us, we are to stand firm, having faith, confident that everything is going to work out. When the children of Israel stood on the banks of the Red Sea and saw the army of Pharaoh giving chase, Moses said to them, 'Do not be afraid. Stand firm and you will see the deliverance the Lord will bring you today.' When confronted with life's problems, we too must remain at peace."

Crossing of the Red Sea by Rosselli.

"Are you not afraid of anything?" Gwyneth asked.

"I would be lying if I said I never feel fear," William admitted. "I am human, after all. But I do not let fear control me."

"How do you mean?" Brandon asked.

"Every day there are battles to be fought and won. Our enemy, the devil, sets many traps for the followers of Christ. However, he cannot overcome God's children except by deception and intimidation. So I choose to stand on the truth of God's Word. For how can Satan deceive someone who recognizes his lies and refuses to believe them? How can he intimidate someone who will not give in to fear? If I stand firm, resisting the devil and avoiding evil in all its forms, then he must flee, utterly defeated."

Brandon said, "But the Holy Ghost stays with you and gives you peace and patience. Right, Will?"

"Yes, and love and joy. And kindness!" Gwyneth added.

"And goodness, faithfulness, gentleness, and self-control," said Lady Isabel.

William smiled and said, "My friends, against such things there is no law."

SAINT GEORGE AND THE DRAGON

Saint George has been venerated as the patron saint of England since the Middle Ages, though little is known for certain about this historical figure. George is believed to have been born to a Christian family in the region of Palestine sometime in the late third century. After both his parents died when he was just a teenager, he went to the Roman emperor Diocletian and asked to become a soldier. George's father had been one of the emperor's finest officers, so Diocletian warmly accepted the young man. George proved an excellent soldier and, by his late twenties, had been promoted to the rank of tribune and was stationed as a guard to the emperor himself.

Diocletian, however, was not a friend to the Christian faith. In the year 302, he issued an edict that required all soldiers to offer a sacrifice to the pagan gods. According to legend, George went before the emperor to object to the new law. The emperor didn't want to lose his best soldier, so he offered George bribes of land, money, and slaves to convince him to renounce his faith. Instead, George proclaimed to his fellow soldiers that he worshiped Jesus Christ and Him alone. The emperor had no choice but to have the tribune executed for his disobedience.

St. George and the Dragon by Riviere.

After the first Crusades in the eleventh century, European soldiers returned from Palestine with legends of the man called Saint George. The most famous of the stories told of a dragon that made its nest by a spring near the city of Silene. The people had to coax the dragon to move so they could get to the water they needed for cooking, cleaning, and drinking. So each day they went to the spring and offered the dragon a sheep to eat. If no sheep could be found, a young maiden was taken instead. The girls were chosen by lottery, and one day the name of the king's daughter was drawn! The king begged the people to spare her life, but the princess was taken and offered to the dragon just as George rode by on his horse. He drew his sword, killed the dragon, and rescued the princess. After George told the people about the One True God who had given him the courage to slay the dragon, the grateful citizens gave up worshiping their false gods.

Eight hundred years later, the soldiers of Richard the Lionheart returned to England from the Crusades wearing the colors of Saint George—a red cross against a white background. Since that time, the flag known as St. George's Cross has flown over England for nearly a millennium.

THINK ABOUT IT

» According to the code of chivalry, what character traits will Brandon need to develop if he is to become a knight of the realm? Which of these traits does Brandon already demonstrate as a page to Sir William and a friend to Gwyneth?

» Why is Quentin upset with Brandon and William? How does he express his anger toward them? How could he express his feelings in a healthier way?

» Before the twentieth century, the Holy Spirit was often called the Holy Ghost, and many people still use this name today. Who is the Holy Spirit? Where can you find Him? How can you know He's there?

» What would it be like to visit the throne room of an earthly king? What kinds of things would you expect to see there?

» What do you imagine it will it be like to stand before God's throne in heaven? What do you expect to see there? How do you think you will feel?

WORDS YOU NEED TO KNOW

» **Fruit of the Spirit**: Christlike attitudes that show the Holy Spirit is working in my life

» **Holiness**: Purity in my heart in everything I think and say and do

HIDE IT IN YOUR HEART

But the fruit of the Spirit is love, joy, peace, patience, kindness, goodness, faithfulness, gentleness and self-control. Against such things there is no law. (Galatians 5:22–23)

I am the LORD your God. Keep yourselves holy for me because I am holy. (Leviticus 11:44, ICB)

WHAT IS THE FRUIT OF THE SPIRIT?

Fruit is mentioned many times in the Bible, as far back as the first instructions given to Adam and Eve in the garden. In fact, the word "fruit" is used more than fifty times in the New Testament alone! Sometimes the Bible is speaking of the kind of fruit you eat—apples, figs, grapes, olives, dates, mulberries, even pomegranates. You will also find many references in God's Word to biological fruit, as in giving birth to children. This is what God was talking about when He blessed the first man and woman and told them, "Be fruitful and multiply" (Genesis 1:28, NKJV).

And then there is *spiritual* fruit. In John 15:8 (ICB), Jesus says, "You should produce much fruit and show that you are my followers. This brings glory to my Father." Is He saying we should give glory to God by planting vineyards and orchards or starting a Christian banana plantation? No. Jesus is talking about being fruitful—living in a way that feeds a spiritually hungry world. Just as the fruit that grows on a tree can feed many people, so the spiritual fruit produced in our lives can feed the souls of the people we come into contact with each day. When we walk and talk and love people the way Jesus did, they will see and hear the gospel and many will believe and give glory to our Father in heaven.

How is this possible? When we commit ourselves to following Christ, God sends the Holy Spirit into our lives to guide us and teach us (John 16:13–15) and give us the strength, desire, and power to do what is right (Philippians 2:13). As the Holy Spirit works within us, we become more and more like Jesus. This is God's desire for your life: to make you more like His Son.

How can you know you are becoming more like Christ? By the "fruit" the Spirit produces in you. According to the apostle Paul, the fruit of the Spirit is love, joy, peace, patience, kindness, goodness, faithfulness, gentleness, and self-control (Galatians 5:22–23). During His life on earth, Jesus exemplified each of these character traits in His words and actions. God wants to see this same fruit growing in our lives—that is His definition of a productive Christian life.

So get to know this fruit and ask God to cultivate it in your life. Love. Joy. Peace. Patience. Kindness. Goodness. Faithfulness. Gentleness. Self-control. Perhaps some of these sound familiar because we've already talked about them in this book. You learned about peace in lesson 3. We talked about patience and joy in lesson 4. And self-control was an important topic of both lessons 4 and 6. Review these chapters later. For now, let's take a closer look at the other fruit of the Spirit.

LOVE

Love is more than just the first fruit mentioned in Paul's list. It is *the* fruit. When asked which commandment in God's law is greatest, Jesus replied, "'You must love the LORD your God with all your heart, all your soul, and all your mind.' This is the first and greatest commandment. A second is equally important: 'Love your neighbor as yourself.' The entire law and all the demands of the prophets are based on these two commandments" (Matthew 22:37–40, NLT). Likewise, all the fruit of the Spirit is an expression of love.

Movies, television shows, and modern music promote many different ideas about what love is. Some of these notions are just plain silly, and many are downright false. So where do we go to find the truth about love? The Bible, of course! Here we find the best description of what love looks like:

Love is patient, love is kind. It does not envy, it does not boast, it is not proud. It is not rude, it is not self-seeking, it is not easily angered, it keeps no record of wrongs. Love does not delight in evil but rejoices with the truth. It always protects, always trusts, always hopes, always perseveres. Love never fails. (1 Corinthians 13:4–8)

Love is patient. Love is kind. Love is joyful. Sound familiar? Once the love of God begins to flow through you and begins touching the lives of others, the other fruits of the Holy Spirit will start to blossom in your life. Paul said, "I may understand all the secret things of God and have all knowledge, and I may have faith so great I can move mountains. But even with all these things, if I do not have love, then I am nothing" (1 Corinthians 13:2, NCV).

Jesus says, "Love your neighbor as yourself." But what if you don't feel love for your neighbor? After all, some people are hard to love. People can be annoying, prickly, abrasive, and just plain difficult to get along with. In fact, everyone is hard to love some of the time, including you and me. Thankfully, Jesus never said we had to *like* everybody, but we do have to love them. The key to obeying this commandment is to remember that love is something you *do*, not just something you say or feel (1 John 3:18).

Love is a choice—a decision you make to put another's needs and desires ahead of your own, no matter how un-lovely that person may be. True love requires action on your part because that is the way God loves us. When we were lost in rebellion and sin, He didn't turn His back on us and leave us to suffer the punishment we deserved. Instead, He made the ultimate gesture of love by giving His only begotten Son to die in our place (John 3:16).

Jesus loved as no person ever loved. His love knew no limits. From the lowliest beggar to the richest king, from the worst of sinners to the greatest of saints, He loved them all. He even loved those who plotted to kill Him, even though they had no intention of making Him feel warm and fuzzy all over. Ephesians 5:2 (NLT) says, "Live a life filled with love, follow-

> *"Love when you expect no love in return. Do good without expecting thanks. Lend when you do not hope for a return. This will make us act like sons and daughters of the Most High."*
> **Henrietta Mears**
> 1890–1963

ing the example of Christ." We need to love others as Jesus loves them, but only the Spirit of God working in our lives can produce that kind of fruit.

KINDNESS

What does the well-dressed Christian wear in public? A jacket and tie? A modest dress cut below the knees? A WWJD bracelet? A clean pair of jeans and a "Got Jesus?" T-shirt? Ask a fashion designer and he or she will tell you that the clothes you wear should say something about you—your personality, your lifestyle, your goals, and your taste. So what does a person wear to tell the world "I am a beloved child of God and a glad follower of Jesus Christ"? In his letter to the church at Colossae, the apostle Paul gives us this important fashion tip:

> *God has chosen you and made you his holy people. He loves you. So you should always clothe yourselves with mercy, kindness, humility, gentleness, and patience."* (Colossians 3:12, NCV)

Paul is saying that when you get up in the morning, you should get dressed spiritually as well as physically. What kind of attitude did you put on this morning? Were you kind to your family at breakfast? Did you offer to help someone with a chore, if only to lighten that person's load a little? If the people you came into contact with today didn't know you, would they be able to tell you're a Christian simply by your words and actions?

Kindness starts with watching and listening for the needs of others. Find out what you can do for someone today and do it. Many times this can be as simple as saying a kind and supportive word. Proverbs 15:4 (CEV) says, "Kind words are good medicine, but deceitful words can really hurt." Another translation of this verse says, "Evil words can crush the spirit" (ICB). You can either heal people or destroy them with your words, so be careful what you say. You can be a member of God's construction crew and build people up, or you can work for Satan's wrecking crew and tear people down. Whom will you serve this day?

Do not wait to show kindness to someone. Galatians 6:10 says, "As we have opportunity, let us do good to all people." When you think something like *I should write a thank-you note to my grandmother* or *I should do something nice for my neighbor*, don't put it off. God may be urging you to show someone kindness because it's exactly what that person needs right now. Help your mom around the house or wash the car for your dad—do something nice today just because you have the opportunity. Everyone you will meet this week—including your family—needs someone to show them a little kindness. Are you ready to meet their need?

> ## MAKE A NOTE OF IT
> Read the story of the Good Samaritan in Luke 10:30–37. The Jewish people of Jesus' time did not like the people of Samaria, and the feeling was mutual. Yet in the story, the Good Samaritan put aside his personal feelings to do the right thing. How did the Samaritan show love and kindness to the Jewish man? Why do you think the Jewish priest and the Levite did not stop to help the man? Think of a person you do not like. How can you show love and kindness to that person?

> *"Kind words are the music of the world. They have a power which seems to be beyond natural causes, as though they were some angel's song which had lost its way and come to earth."*
> **Frederick William Faber**
> 1814-1863

GOODNESS

Mark Twain once wrote, "Always do right. This will gratify some people and astonish the rest." Why should anyone be astonished when you do the right thing? Because, despite what you may have heard on a touchy-feely TV talk show, people are not good by nature. Isaiah 53:6 says that every one of us has departed from God's path to go our own way. Indeed, the Bible makes it clear: Only God can truly be called good (Mark 10:18).

History shows that people find it hard to do good things even when they know the right thing to do. Despite being the most educated and technologically sophisticated generation ever, we still have wars and famine and crime, and people still hate others who are different from them. That's because people are born selfish and sinful (Romans 5:12). Even the apostle Paul said that no matter how hard he tried, he couldn't make himself do right. He wanted to be good, but he couldn't. And when he tried not to do wrong, he did it anyway! Read it for yourself in Romans 7:14–25 (NLT). In verse 24, Paul cries out, "Oh, what a miserable person I am! Who will free me from this life that is dominated by sin and death?"

The answer, of course, is Jesus Christ. (As Paul says, "Thank God!") Because we have chosen to follow Christ, we now belong to Him. And because we belong to Him, the power of the Holy Spirit has freed us from the power of sin (Romans 8:1–2). As a result, we can now live fruitful lives for God. That's because the Spirit is working in us, giving us "the desire and the power" to do what is right and good (Philippians 2:13, NLT).

THE LOVE BUG

The artist Robert Indiana was born Robert Clark in New Castle, Indiana, in 1928. When he was twenty-six, Clark changed his name and moved to New York City where he joined the growing Pop Art movement. Pop art often took its imagery from the popular culture of the day. For example, Andy Warhol based one of his most famous works on an advertising icon, the Campbell's Soup can, while Roy Lichtenstein drew his imagery from the world of comic books. Unlike these painters, Robert Indiana was a sculptor who created bold, simple images, usually made up of numerals or short words like EAT and HUG.

Love by Robert Indiana. Photo: Hu Totya.

Then in 1964, Indiana produced a work that would become a worldwide sensation. Originally designed as a Christmas card for the Museum of Modern Art, his piece LOVE would be presented as a full-size steel sculpture six years later. The design is deceptively simple. The capital letters L and O are mounted atop the letters V and E, with the O whimsically canted sideways. The public reaction was immediate and overwhelmingly positive. In 1973, the United States Postal Service featured Indiana's design on the very first of what has become a tradition—LOVE stamps, which are issued every year around Valentine's Day.

Today, the original twelve-feet-tall LOVE sculpture is located at the Indianapolis Museum of Art in the artist's home state, but at least thirty versions of the work are on display in a variety of colors in museums and parks and in public locations around the world, including Tokyo, Lisbon, Bangkok, Shanghai, Montreal, Derbyshire in the United Kingdom, New York, New Orleans, and Provo, Utah. There's even a version in which the Hebrew word for "love" is spelled out in Hebrew letters and displayed at the Israel Museum in Jerusalem!

FAITHFULNESS

In 1933, "The Lone Ranger" premiered on a Detroit radio station and soon was heard in homes across America. The theme music, the finale of Gioachino Rossini's *William Tell Overture*, is now forever linked with the masked man. The title character is an Old West lawman who is left for dead after his entire posse has been ambushed and killed. When he is rescued by a childhood friend, a clever and resourceful Native American named Tonto, our hero chooses to let the world believe he died along with his posse. He puts on a mask and, accompanied by Tonto, rides throughout the West on his horse, Silver, fighting injustice and right-ing wrongs as the Lone Ranger.

The Lone Ranger and Tonto lived by a strict moral code that guided their actions. Their creed, or statement of beliefs, was written by one of the show's writers to help young fans live a life of goodness, fairness, and decency, just like their heroes. The creed began, "I believe that to have a friend, a man must be one." Tonto often called the Lone Ranger "Ke-mo sah-bee," which was said to mean "trusty scout" or "faithful friend" in his native language.

To be faithful means to be trustworthy and dependable. Proverbs 20:6 (NLT) says, "Many will say they are

loyal friends, but who can find one who is truly reliable?" It's not easy to find a friend who can really be counted on in both good times and bad. Proverbs 25:19 (ICB) says, "Don't trust unfaithful people when you are in trouble. It's like eating with a broken tooth or walking with a crippled foot." That's because unreliable people can cause a great deal of pain for those who depend on them.

Do you have a reputation for being a faithful friend? Do you keep your promises? Do you always do what you say you will do? Do you take care of the things you borrow from others? Do you remain loyal to your friends, even when they're in trouble or someone else says something bad about them? You may be bright, funny, and talented. But if you're not dependable, you're going to find that friends are in short supply.

The best place to begin developing faithfulness is at home, and the best time to start is now. When you are assigned a chore, do it to the very best of your ability. When it's time to go to church or run errands or go to a movie, be ready on time. Don't make everyone else wait on you. Always tell the truth and take responsibility for your actions when you do something wrong. Pray, study your Bible, and meditate on God's Word every day.

Jesus said, "Whoever can be trusted with very little can also be trusted with much" (Luke 16:10). Life is largely made up of little things. Make a habit now of being faithful in the little things, and you will be faithful when people are depending on you most.

> *"It is better to be faithful than famous.*
> **Theodore Roosevelt**
> 1858-1919

GENTLENESS

Since the early 1600s, the nation of India had come under the increasing influence of the British. But by the 1800s, the people of India became seriously displeased with oppressive British policies. A violent uprising in 1857 resulted in the deaths of at least 100,000 Indians but failed to overthrow the colonial government. Then in the early twentieth century, a man named Mohandas K. Gandhi united the people of India in a renewed struggle for independence. Under Gandhi's leadership, India successfully won its freedom and became an independent country in 1947.

Mohandas K. Gandhi.

Perhaps you're thinking Gandhi must have been a great warrior, a brilliant military strategist who, like George Washington, inspired people to fight for the cause of freedom. But this wasn't the case. In fact, almost the opposite was true. Gandhi was a simple country lawyer who taught his people *not* to fight back. Yes, he courageously rejected the unjust policies of the British and encouraged his followers to do the same, but he did so without the threat of violence. With the whole world watching, he chose to go to prison for his people's disobedience and fasted in protest. But he refused to raise his fists or wave a weapon in anger. Gandhi once said, "In a gentle way, you can shake the world." And so he did. Gandhi died only a year after his country won its independence, but to this day, the Indian people call him Mahatma, or "The Great Soul."

Philippians 4:5 (CEV) tells us to "always be gentle with others." Does this mean we are supposed to crawl through life, being timid and weak? No. Gandhi was gentle, but he was neither timid nor weak. He spoke boldly against injustice as the political and spiritual leader of one of the most populous nations on earth. Deborah was called "a mother to Israel" (Judges 5:7, NCV), but she was no shrinking violet. She led God's people to victory in battle, paving the way for forty years of peace. As a man, the Lord Jesus was gentle, but He was no weakling. A carpenter by trade, Jesus was strong, assertive, and unafraid, as when He fashioned a homemade whip and drove the moneychangers from God's temple (John 2:13–17).

These days, gentleness, or meekness, is often confused with weakness. But true gentleness is defined by a quiet strength, an expression of love by a person who brings his or her power under control. A mighty river can be wild and destructive, but when brought under control it can be used to generate electrical power for an entire city. Fire can be deadly, but when brought under control it can be used to cook a meal for the homeless or heat an office building in winter. This is the idea conveyed by the biblical word *gentleness*—strength under control.

Giving the Spirit control in your life will make it possible for you to always be gentle when dealing with people. Here are just a few pointers for showing quiet strength:

» When someone corrects you, listen. Be teachable. Do not jump to defend yourself, but be willing to learn and accept correction. James 1:19 says, "Be quick to listen, slow to speak and slow to become angry."

» If you feel the need to correct someone, do so with kind words. Whenever you feel tempted to judge another person harshly, stop and think about how much God has forgiven you.

» When someone disagrees with you, remember, "A gentle answer turns away wrath, but a harsh word stirs up anger" (Proverbs 15:1). If you remain calm and respond quietly, the other person is much more likely to stop and consider what you have to say (2 Timothy 2:24–25).

» If you are bigger and stronger than someone else, do not use your size to your advantage. Instead, ask that person what you can do to help him or her. You will make that person's day!

You may never walk the human corridors of power. You may never become a great leader of men and women. You may never rule a nation or become the chief executive of a large corporation. But you can be certain that one day the meek *will* inherit the earth (Matthew 5:5). And you will stand beside Jesus Christ as His co-heir for all eternity (Romans 8:17).

MAKE A NOTE OF IT

Read chapter 2 from the book of Ruth. Had she come to another field, Ruth might have been harassed by the workers. Her life may even have been in danger. How does Boaz demonstrate gentleness, or "quiet strength," toward Ruth? How do you treat the new girl on the block? What about the boy who doesn't quite fit in with the other kids? Do you stand up for the girl who is being teased or bullied? If you see a small boy who has fallen off his bike, do you stop to help him? What do you think your gentleness and kindness might mean to these kids?

HOW DOES YOUR GARDEN GROW?

So how do we come by all these wonderful character qualities? When you become a Christian, the Holy Spirit moves in, but that doesn't mean you automatically reap the fruit of the Spirit. All Christians have God's Spirit in their lives, but not all Christians have God's power in their lives. That's because many Christians do not tend their "gardens" carefully.

In John 15:5 (NCV), Jesus said, "I am the vine, and you are the branches. If any remain in me and I remain in them, they produce much fruit. But without me they can do nothing." The branch of a grapevine is totally dependent on the main vine to grow fruit. If the branch breaks from the vine and falls to the ground, it can produce nothing by itself. Without the supply of nutrients it receives from the vine, the branch quickly withers and dies. So are you staying connected to the True Vine? Are you depending on His Spirit? Are you obeying His Word?

Think of your life in Christ as a garden planted by the Holy Spirit. This garden will flourish, producing much fruit and providing nourishment and beauty to a world desperate for these things—*if* the garden is tended properly. Here are three important ways you can make sure your garden grows in a way that brings glory to God.

GROWING STRONG ROOTS

The magnificent saguaro cactus is native to the Sonoran Desert of Arizona, California, and Mexico. Although the desert has the benefit of two rainy seasons, the Sonoran may receive as little as three inches of rainfall per year. Meanwhile, during the summer months, temperatures in the region frequently exceed 120 degrees! Yet the saguaro cactus thrives in this environment, growing anywhere from fifteen to fifty feet in height and living for 150 years or more. How is this possible? The cactus collects and stores water in its extensive root system, which spreads out in a radius that equals the cactus's tremendous height! These same roots wrap about the desert rocks, providing a firm anchor when the cactus is buffeted by strong winds.

All of us experience difficult times in our lives, times of heat and drought when nothing seems to be going right and we start to wonder just how much more we can stand.

Saguaro cactus. Photo: Grombo.

If you don't have good roots, your faith won't survive these tough times. Jeremiah 17:7–8 (NLT) says:

> *Blessed are those who trust in the LORD*
> *and have made the LORD their hope and confidence.*
> *They are like trees planted along a riverbank,*
> *with roots that reach deep into the water.*
> *Such trees are not bothered by the heat*
> *or worried by long months of drought.*
> *Their leaves stay green,*
> *and they never stop producing fruit.*

So how can you cultivate good roots? Notice that the above scripture speaks of a tree planted by the river. Jesus described Himself as the source of "living water" (John 4:10; 7:37–38). You grow good roots by providing them with a constant source of water. Therefore, spend time with Jesus daily. Pray and talk with Him about everything. Psalm 1:2–3 tells us that we set down strong roots by reading and meditating on God's Word. Roots grown in this way will not wither and die during difficult times. Nor will they dry up and blow away when we're challenged by the harsh, changing winds of the world and the angry words of those who oppose Christ. Proverbs 12:3 tells us that "the righteous cannot be uprooted."

Start by telling God you want to be a fruitful, productive Christian, that you want to follow His plan for your life. Plant yourself deep in the nutrient-rich soil of God's Word, and ask God to use His Word to change the way you think. Ask Him to help you respond to difficult people and unpleasant situations the way Jesus would. Then invite the Holy Spirit to have free rein in your life. Don't withhold any part of your life from Him. Be aware that God is always with you, in you. Talk to Him constantly about every decision, every need, every concern, and every friendship. Soon you will begin to see the fruit of the Spirit growing abundantly in your life.

SUBMITTING TO GOD'S PRUNING

In John 15:1–2, Jesus says, "I am the true vine, and my Father is the gardener. He cuts off every branch in me that bears no fruit, while every branch that does bear fruit he prunes so that it will be even more fruitful." Pruning sounds painful, but it's an important part of gardening. Pruning involves cutting off the dead branches and cutting back the living branches, both to shape the tree or vine and to stimulate new growth. If you don't cut the excess leaves and branches from a rose bush in winter, the bush will direct so much of its available water and nutrients to the maintenance of these leaves and branches that little will be left for the production of beautiful new roses in the spring.

Several years ago, we moved into a home with an apricot tree in the back yard. For one long winter, visions of apricot pastries, fresh fruit cobbler, and apricot-glazed hams danced in our heads. Do you know how many apricots we harvested the following summer? Zero. Zip. Nada. So my wife did some research on apricot trees, and the following winter she got out the pruning shears. She lopped off dead limbs and cut back the healthy branches until the tree was little more than a collection of nubs on a trunk. Yet the following summer, we had so many apricots that we were able to share bags full of delicious fruit with the neighbors on our block.

One of the ways God prunes us is to remove the sinful stuff—the deadwood—from our lives. But He also sometimes cuts back those things in our lives that appear to be healthy and strong. In this way He encourages even greater growth and more fruitfulness. This can be confusing, even frustrating, especially when He lops off something that has been a blessing in your life. For example, your best friend suddenly must move with his or her family across town or across country. The two of you were very close: You played together, went to church together, and encouraged one another in your faith. But perhaps God wants to introduce you to a new friend who needs encouragement, or to someone who will challenge you to develop your God-given talent or make a deeper commitment to growing His kingdom.

Pruning is never fun and it's not pretty, but it is absolutely essential for spiritual growth. God is glorified when we bear "much fruit" (John 15:8), and that requires pruning. We must keep in mind that the loppers are in the hands of our loving God. He knows exactly what He is doing, and He always wants what's best for us.

GETTING RID OF THE WEEDS

Merriam-Webster's dictionary defines a weed as "a plant that is not valued where it is growing and is usually of vigorous growth; especially one that tends to overgrow or choke out more desirable plants." Without constant vigilance and work on the part of the gardener, unwanted weeds can quickly overrun the most beautiful of gardens. Weeds compete with garden plants for water, light, and nutrients and often invite in new pests and diseases. The gardener needs to eradicate these weeds before they choke the life out of the more delicate flowers.

Likewise, we need to eliminate the weeds in our lives in order to grow the spiritual fruit God wants us to produce. Remember the parable of the sower? In Luke 8:14, Jesus explained, "The seed that fell among the thorny weeds is like those who hear God's teaching, but they let the worries, riches, and pleasures of this life keep them from growing and producing good fruit" (NCV). If you want your life to be fruitful, you must get rid of the weeds that choke off the precious resources you need to bear good fruit.

What are the weeds in your life? What are the activities, distractions, and worries that eat away at your time, energy, and joy and keep you from living a productive Christian life? The Internet? Video games? Food? Fashion? Gossip? A poor attitude? An inappropriate friend? Any worldly thing that preoccupies your thinking can be a weed that keeps you from growing spiritually.

If these or other desires and concerns are crowding time with Jesus from your life, it's time to pull the weeds and plant some seeds. Go back to Romans 12:2 and Philippians 4:8 and renew your mind by spending your time thinking about whatever is true, whatever is noble, whatever is right, whatever is pure, whatever is lovely, whatever is admirable, and anything that is excellent or praiseworthy.

Make a Note of It

Make a list of the fruit of the Spirit—love, joy, peace, patience, kindness, goodness, faithfulness, gentleness, and self-control. Now talk with a parent to determine which of these are currently strongest in your life. Which ones need more water and work? How can you go about cultivating these attitudes in your life?

What Should I Do?

God is holy, meaning He is completely without sin. He is absolutely pure, intolerant of sin, and morally (and in all other ways) perfect. And because we are made in His image, God commands us to be holy, too (Leviticus 11:44). This may sound like a tall order for imperfect humans, but in His boundless mercy and amazing grace, God has provided us "everything we need to live a life that pleases God" through our knowledge of Christ so that we may "escape our evil desires and the corrupt influences of this world" (2 Peter 1:3–4, CEV). Keeping a pure heart in everything you say and do will help you to grow the fruit of the Spirit, just as bearing much fruit will help you and encourage you to be holy.

A Prayer

Dear God, thank you for coming to live inside me. Thank you for helping me to become like your Son, Jesus. Help me to be a fruitful Christian and live a life that is pleasing to you. Jesus, help me to love people and see them the way you do. Holy Spirit, help me to grow your fruit in my life so that when people see me they will see Jesus. I ask these things in His name. Amen.

Photo: NASA.

WORLDVIEWS IN FOCUS

MEET JIN-HO

Jin-Ho is a twelve-year-old boy who lives in Pyongyang (pronounced "pyawn-YANG"), the capital city of the Democratic People's Republic of Korea, better known around the world as North Korea. Jin-Ho lives with his mother and father, and he has one older brother, Jin-Yong, a soldier who is stationed away from home.

Jin-Ho's full name is Kim Jin-Ho. In Korea, a person's surname, or family name, comes first to honor the family. Today, only about 250 Korean family names are in use—almost half the population of North Korea is named Kim, Lee, or Park. Family is very important to Koreans, and Jin-Ho does everything he can to show respect to his parents and grandparents.

Jin-Ho's father has a job with the Korean Workers Party, the communist ruling party of North Korea led by the current president, who is called the Great Leader. Jin-Ho's father says that without the leadership of the Great Leader and his late father, who is known as the Eternal President, North Korea would not be the country it is today. To honor their president, all North Koreans wear a political pin over their heart showing a picture of the Great Leader. Jin-Ho's father makes sure he never leaves the house without it!

The department where Jin-Ho's father works is responsible for overseeing agriculture and farming in the Pyongyang province. Food is scarce throughout North Korea. Because almost eighty percent of the country's land is mountainous, North Korea doesn't have enough farmland to grow enough rice and corn to keep its people fed. Also, in recent years North Korea has suffered many floods that destroyed precious farmland, causing severe famines that killed as many as 3 million people. Jin-Ho's father says that his work is important in rebuilding farms and making North Korea into a self-sufficient nation. He also helps distribute the food and grain that nations like China and South Korea send to the North Koreans.

Jin-Ho's mother works at the Grand People's Study House, the largest library in North Korea. Her job is to preserve the knowledge and culture of the Korean people. She dresses for work in a traditional Korean *hanbok*, a high-waisted dress with a full skirt and a bow at the collar. Sometimes foreigners visit the library on guided trips. This is a big treat for Jin-Ho's mother and her fellow librarians because very few outsiders are allowed to visit North Korea.

Korean women wearing traditional *hanboks*.

Because Jin-Ho has scored well on academic tests—and because his father works for the Korean Workers Party—he has been chosen to attend special classes at the Schoolchildren's Palace in Pyongyang. In North Korea, the state (the government) provides free education, including school supplies and uniforms. All children are expected to attend at least eleven years of school, as well as several years of college or technical school. The state wants to make sure that everyone is productive so the country will prosper. North Koreans are proud of the fact that almost everyone in their country can read and write.

Every morning, Jin-Ho dresses in his school uniform—navy-blue pants and a crisp white shirt with a red scarf tied around his neck. Jin-Ho thinks his school uniform makes him look more intelligent, even if his ears do stick out from under his short haircut, earning him the nickname *Kokiri*, which means elephant. By the time he is dressed and ready, his mother has breakfast on the table. Jin-Ho's favorite breakfast is rice and *kimchi*, a spicy vegetable rel-

A government mural in one of the Pyongyang Metro stations. Photo: Gilad Rom.

ish his mother makes from scratch. Sometimes, if she has been lucky enough to find eggs at the market, Jin-Ho's mother will also make them just the way he likes them.

After breakfast, Jin-Ho and his mother walk to the nearest subway station and ride the Pyongyang Metro to the stop between the Schoolchildren's Palace and the Great People's Study House. Each of the seventeen stations of the Pyongyang Metro is named for a different nationalistic theme, such as Glory, Victory, and Renewal. While he and his mother wait for the train, Jin-Ho likes looking at the murals and posters that proclaim the strength of North Korea and the wisdom and benevolence of the Great Leader.

When they reemerge on the street, Jin-Ho says good-bye to his mother and walks the last few blocks alone to school. His favorite sight on the morning walk is the Juche Tower on the opposite bank of the Taedong River, which runs through the middle of Pyongyang. At night, the top of the tower is lit so that it looks like a giant torch. This monument represents the North Korean ideal of *juche*, or self-reliance. Jin-Ho's father explains that juche means "man is the master of everything and decides everything" and that Koreans must decide what is right for their own country without outside interference.

Juche Tower. Photo: Mark Scott Johnson.

At school, Jin-Ho takes classes in math, music, and Korean language and grammar, and he is also learning English. Jin-Ho's teachers make sure he understands communist principles and shows proper reverence for the Great Leader. His teachers say that communism—which means having the state control and provide everything the people need, like food, clothing, housing, and jobs—keeps their country strong and independent.

Jin-Ho learns in school that the communist system is designed to make sure everyone is treated equally and receives the same amounts and quality of necessities like food, education, and medical care. He learns that if everyone works together, then they can all share together. Jin-Ho's teacher explains that communism was created at a time when a few rich people owned everything and made lots of poor people work hard for next to nothing. To combat this inequality, communist leaders force everyone to share everything. If one person has too much, it is taken away and given to someone who has less.

On the other hand, Jin-Ho knows that his father's position in the Korean Workers Party gives his family access to extra privileges. For example, he probably would not have been picked to attend special classes without his father's influence. They also enjoy better food and more reliable electricity in their home. Yet many children wander the streets of Pyongyang without homes or food, and Jin-Ho wonders why the state isn't taking care of them. As it is, Jin-Ho sometimes feels like *he* is always hungry.

After his regular classes are over for the day, Jin-Ho and his friends attend special activities in another part of the Schoolchildren's Palace. Sometimes they listen to a lecture given by one of the teachers or a mock debate between older students. Other times he and his class watch political films. The state wants to make sure that every Korean knows how to be an obedient and productive citizen. Afterward, Jin-Ho meets up with his mother when her workday has ended.

This afternoon they take a detour before going home, riding an electric streetcar to the open-air market. Jin-Ho's father brings rice home each week from work so they don't have to pay the state-dictated prices at the market. But Jin-Ho's mother wants to surprise her husband tonight by serving grilled beef ribs, called *galbi*. She is also hoping some brave farmers will be there selling fresh vegetables. Although the state is supposed to receive all produce from the local farms so that it can be distributed throughout North Korea, sometimes farmers sell some of their vegetables at the market to make a little extra money. Today Jin-Ho's mother is hoping to find cucumbers, radishes, or spinach to go with their meal.

After bartering with a farmer at his stall and trading a handful of Korean *won* (the national currency) for a bag of vegetables, Jin-Ho and his mother catch another tram for the ride back to their apartment, glad that the electricity is running this evening so they don't have to walk. Jin-Ho has never been in a car. Automobiles in North Korea are mainly reserved for important state officials, so most citizens ride subways, buses, and trams to get around. As the streetcar rumbles toward his home, Jin-Ho likes to watch the robotic movements of the traffic girls, who stand at the center of major intersections in their smart uniforms and crisply direct traffic during peak commuting hours. The traffic girls help North Korea save electricity that would otherwise be used to power stoplights.

A traffic girl at work. Photo: John Pavelka.

Once home, Jin-Ho works on his school assignments at the kitchen table, while his mother grills the galbi in a spicy sauce, fries up the vegetables, and cooks rice. Although most Koreans like their rice moist and sticky, tonight's rice came from China as part of a famine-relief shipment and is too dry to prepare correctly. Most Korean meals are made up of one main bowl of rice surrounded by several side dishes of vegetables, meat, and seafood, collectively called *banchan*. There are also bowls of different sauces flavored with chilies, garlic, ginger, and soy sauce. Another of Jin-Ho's favorites is *jeon*, thinly sliced vegetables or meats stirred into a batter and fried like a pancake.

When Jin-Ho's father arrives home, the family sits down at the table to eat quietly. In the Korean culture, it is considered very bad manners to talk and eat at the same time! Jin-Ho can tell that his father likes the ribs and gives his mother a conspiratorial smile. After the meal, his mother cleans up while Jin-Ho and his father watch television. Because the electric grid throughout North Korea is shut down most of the night, the Kims use a car battery to power their television set.

While Jin-Ho connects the battery, his father makes sure the curtains are shut tightly so their neighbors will not see the light from the television. Very few North Koreans own a television. Jin-Ho's father jokes that he will one day be important enough that they will have their own telephone too. But from the kitchen, Jin-Ho's mother quickly shushes him, telling him it is bad luck to talk this way.

After a few hours of watching the educational and political programs available on the

Ryugyong Hotel. Photo: Myouzke.

four state-run channels of Korean television, Jin-Ho and his parents get ready for bed. Nearly everyone in Pyongyang lives in small apartments—the Kim's apartment has three rooms and a small bathroom. Jin-Ho's father is proud that he is able to rent a home so close to the city's center. From their tiny balcony, Jin-Ho and his parents can look out over the city and see the spire of the Ryugyong Hotel, by far the tallest building in Pyongyang, even though it is still under construction

after many years. Jin-Ho's parents sleep in the apartment's only bedroom. Jin-Ho sleeps on the sofa.

Jin-Ho is looking forward to this weekend because his brother Jin-Yong will be home for a few days on leave. Jin-Yong has been stationed at the southern border between North and South Korea. This border is called the Demilitarized Zone, or the DMZ. Once a single nation called Korea, the Korean peninsula has been divided into two nations since 1953. More than 2 million North Korean troops are stationed on the north side of the four-kilometer-wide border. Jin-Yong tells his brother that the soldiers, fences, and weapons have been placed along the border to keep enemies out. Jin-Ho is confident that his country will be safe while his big brother is a soldier!

In preparation for Jin-Yong's visit, his mother has put away the small statues of Buddha surrounding her prayer shrine and prominently displayed the pictures of the Eternal President and the Great Leader over the television. Although Jin-Ho's father tolerates his wife's devotion to the old Buddhist religion, her beliefs anger her oldest son. He says that religious ideas like God and Buddhism and ancestor worship have no place in a modern communist country. Jin-Yong believes religion is a lie devised by the rich and powerful people of this world to keep the poor from achieving success. Jin-Ho's mother will not give up her beliefs, but she doesn't want to spend Jin-Yong's visit fighting about religion.

Although Jin-Ho is looking forward to seeing his brother, he can't wait to see the present Jin-Yong is bringing him. Somehow, Jin-Yong was able to trade for a CD player from China and has promised to bring it home. Jin-Ho is very excited to be able to show off his new toy to his friends. He must be very careful, though, to play only approved music on it. The state will not tolerate anything from the outside world that may taint the purity of North Korean culture, so there are harsh penalties for listening to foreign music, watching foreign films, or reading foreign books or pamphlets. Jin-Ho's father tells him that this is because foreign powers will say anything to undermine the work of the Great Leader, who has set these rules to protect his people.

As a reward for all his hard work on behalf of the party, Jin-Ho's father has been given tickets to the Mass Games to be held in April. The Mass Games are held each year in Pyongyang to celebrate the birthday of the Eternal President. The giant May Day Stadium, located on Rungra Island in the midst of the Tae-dong River, can seat 150,000 people! At the Mass Games, tens of thousands of gymnasts and dancers perform the history of communist North Korea on the stadium floor, while in a special section of the seats, 20,000 trained schoolchildren hold up a succession of large cards to create a mosaic backdrop spelling out

The Mass Games. Photo: Kok Leng Yeo.

words and forming massive images and landscapes in perfect unison. There are even acrobats who do aerial tricks while suspended from the ceiling on wires. The performers train and practice for this event all year round. For many, this is their career.

Things like the Mass Games and the glorious statues and monuments scattered around Pyongyang make Jin-Ho glad to be a North Korean. Although he and his family must do without many luxuries, Jin-Ho thinks it is worth it to live in such a united country. Sometimes, though, he worries that with all the rules governing life in a communist country, he will not be able to live up to the ideal of perfect citizenship the way his brother has. Jin-Ho is much more interested in reading than in being a soldier. But he hopes that one day he will be able to do something important to help the Great Leader fulfill his goal of making North Korea strong, independent, and self-reliant.

WHAT'S THE DIFFERENCE?

- How is the way Jin-Ho lives different from the way you live? How are your lives similar?

- Why do you think Jin-Ho's father is so careful to wear his Great Leader political pin in public?

- The communist worldview generally teaches that all people are equal and must share their resources equally. How is this different from the system of government where you live?

- The president of North Korea is said to live in a seven-story palace while the average worker in his country earns less than $1,000 per year. Meanwhile, some government officials receive better food and greater benefits than the average citizen. Why do you think some citizens are treated as "more equal" than others under communist rule?

- Some North Koreans believe their president has the ability to control the weather based on his mood. What would that be like, having the weather depend on the emotions of a human being? Who do you believe controls the weather?

- Although the North Korean constitution permits religious freedom, the communist government promotes atheism—the belief that there is no God—and imposes strict control over the religious activities of its people. Possession of Bibles and other religious materials is reported to be illegal and may be punished by imprisonment or even execution. What would you do if your country's government said you could no longer worship God or tell others about Jesus? Why?

WHO DO YOU THINK YOU ARE?

> JUST AS YOU RECEIVED CHRIST JESUS AS LORD, CONTINUE TO LIVE IN HIM, ROOTED AND BUILT UP IN HIM, STRENGTHENED IN THE FAITH AS YOU WERE TAUGHT, AND OVERFLOWING WITH THANKFULNESS.

COLOSSIANS 2:6-7

THE BIG IDEA

In J. R. R. Tolkien's *The Lord of the Rings,* four hobbits set out from their beloved and peaceful Shire and undertake a perilous journey across Middle-earth. Early in their travels, they stop at a pub at the edge of the Shire. There the diminutive hobbits meet a weather-beaten man called Strider. He's lean and tall with dark shaggy hair, travel-stained clothing, and mud-caked boots. The locals think Strider is a vagabond, an eccentric drifter, a loner. But the hobbits soon discover that he is, in fact, a warrior who roams the countryside and keeps the Shire safe, unbeknown to those whose lives he protects.

Strider offers to travel with the hobbits as their guide and protector, and bit by bit, as the journey becomes more dangerous, more of Strider's true nature is revealed. His name is really Aragorn, and he is a man of wisdom, skill, and courage. He is respected in the halls of power and feared by the forces of evil. But even these admirable traits do not prepare his fellow travelers for the truth that Aragorn is the rightful heir to the throne of all Middle-earth! This scruffy, hard-bitten man whom the hobbits once feared and mistrusted is in reality the great king whose coming has been foretold, and it is his destiny to banish evil from the land and restore harmony and prosperity to the kingdom.

Like Strider, there is much more to you than meets the eye. If you are in Christ, then you are a child of God and you must begin thinking differently about yourself. What you truly are has not yet been made known to the world (1 John 3:2). To those unaware, you might look like anybody or nobody. But you are someone very special indeed. If you are a child of God, you are a co-heir of glory with Jesus Christ, and you have every right to enjoy a special relationship with your heavenly Father. Your privileges include unrestricted access to the throne room of Almighty God (Hebrews 4:14–16). You can go boldly before Him and ask anything in His Son's name according to His will, and it will be done for you (John 16:23). You can also rest assured that, whatever your circumstances, God will use them for your good (Romans 8:28). And you can walk through life with confidence and grace, knowing that you can do all things through Christ, who strengthens you (Philippians 4:13).

Are you a child of God? John 1:12 says that all who believe Jesus and receive Him are children of God. Have you accepted Him as the Lord of your life? If not, do not hesitate a moment longer, for no one knows what will happen tomorrow (James 4:13–14). Do you believe Jesus is who He says He is? Will you accept His free gift of forgiveness and salvation? You can do this simply by praying a prayer like this one to express your faith in Christ:

> *Dear God, I believe that Jesus Christ is your Son. I believe you sent Him to earth to die on the cross to take the punishment I deserve for my sins. I believe He was resurrected from the dead so that I may live with you forever. Please forgive my sins and make me a new creation. Send your Holy Spirit to live inside me and work in me to make me more and more like your Son every day. Thank you for this precious gift. In Jesus' name I pray. Amen.*

WHAT YOU WILL DO

» You will learn what it means to be "in Christ."
» You will examine six important characteristics you possess as a child of God.
» You will recognize the lordship of Jesus Christ and begin to embrace His authority over every area of your life.

PETER AND THE WOLF

Russian composer Sergei Prokofiev (SAIR-gay pro-KO-fee-ev) wrote his first piece of music when he was just five years old. He composed an opera when he was nine. In 1936, at the age of forty-five, Prokofiev wrote the story and music for *Peter and the Wolf*, calling it "a present for the children of Moscow." Although in the composer's words, the work "failed to attract much attention" when it debuted, over the years the symphony has delighted and inspired generations of children and adults.

Peter and the Wolf was written to be performed by a narrator and an orchestra. The narrator tells the story, while each character in the story is represented by a different musical instrument. Peter, a young boy who lives with his grandfather near the forest, has a warm, sprightly theme played by the strings—violins, violas, cellos, and basses. The deep, gruff theme for Peter's grandfather is played by a bassoon. The little bird is represented by a chirpy flute, the duck by a melancholy oboe, and the cat by a cool clarinet. The wolf is around whenever the mysterious French horn sounds. The hunters chasing the wolf are represented by the woodwinds, and their gunshots are made by the timpani and bass drum.

In the story, Peter ventures out past the garden gate one day into the meadow beyond. He meets a bird singing in a tree and a duck swimming in a pond. A cat comes by, ready to pounce on the bird, but Peter scares the cat away and saves the bird. Peter's grandfather comes and scolds him for going out to the meadow when there's a wolf lurking about. After Peter and his grandfather return home, the wolf does indeed appear and chases the duck. Peter fetches a rope and climbs over the garden wall into the tree. He asks the bird to fly around the wolf's head to distract him. Letting down his rope, Peter catches the wolf by the tail. When the hunters who have been tracking the wolf arrive, they join Peter in a grand procession in which the captured wolf is taken to the zoo.

Prokofiev's *Peter and the Wolf* has inspired several film and television versions and has even been staged as a ballet. Numerous recordings of the symphony have been made, featuring such diverse narrators as Boris Karloff, Sir Alec Guinness, Sean Connery, Sophia Loren, William F. Buckley, Sting, and "Weird Al" Yankovic!

THE CEREMONY

"Gwyn!" Brandon rapped lightly on Gwyneth's door once more, hoping not to wake the other ladies in waiting. The hour was midnight, and everyone had retired early in preparation for William's knighting ceremony in the morning. Brandon whispered again, *"Gwyn!"*

A light suddenly appeared in the hall behind Brandon. "Brandon, what are you doing here?" Gwyneth asked, holding a candle and coming up behind him in her nightgown.

"Oh, Gwyn, there you are. Something terrible has happened. William's sword—it's gone!"

"Gone? But William never lets that sword out of his sight. Where is he?"

"He's praying all night in the chapel and cannot be disturbed. He entrusted the sword to my keeping, but it's disappeared! The ceremony is only hours away! What am I going to do?"

"Well, first you need to calm down and catch your breath," Gwyneth said. "When did you last see the sword?"

Brandon replied, "I was polishing the sword when Quentin came to my room and sent me to fetch water. When I returned, the sheath was still there but the sword was gone. Where could it be?"

"Quentin! I was running an errand for Isabel in the kitchen when I saw him out the window. He was carrying something under his cloak and headed into the forest."

"But why would Quentin take Will's sword?"

"How will it look if William shows up for the ceremony without his sword? What do you think the baron will say then about Will's choice of you for his squire? What do you think the king will say?"

"I'm not worried about me, but I'm not going to let Will down. We've got to find Quentin. Will you help me?"

"Of course. Let me get my cloak."

Because the young friends did not wish to be seen leaving the castle, they did not carry a torch. The full moon was high and they relied on its light to guide them to where Gwyneth had seen Quentin entering the forest.

Somewhere deep in the darkness, a wolf howled. Gwyneth shivered, and Brandon put a reassuring hand on her shoulder. "Don't worry, Gwyn. We'll be all right."

Gwyneth decided to change the subject. "So why is William praying all night?" she asked in a hushed voice as they made their way tentatively through the woods.

"He called it a *vigil*. It's part of the knighting ceremony. First, Will fasted all day. Then he took a special bath. He said it's a symbol of being cleansed by Christ and given a pure heart, but I think he just wanted to smell good for the king."

Gwyneth stifled a giggle.

Brandon said, "Then I helped him dress in a white cloak, a red robe, and black shoes. Now he's alone in the chapel, where he'll pray silently for ten hours before morning Mass. Then

John Pettie. *The Vigil*. Exhibited 1884. Oil on canvas, 115.8 x 170.3 cm. Tate Gallery, London, Great Britain.
Photo Credit: Tate, London / Art Resource, NY

comes the ceremony, where the king is to knight Will and formally present him with his sword. We've just got to find it, Gwyn."

"Brandon, we need to follow Will's example. Let's stop and pray right now and ask God to help us find the sword. The Bible says that when two or three are gathered in Christ's name, He will be there with us."

"I don't know why I didn't think of that before." Brandon fell to his knees, and Gwyneth knelt beside him. Brandon prayed, "Lord, thank you for my friends Will and Gwyn who are teaching me so much about you and your Word. And thank you for being my Father because I have no father. I'm in trouble, God, and I really need you. Please help me to find Will's sword and have it ready in time for the ceremony. I ask this in Jesus' name. Amen."

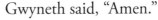

Gwyneth said, "Amen."

Brandon looked up then and spotted a glint of something in the moonlight fifty yards away. He and Gwyneth got to their feet and began to run toward the shiny object, but twenty yards away they stopped suddenly. There it was: William's sword leaning against a tree in the clearing. Fifteen feet overhead was Quentin, clinging to a tree limb and whimpering. At the foot of the tree was a large, gaunt grey wolf, pacing back and forth. Having treed its quarry, it seemed to be biding its time, waiting for the branch to give out or for Quentin to attempt an escape.

Brandon and Gwyneth crouched behind a tree, and Gwyneth whispered, "If I fetch Will's longbow, could you fell the wolf from here?"

"Maybe," Brandon said. "But if I manage to only wound it with the first shot, the wolf will become even more dangerous." He thought for a moment. "I've got an idea. Run back to the castle. Grab some pots and pans and spoons and any kitchen staff you can find and bring them here. I'll keep watch."

"I'll hurry." Gwyneth hiked up her nightgown and ran as quickly as she could. She returned fifteen minutes later with a scullery maid and two eight-year-old pages who had been sleeping by the kitchen fireplace. All of them carried pots and spoons, including one of each for Brandon.

It's not much of an army, Brandon thought, *but it will have to do*. He said, "I want everyone to spread out in a semicircle south of the clearing.

237

Remain silent and stay out of sight. When I shout, everyone jump out and yell as loud as you can and bang the pots with your spoons."

No one said a word but merely nodded, their eyes wide in the moonlight. Brandon smiled and placed a reassuring hand on the shoulder of one of the small boys. Gwyneth motioned for the boys and the maid to follow her, and she stationed each one behind a tree not far from the clearing.

The wolf growled menacingly as though it sensed their presence.

Once everyone was in position, Brandon said a silent prayer. Then he leaped from his hiding place and shouted, "A sword for the Lord and for the king!" At this, Brandon and his four recruits began yelling and banging on the pots and pans with all their might.

At first, the wolf turned in quick circles, clearly confused by the commotion. Then it yelped, turned tail, and ran off in the opposite direction.

The yelling turned to cheering as the small band emerged from their hiding places. Quentin dropped out of the tree and picked up William's sword. Then he knelt before Brandon and with both hands offered him the sword. "I'm ashamed of the way I've acted. I was angry and jealous, and I wanted you to fail. My behavior was not worthy of the knights we serve. Can you ever forgive me?"

"Of course, varlet," Brandon said, pretending to be haughty. But he was unable to keep a straight face and broke into a huge grin.

Quentin and the others laughed heartily. As they began walking back to the castle, Quentin slapped Brandon on the back and said, "That was brilliant how you chased away the wolf. What made you think of it?"

"Well, I remembered the story of Gideon in the Bible. One day when he was working, the Angel of the Lord appeared to him and said, 'The Lord is with you, mighty man of valor!' Gideon didn't feel much like a warrior, but he trusted God."

"I know that story," Quentin said. "God sent Gideon and a few hundred men against an entire army in the dead of night armed with nothing more than torches, water pitchers, and trumpets.

Gwyneth said, "Yes, and on Gideon's signal, the men broke the pitchers, shouted, and blew their trumpets. The enemy was so terrified, many of them killed one another and the rest fled. But how did you know the wolf would run away?"

"You taught me that the Lord is always with me, Gwyn. Besides, wolves are tough when they hunt in packs, but this one is a rogue come down from the north. A lone wolf will usually run when it's outnumbered. I was just hoping to fool it into thinking there were more of us than there really were."

Quentin said, "Brandon, I was wrong about you. You're going to make a great knight, and I will be proud to fight at your side one day. I don't know how I can ever thank you."

"Right now, I need to get this sword cleaned and ready for William's ceremony. Will you help me?"

"I would be honored . . . Squire Brandon."

Great excitement filled the air as the lords and ladies and knights talked among themselves in anticipation of the king's arrival. An empty throne waited upon the dais, surrounded by too many glowing candles to count. The walls of the great hall were specially hung with large banners displaying St. George's Cross, the fleur-de-lis of France, and the colors of the king.

Engraving of Edward III.

Brandon stood nervously along the wall, next to Gwyneth and Isabel, who were discussing the finery worn by the ladies of the court. William was near the front of the gathering, talking with his fellow knights. Brandon caught his eye, and William gave him a smile and a quick nod.

Suddenly, the assembly was hushed by a fanfare of trumpets. A herald entered from the back of the hall and announced, "His royal highness, Edward the Third, by the grace of God, King of England and France and Lord of Ireland!"

Every person bowed deeply as the great king entered and led a small procession up the aisle, including the Baron John de Lisle, William's patron and lord of the castle in which they stood. Accompanied by more fanfare, the procession mounted the three steps to the dais, and the king took his seat upon the throne.

The trumpets were silenced, and the king spoke. "I call to order the Knights of the Garter. Draw near and be heard."

The assembly rose as one, and the Baron de Lisle stepped forward. He said, "Your

Majesty, I beg to inform you that our numbers are not complete. There is one who by his deeds and his demeanor has the right to a place in our company, a place for which he has shown himself worthy."

The king replied, "Then let him come forward."

The baron took his place to the right of the king, and William stepped into the aisle and knelt upon the first step.

The king leaned forward and, with a glint in his eye, said to William, "For what purpose do you desire to enter the Most Noble Order of the Garter? If it be for riches or to take your ease and be held in honor without bringing honor to your God and country, then you are unworthy of it."

William stood and responded, "I do not desire earthly riches or honors for myself. I seek only to serve my king, to defend the laws of Almighty God and of this realm, and to give all glory to Christ our Lord, who has crowned me with glory and clothed me with His righteousness."

Then the king spoke to the assembly. "A knight of the realm is charged at all times to protect the weak, defend the defenseless, help the needy, and put right every injustice he sees. He must draw his strength and sustenance from the Word of God. A knight must keep a pure heart,

Edward III inducting the Black Prince into the Order of the Garter.

a healthy body, and a disciplined mind so that he stands ready to meet every challenge, never bringing shame upon the name of our Lord or his brethren, whom are called by our Savior's name." The king's gaze turned once more upon William. "Are you willing to give your dying breath in the service of our Lord? Will you shrink in fear from the enemies of Christ, both seen and unseen; or having done all, will you stand, steadfast in your faith, to defend all that is holy?"

Brandon prayed silently for his friend to answer well. There were no words prescribed for this part of the ceremony. The knight was expected to respond from the fullness of his heart.

Sir William paused only a moment, then boldly proclaimed, "If God is for me, who can be against me? As for my brethren, 'Who shall separate us from the love of Christ? Shall trouble or hardship or persecution or famine or nakedness or danger or sword? Nay, in all these things we are more than conquerors through Him who loved us. For I am convinced that neither death nor life, neither angels nor demons, neither the present nor the future, nor any powers, neither height nor depth, nor anything else in all creation, will be able to separate us from the love of God that is in Christ Jesus our Lord.'"

The king smiled, then stood. "Let the sword be brought forward," he said.

Sir Thomas Holland, a knight of the order, stepped forth, carrying William's sword upon a large velvet pillow. Brandon grinned, as the sword gleamed like never before beneath

the light of the thousand candles surrounding the dais. He was nervous for just a moment as the king examined the sword for flaws or blemishes, but finding none, he nodded his approval.

The king turned to the assembly and said, "The sword represents the knight's authority to dispense justice. The double edge of the blade reminds the knight to always temper justice with mercy. As the steel of the sword must be purified and strengthened in fire and water, so must the soul of the knight be purified and strengthened by adversity and compassion." He then offered the sword to William and said, "Never draw this sword in anger."

William bowed his head and, with both hands held out before him, received the sword. A flowing velvet robe of deep blue was brought forward and placed on his shoulders.

The king then drew his own sword and said, "Kneel, my son."

He lay the sword first on William's right shoulder, then on his left. As he did so, he announced, "I dub thee Sir William, Knight of the Garter. Arise, Sir William, and enter into the joy and service of our Lord and join the glad fellowship of the order!"

The hall erupted with boisterous cheers from William's fellow knights, Brandon, Gwyneth, Lady Isabel, and all in attendance.

A great feast was held that afternoon, to be followed by games in which Sir William and his fellow knights would display their skills with the sword and lance before the king and the lords and ladies of the court. Food and drink flowed continuously from the castle's kitchen, while entertainment was provided by a troupe of strolling musicians, acrobats, and jugglers.

Brandon, Quentin, and Gwyneth were standing together laughing when Sir William and Lady Isabel walked up and William said, "Everybody friends now?"

Quentin said, "Yes, Sir William. But, sir, I owe you an apology."

William held up a gloved hand. "No apology necessary. Everything has worked out for the best. This is a day of celebration, and all is forgiven. I am confident that one day, Quentin, you too shall kneel before the king and join me in the brotherhood of knights."

"I do hope so, sir."

"For now, I must steal Brandon from your company, for we must prepare for the tournament. I fight today for the favor of my Lady Isabel."

Isabel blushed and said, "You have that already, rascal. You just be careful out there, lest your knighthood prove historically brief."

William laughed and walked off, his arm around Brandon's shoulders.

"Will," Brandon said, "I too owe you an apology."

"And what offense did you commit against my person?"

"I lost your sword, which you entrusted to my keeping."

"Isabel told me all about your midnight adventure. It seems you woke up half the castle with all your shouting and banging. But your courage showed that I could not have left my sword in better hands. All I have to say to you is this: Well done, good and faithful servant. You are a friend indeed. And a resourceful one at that."

Brandon grinned. "Thanks, Will," he said.

"Now," said William, "there's someone I'd like you to meet. Brandon, allow me to introduce you to his royal highness, Edward the Third, king of England."

"And of France," the king reminded him, pretending to be offended.

The baron, who was standing beside the king, chuckled.

Brandon gasped and fell to his knees. "Your majesty" was all he could say.

"And of course, you know the Baron John de Lisle," William said.

"Yes, Wi— I mean, Sir William." He bowed his head once more.

"Sires," William said, "this is the lad I was telling you about. Though Brandon is but twelve, no knight ever had a better friend or servant. With your approval, I wish to make him my squire."

"Done!" the king cried good-naturedly. "Brandon, I don't suppose you remember me?"

Brandon climbed to his feet. "No, your majesty. I've never met a prince before, let alone a king."

"Ah, but you have! Your father was my servant and best friend when we were children. We grew up together at court, and I was there at your birth. Tragically, your mother and father both died in a fire when you were but two years of age. I was at war in our French provinces at the time, or I might have raised you as my own. Instead, I made arrangements for you to be brought to the household of the baron. Only he and his wife knew of your palace origins. My instructions were that you be treated as a servant so that you might learn humility, mercy, and grace. At the age of seven, you were made a page so that you might learn patience, faithfulness, and the value of work."

Brandon glanced at William, but he seemed as surprised as Brandon.

King Edward said, "Sir William knew nothing of this. Yet he has wisely chosen you from among the baron's servants to be his squire. From him you will learn duty, honor, and godliness before you take your place on the roll of knights alongside the baron, Sir William, and my son the Black Prince."

"Your majesty," Brandon said, "who am I that you should remember me? My parents were but servants, and they are dead. Why should you, a great king, care what happens to me?"

The king said to Brandon, "Your father was a loyal and trusted companion. Good friends are rare things and are to be treasured. Sir William tells me that you too have proven yourself a true friend. I am glad to hear it. From this day forward, Brandon, you shall be known as my own son. You are now adopted into the house of Plantagenet, with all the privileges thereof. You will defend the kingdom and share in my glory. And when you are grown, you will come to live in my palace."

The king then turned to his newest knight. "Sir William, I charge you with the education and training of this child of the king. It is my desire that he one day serve England as one of her mightiest and most righteous of knights. Do you accept this charge?"

William smiled broadly at Brandon. "Sire, I can think of no greater honor."

THE HUNDRED YEARS' WAR

Near the end of the Middle Ages, England and France fought the Hundred Years' War to determine who would rule France. King Philip IV had died, leaving no heir to the throne. So the officials of France crowned King Philip's nephew. But Edward III of England believed he had a stronger claim to the throne because he was Philip's grandson, and in 1337 Edward went to war with France to win back his birthright.

Edward III led the English armies against France for more than twenty years, winning back much of the territory his ancestors once ruled. During this period, two major battles of the war took place: the Battle of Crecy in 1346 and the Battle of Poitiers in 1356, which was fought by Edward's son, the Black Prince. Both battles were monumental victories for England, which used archers with longbows to defeat a much larger force of French knights. The military tactics used in these two battles changed the way wars were fought.

By the early 1400s, however, France had won back much of its conquered land. The new English king, Henry V, decided to renew the campaign. On St. Crispin's Day in 1415, his forces engaged the French at the Battle of Agincourt, despite being badly outnumbered. In William Shakespeare's play *Henry V*, before the battle, the king rallies the troops with a stirring speech:

Joan of Arc by Lenepveu.

> *And Crispin Crispian shall ne'er go by,*
> *From this day to the ending of the world,*
> *But we in it shall be remembered;*
> *We few, we happy few, we band of brothers;*
> *For he today that sheds his blood with me*
> *Shall be my brother . . .*

Once again, the English triumphed, losing only a handful of men but costing the French many thousands. Victorious, Henry made a treaty with the French, who promised that his son would be declared king of England and France. For a while, it seemed that all of England's dreams for gaining power in Europe were coming true.

But Henry died while his son was still a baby, and instead of gaining power, England lost it. The final blow came when a young girl named Joan of Arc helped to rally the French troops, who believed she was sent by God to lead them to victory. Although she was eventually captured and executed by the English, the tide of the war had turned. After a war that had lasted 116 years, the French succeeded in driving England out of France for good.

THINK ABOUT IT

» Where does Brandon get his idea for chasing away the wolf? Looking back over Brandon's adventures, how is young Brandon like the biblical Gideon?

» Brandon has learned much about himself and his identity. How is his position as a child of God mirrored by his adoption as a child of the king of England? How might the king's revelation change Brandon's thinking about himself and his future?

» How are you like a knight in the service of the King of all kings?

WORDS YOU NEED TO KNOW

» **Justified:** To be declared innocent or free from guilt

» **Saint:** A person who has been justified through faith in Jesus Christ

» **Church:** The community of everyone who has been called out from the world by God to live as His people under the authority of Christ

» **Ambassador:** My position as an appointed representative of Christ whose job it is to share His gospel with the people of this world

HIDE IT IN YOUR HEART

Therefore, if anyone is in Christ, he is a new creation; the old has gone, the new has come! (2 Corinthians 5:17)

Therefore God exalted him to the highest place and gave him the name that is above every name, that at the name of Jesus every knee should bow, in heaven and on earth and under the earth, and every tongue confess that Jesus Christ is Lord, to the glory of God the Father. (Philippians 2:9–11)

WHAT DO YOU SEE WHEN YOU LOOK AT YOURSELF?

At the dawn of creation, Adam and Eve enjoyed a wonderful relationship with God. They walked with Him and talked with Him in the cool of the garden, and God talked with them. He provided for their every need. He instructed them and gave them important responsibilities in caring for His creation. Adam and Eve also enjoyed a relationship of harmony within themselves. The first man and woman knew who they were and why they were created. They loved themselves in the right way, and they knew nothing of fear or anxiety or shame. Then Adam and Eve chose to disobey God, and everything changed.

Today, many people are largely unhappy with their lives. Because they are not at peace with God, they no longer look to Him to fill the great big God-shaped void in their lives. Instead, they try to plug this hole with jobs, money, school, cars, food, clothes, houses, vacations, and endless activities. Because they are not at peace with themselves, they no longer look to God to tell them who they are. Instead, they constantly compare their lives to the lives of others, hoping the cosmic scales tip in their own favor. As a result, they tend to see themselves not as they really are, but how they think others see them. *Am I good enough?* they wonder. *What do people say when they talk about me? Do I meet with their approval? Do people make fun of the way I talk or the way I dress? Do they think I'm cool enough? Pretty enough? Smart enough? Does anybody love me?*

Even as Christians, we are not immune to this way of thinking. We look in the mirror for signs of greatness, but we see only the glaring new pimple or the makings of a bad hair day. Every time we make a mistake, every time we're not invited to a party or picked for a team, every time someone calls us a name, every time we sin, doubt and discouragement creep in, and we think less of ourselves. Sometimes we begin to feel so inferior, so worthless, we can't believe anyone could *like* us, let alone love us. We couldn't be more wrong.

As a child of God, you are not just the person you see in the mirror. If you want to know who you really are, what you are truly worth, stop looking in the mirror and spend more time looking in God's Word. It's all written there—who you are, who you were meant to be, and who you are becoming.

> *I am His daughter. He said so. Oh, the infinite gentleness of my God!*
> **Margaret of Cortona**
> 1247–1297

YOU ARE SOMEONE NEW!

When you were born, your parents gave you a name. Perhaps you were given the name of a beloved relative. Maybe you were named after a famous athlete or actor or a character in a book. Or maybe your parents plucked your name out of a baby-name book or chose it from the Bible because they liked the way it sounds or what it means. Your name is one of the first things you learned as a small child. It's part of your identity—it sets you apart from other people. When you were "born again" (John 3:3)—when you accepted Jesus as your Lord and Savior—you received a new name: Christian. This name means "follower of Christ."

As a follower of Christ, you are a brand-new creation: "Therefore, if anyone is in Christ, he is a new creation; the old has gone, the new has come!" (2 Corinthians 5:17). You not only have a new name, you also have a new identity. Romans 6:6 says that your old self

was "crucified" with Christ. You're not the same old person walking around in new clothes. The person you once were is dead and gone, and only the new person remains. A butterfly isn't a caterpillar with wings; it's a new creature with a new identity. The caterpillar once crawled in the dirt, devouring everything in its path and sometimes causing great damage. But now that it's a butterfly, it soars on brightly colored wings, sipping nectar from flowers and (through pollination) spreading life and beauty wherever it goes. The caterpillar had no part in this transformation—its Creator did it all. This same process of change occurs in every person who is in Christ.

Just who is this new creation you've become? What does it mean that you're "in Christ"? Some people think being a Christian is about going to church on Sundays or driving around with a "Beam Me Up, Jesus!" bumper sticker on your car. Many people (including some Christians) think it's about following a list of rules or trying to be good all the time. But being a Christian is not defined by rules or rituals or even religion. Remember, it's not *what you do* that determines who you are; it's *who you are* that determines what you do.

You need to understand who you truly are in Christ—to see yourself the way God sees you. Of course, you can instead try to "act" the way you think a Christian is supposed to behave. You can dress the part and put on a good show for your friends. But you cannot consistently live and think and act in a way that's different from how you really see yourself. If deep down you think you're worthless, you will probably live as if you *are* worthless. If you think you're a loser, you'll probably live as though you *are* a loser.

Satan can do nothing to damage your position as a child of God. But if he can deceive you into believing his lies—that God wants nothing to do with you, you're nobody, and you will never amount to anything as a Christian—then you will stumble through life, acting like you're nobody special. If the devil can make you believe you're no different from the rest of the world, then you will behave no differently from those who reject God. However, if you see yourself as a child of the Most High God—if you believe and accept all that this means—then you will be able to live in victory and overcome this world (1 John 5:3–5)!

So who are you going to believe—God or the devil? The Bible has a great deal to say about who you are in Christ. Let's examine together some of what God says is true about you.

> *Not only do we only know God through Jesus Christ, but we only know ourselves through Jesus Christ.*
> **Blaise Pascal**
> 1623–1662

YOU ARE JUSTIFIED

The prophet Ezra prayed, "I am much too ashamed to face you, LORD God. Our sins and our guilt have swept over us like a flood that reaches up to the heavens" (Ezra 9:6, CEV). When the prophet Isaiah experienced a vision of God sitting upon His throne, he cried out, "I am doomed, for I am a sinful man. I have filthy lips, and I live among a people with filthy lips. Yet I have seen the King, the LORD of Heaven's Armies" (Isaiah 6:5, NLT). Ezra and Isaiah knew that a holy God can have no part of sin, and only perfect people who are without sin can stand in His presence.

Christ on the Cross by El Greco.

Yet because we are in Christ, you and I may go before God "with freedom and confidence" (Ephesians 3:12). That's because we have been **justified** in the sight of God. When Jesus was nailed to the cross, God placed all our sins on Him and then declared us to be without sin. To be justified means God has removed our sins completely. He does not just cover up our guilt or overlook it. God does not say, "Well, you're still guilty, but I'll let you off the hook." He says, "You're not guilty"!

As a result of this gracious gift, "we have been justified through faith" and are at "peace with God" (Romans 5:1):

Therefore, there is now no condemnation for those who are in Christ Jesus. (Romans 8:1)

So let us come near to God with a sincere heart and a sure faith. We have been cleansed and made free from feelings of guilt. (Hebrews 10:22, ICB)

Let us therefore come boldly to the throne of grace, that we may obtain mercy and find grace to help in time of need. (Hebrews 4:16, NKJV)

YOU ARE A SAINT

Throughout the New Testament, the followers of Jesus are called "saints." The word *saint* literally means "holy person." Many people think a saint is someone who has earned this lofty title by living a good life or doing good works or even performing miracles. But God says that every Christian is a saint! He doesn't call us sinners or even former sinners. Instead, He calls us holy ones. That's because He has removed our sins through our faith in Jesus Christ.

To be holy means to be "blameless, pure, [and] set apart" for God's purposes, as Jesus was (Hebrews 7:26). Psalm 4:3 says, "The Lord has set apart the godly for himself." As His image-bearers, we are meant to set ourselves apart

> *Holiness is the everyday business of every Christian.*
> **Chuck Colson**

from sin and set ourselves apart *for* Him. Therefore, "we should stay away from everything that keeps our bodies and spirits from being clean. We should honor God and try to be completely like him" (2 Corinthians 7:1, CEV).

In Christ we have been "put right with God, and have been made holy, and have been set free from sin" (1 Corinthians 1:30, NCV). Does that mean you will never sin again? No. Sin and Satan are still around, and they are strong. So if you are sorely tempted to sin, run away (2 Timothy 2:22). Instead of giving in to temptation, give yourself completely to God. Stand firm in your faith against the devil, and *he* will flee from *you* (James 4:7).

MAKE A NOTE OF IT

Think of the Bible as a personal love letter from God to you. Insert your first name into each of the following verses and write them out in your notebook: 2 Corinthians 5:17–19, Psalm 4:3, Romans 8:1, 2 Corinthians 7:1, Ephesians 3:12, 1 John 5:5, and 1 Peter 2:9. For example, "The Lord has set apart Jane for himself" (Psalm 4:3). Give this page a title: "What the Bible Says About Saint (Your Name)."

YOU ARE A CITIZEN OF HEAVEN

Being a citizen means you are a resident or member of a particular city, state, or country. A citizen owes his or her allegiance to the government and is entitled to its protection. Every ten years, the United States government conducts a census to count its citizens. By knowing how many people are in each household and where they live, the government can better plan and provide services for all its people. A list of citizens is kept in heaven, too. This list is called the Book of Life (Revelation 3:5). And as a follower of Christ, your name is written in that book.

THE STORY OF SEABISCUIT

During the Great Depression of the 1930s, an unlikely success story captured the hearts of a weary nation. Seabiscuit was an undersized, knobby-kneed racehorse that walked funny and liked sleeping and eating more than he did racing. However, the horse was the "grandson" of the legendary Man o' War, and Seabiscuit's owner expected him to become a champion. But after he lost ten races in a row, his owner decided to sell him.

Seabiscuit racing at Santa Anita Park in 1940. Photo: Seabiscuit Heritage Foundation.

The horse's new owner, Charles Howard, had a weakness for lost causes. Howard had almost single-handedly saved the struggling automobile business in turn-of-the-century California. When he decided to breed racehorses, Howard found trainer Tom Smith living out of a horse stall in Mexico and hired him. Smith had taken a liking to the little horse with the comical gait and convinced Howard to purchase Seabiscuit. Smith put the horse on a special training program and hired unheralded jockey Red Pollard to ride him. Although Pollard was an experienced jockey, he had been frequently unemployed and was even blind in one eye. In their first race together, Seabiscuit and Pollard did not finish well. But they quickly improved.

Seabiscuit with trainer Tom Smith.
Photo: Seabiscuit Heritage Foundation.

Slowly, race after race, Seabiscuit began making a name for himself. Seabiscuit was the leading money winner in the United States in 1937 and was named Horse of the Year in 1938. By now the horse was a huge celebrity, drawing record crowds to racetracks from coast to coast. The "little horse that could" had become a symbol of enduring hope to a nation badly in need of it. Then, at the height of their careers, both Seabiscuit and Red Pollard were injured in separate accidents.

It looked like Seabiscuit was finished. But after a year of careful training with Smith, both horse and jockey came back, determined to win the race that had thus far eluded them: the Santa Anita Handicap, with one of the richest purses in America. Stuck in the pack at the beginning of the 1940 race, it looked like Seabiscuit would fall short. But at the last moment, he surged ahead, winning the race to the cheers of a nation. Today, a life-size bronze statue of Seabiscuit is on display at Santa Anita Park.

When God called us out of the world to join His family, we were all broken-down underachievers who had fallen short of God's glory (Romans 3:23). But He brought us together to love one another, train one another, and build one another up, and He made us far more than we could ever hope to be separately.

The Bible says that your citizenship is in heaven (Philippians 3:20). Heaven is a real place for real people, and your true home is in that glorious place! In fact, Jesus is there now, preparing a spot just for you (John 14:2). You are a member of God's household (Ephesians 2:19), and you live under His protection (1 John 5:18). As a child of God, you can confidently sing the old hymn that says, "When the roll is called up yonder, I'll be there."

Colossians 3:1–2 (NLT) reminds us to "set [our] sights on the realities of heaven. . . . Think about the things of heaven, not the things of earth." When you spend time thinking about the things of heaven, you will be better prepared to help the people of this world. C. S. Lewis wrote in his classic book *Mere Christianity*, "If you read history, you will find that the Christians who did the most for the present world were just those who thought most of the next. The apostles themselves . . . the great men who built up the Middle Ages, the English evangelicals who abolished the slave trade—all left their mark on earth precisely because their minds were occupied with heaven."

YOU ARE A MEMBER OF GOD'S FAMILY

If someone from another planet were to ask you what a church looks like, you might draw them a picture of a pretty white building with a tall, elegant steeple topped by a belfry and a cross. Or you might draw a towering gothic structure like Notre Dame de Paris or St. Patrick's Cathedral in New York City. Church buildings come in all shapes and sizes, from the one-room prairie churches of the Old West to the futuristic Crystal Cathedral in Southern California, which seats almost 3,000 people and was constructed using more than 10,000 panes of glass.

The Crystal Cathedral. Photo: Concord.

However, when the New Testament authors spoke of the church, they weren't talking about buildings with flying buttresses and stained glass. When Jesus said He would build His church upon this rock (Matthew 16:18), He didn't have pulpits and communion tables in mind. That's because the church is not a building. It's people. The word "church" comes from the Greek term *ekklesia*, which is formed from two words meaning "an assembly" and "called out." The **church** is made up of everyone who has been called out from the world by God to live as His people under the authority of Jesus Christ (Ephesians 1:22–23). Whether you meet with other believers in a home, a warehouse, or a state-of-the-art auditorium, you don't just *go to* church. You *are* the church.

The Bible calls the church a family (Ephesians 2:19), for we are "all children of God through faith in Christ Jesus" (Galatians 3:26, NLT). As brothers and sisters in Christ, we are commanded to love one another (John 13:34), honor one another (Romans 12:10), serve one another (Galatians 5:13), encourage one another (1 Thessalonians 5:11), teach one another (Colossians 3:16), and gather together to worship and pray (Acts 2:42–47; Hebrews 10:25). In this way we will be built up "until we all come to such unity in our faith and knowledge of God's Son that we will be mature in the Lord, measuring up to the full and complete standard of Christ" (Ephesians 4:13, NLT).

YOU ARE AN AMBASSADOR FOR CHRIST

An **ambassador** represents his or her country by carrying official greetings and messages from the nation's leaders to the government of another nation. As a citizen of heaven, you are an appointed representative of a "holy nation," and it's your job to deliver the message of God's plan of salvation to the rest of the world:

You are a chosen people, a royal priesthood, a holy nation, a people belonging to God, that you may declare the praises of him who called you out of darkness into his wonderful light. (1 Peter 2:9)

[Jesus said] "And you will be my witnesses, telling people about me everywhere—in Jerusalem, throughout Judea, in Samaria, and to the ends of the earth." (Acts 1:8, NLT)

Through Christ, God made peace between us and himself, and God gave us the work of telling everyone about the peace we can have with him. (2 Corinthians 5:18, NCV)

The Ambassadors by Hans Holbein the Younger.

As an ambassador for God, you must be careful to represent Him accurately. You are a child of light, so make your light shine so that others will see the good deeds you do and praise your Father in heaven (Matthew 5:16). And be ready to explain your faith and hope in Jesus to others, but always with love, gentleness, and respect (1 Peter 3:15–16).

YOU ARE A WINNER

On the night Jesus was arrested, He warned His disciples that their lives were about to become difficult, even dangerous. As His followers, they would be hated by many because they refused to conform to the behavior and attitudes of this world. Some of them would even die for their beliefs. Jesus then comforted them, saying, "I have told you all this so that you may have peace in me. Here on earth you will have many trials and sorrows. But take heart, because I have overcome the world" (John 16:33, NLT).

The Greek word translated "overcome" in this passage is *nenikayka*, which means "to conquer" or "to have victory." You're probably more familiar with the noun form of this word: *nike*. Nike was known as the Greek goddess of victory, and the athletic shoe company Nike was named for her. Since 1928, every Summer Olympics medal has depicted the goddess holding a palm frond in her right hand and a winner's crown of laurel in her left.

> *Our confidence in Christ does not make us lazy, negligent, or careless, but on the contrary, it awakens us, urges us on, and makes us active in living righteous lives and doing good. There is no self-confidence to compare with this.*
> **Ulrich Zwingli**
> 1484–1531

Jesus was telling us that although we will experience disdain and persecution because of our faith, we must remain glad at heart because we share in His total victory over sin and death. We can always be at peace—not because we don't have troubles, but because the battle has already been won! The difficulties of this life are only temporary and are actually preparing us for eternity (James 1:2–4). In the meantime, we are called to overcome this world by standing firm in our faith against the power of the enemy and the temptations of our desires: "Do not be overcome by evil, but overcome evil with good" (Romans 12:21).

You don't have to be physically strong to overcome the enemy, and it doesn't matter if you are only a child. The war we fight is a spiritual one (Ephesians 6:12), and Jesus has given you the authority "to overcome all the power of the enemy" (Luke 10:19). But you do need to have a strong mind and a sturdy faith that will endure the tough times that are sure to come. Therefore, study God's Word and apply it to your life on a daily basis. Take your example from David, Gideon, Samson, Daniel, and the prophets who by faith "overthrew kingdoms, ruled with justice, and received what God had promised them. They shut the mouths of lions, quenched the flames of fire, and escaped death by the edge of the sword. Their weakness was turned to strength. They became strong in battle and put whole armies to flight" (Hebrews 11:33–34, NLT).

Remember, if God is for you, who can stand against you? Nothing can separate you from His love. Not trouble, suffering, hunger, danger, or death. Nothing. In every circumstance, you are more than a conqueror because you are in Christ (Romans 8:31–37). And Jesus gives you this guarantee: "Those who are victorious will sit with me on my throne, just as I was victorious and sat with my Father on his throne" (Revelation 3:21, NLT).

As a child of God, you can walk through life with your head held high, not in haughtiness but in confidence, secure in the knowledge that you can do all things through Christ who strengthens you (Philippians 4:13).

> *For the LORD God is a sun and shield;*
> *the LORD bestows favor and honor;*
> *no good thing does he withhold*
> *from those whose walk is blameless.*
> Psalm 84:11

MAKE A NOTE OF IT

Title this page "What Can God Do for Me?" Make a complete list of all the problems, large and small, that you or other family members are facing right now. Now, put a checkmark next to all of the problems that are so big and terrible that Jesus' victory on the cross could not overcome them. Look at your list one more time and know that because Jesus has overcome the world, you do not need to worry or be afraid of any situation in your life.

WHAT SHOULD I DO?

Because Jesus humbled Himself in obedience to the Father and died a criminal's death on the cross, "God elevated him to the place of highest honor and gave him the name above all other names" (Philippians 2:9, NLT). He has been given "all authority on heaven and on earth" (Matthew 28:18). When we call Him "Lord," we are declaring His rightful place as King of the universe and saying that He has the authority to tell us how to live our lives.

It is very important that you give Jesus lordship over every part of your life. After all, no one is more knowledgeable or capable, and no one loves you more than He does. So give yourself to Him, body and soul. Don't hold anything back. Give Him complete authority over your time, your money, your work, your school, and your relationships. Obey Him and honor Him in all things, and you will walk in His peace, looking forward to that glorious day when "at the name of Jesus every knee should bow, in heaven and on earth and under the earth, and every tongue confess that Jesus Christ is Lord, to the glory of God the Father" (Philippians 2:10–11).

A PRAYER

Dear God, thank you for choosing me to be your child. I love you, Father. Thank you for helping me see myself the way you see me. Help me to be a good ambassador and tell many people about your Son. I choose to give every part of my life to Jesus. He is truly the Lord of everything. In His name I pray. Amen.

Photo: NASA.

WORLDVIEWS IN FOCUS

MEET MEI

Mei (pronounced "may") is a twelve-year-old girl who lives in a small apartment in Tianjin, China, with her father, mother, and baby sister, Lin. Her parents both come from rural areas of China. They met when they moved to the city to find work. After getting married, they decided to stay in Tianjin and raise their children there. Tianjin (tyen-CHIN) is about a hundred miles southeast of Beijing, the capital of China.

Mei's father works at a factory as an engineer, and Mei's mother works as a seamstress. During work hours, they leave baby Lin with an elderly neighbor. The neighbor, who is from Taiwan, asks Mei to call her Ama, which means "grandma" in her native dialect. In return for her babysitting services, Mei and her mother clean Ama's apartment and prepare dinner for her every night. Ama doesn't see her own son and grandson very often because they are always working, so she greatly appreciates the time she spends with Mei and Lin.

In China it is rare for a family to have more than one child. China is home to 1.3 billion people—one fifth of the world's entire population! The government wants to make sure that it has enough resources to take care of every person, so Chinese law says that each couple is allowed to have only one child. Recently, however, a new law was passed that allows couples without brothers and sisters to have two children. Because Mei's parents are both only children, they were allowed to take advantage of this new law. Mei's little sister was born a year later.

Boys are considered more important than girls in China because they are thought to be more helpful in farm work and, as adults, are able to provide for their aging parents and carry on the family name. Because of this traditional preference, many families want their child to be a boy. So baby girls are sometimes put up for adoption, abandoned, or worse. When Mei's mother was pregnant with her, the doctors suggested that she terminate the pregnancy and try again to become pregnant with a son. But Mei's parents told the doctors they were going to keep her and thank God for the precious gift He had sent them.

Mei is grateful that her parents' beliefs allowed her to be born. Her parents are Christians—a rarity in China—and now she is a Christian, too. When she was young, her parents told her about Jesus, the Son of God, who came to earth as a man to die for the sins of all people. Mei's father taught her that Jesus took her sins upon Himself and was killed so that she wouldn't have to be punished for her sins. Even as a child, Mei's soft heart understood that Jesus had been hurt for her, and she chose to love and follow Him to honor His sacrifice. Now Mei can't wait for Lin to grow old enough so she can share the story of Jesus' love with her, too.

The People's Armed Police. Photo: BrokenSphere.

Being a Christian in China is not easy. The communist government wants to control what the people believe, to keep their energies focused on creating a unified country. Chinese officials believe that Christianity is dangerous, and they do everything they can to control its growth and possibly even stamp it out altogether. Today, some of the worst persecution of Christ's followers happens in China. Mei and her parents and their Christian friends know they are making a brave choice by deciding to follow Christ. They expect to run into problems for their beliefs because the Bible says those who believe in Jesus Christ will be hated by the world, just as Jesus was hated. Mei's parents say they are willing to die rather than renounce, or give up, their beliefs.

Last year, one of the young men in Mei's church was arrested after sharing his faith with a friend at the factory where he worked. After several weeks of interrogation and torture, the young man was executed because he would not renounce his belief in Jesus. Although Mei was very sad to hear of his death, his example only strengthened her faith. She hopes that if the time ever comes when she is asked to deny Jesus, she will be able to stand firm in her faith regardless of the consequences.

Despite the government's persecution of Christians, Mei is proud to be Chinese. She has learned in school about China's rich heritage, which stretches back thousands of years. Her father says there are many things about China to be proud of, such as introducing the world to paper, woven silk, the magnetic compass, fireworks, kites, ice cream, and an early form of the printing press. Mei's favorite hobby is Chinese calligraphy. Using a soft brush and ink, she carefully writes Chinese characters in neat columns, trying to copy the flowing grace of the master calligraphers. The ink comes in a stick that must be rubbed into water in a special inkstone. Mei's grandfather has taught her the right way to rub the ink stick and mix it with water so the ink forms just the right consistency. Mei practices whenever she has the chance. Her mother jokes that it's a good thing paper is inexpensive!

Mei is using her calligraphy skills to create scrolls for the upcoming celebration of Chinese New Year. Also called Spring Festival, Chinese New Year is based on the lunar calendar and is celebrated by people of Chinese heritage around the world. They decorate their houses with brightly colored paper lanterns and scrolls with sayings of prosperity and success. There are also dragon dances through the streets, where dancers stomp their feet to the beat of drums beneath a long, colorful dragon costume.

Dragon dancers at a Chinese New Year festival. Photo: Caseman.

The night before the new year arrives, families gather for a festive meal. Every year, Mei's mother roasts a whole fish and sets out oranges, seafood salad, and lots of sweets. Mei's favorite dessert is fried New Year's Cake, called *nián gao*. Mei and her family buy small presents for each other to celebrate another year of life. Then everyone bundles up in warm clothing (because Chinese New Year falls in January or February, depending on the year) and goes outside to watch the fireworks displays. The next morning, Mei's parents give her a red envelope with a little spending money in it. This year she is thinking of purchasing another calligraphy brush.

Nián gao.

To prepare for the new year, Mei also helps her mother scrub their apartment clean, thus getting rid of all the dirt from the old year. Mei's mother says that many Chinese clean their homes because they believe they are ridding the house of evil spirits and bringing in luck for the upcoming year. But Mei's family does it to symbolize renewal, reminding them that becoming a Christian washes away a person's sins in God's eyes. Besides, her mother says, the apartment can always use a thorough cleaning!

Mei has just started seventh grade and now attends middle school. In China, students are expected to attend at least nine years of school, but many drop out before finishing, usually because their families are poor and the children need to work to help bring in money. This is especially true in rural areas where families must work year round on their farms to have enough to eat. Even those young adults who move to the cities to work barely make enough to live on *and* send money back home so their parents can eat. With this kind of poverty in China, it is hard for most families to scrape together enough to pay for extra things like clothes and books so their children can stay in school.

A classroom in a Chinese school. Photo: flickr.com user Rex Pe.

Since many students remain in school for only a few grades, high school is taken very seriously in China, almost like college in other countries. Students must take a big test at the end of ninth grade to determine whether they can attend high school. Those who are fortunate enough to finish high school are considered well educated. Only wealthy people in China can afford to send their children to university.

Mei wants to become a teacher when she grows up and teach the many poor children in rural areas who cannot afford an education. But to qualify for a teacher's certificate, she will need to graduate from high school. She must score well on her entrance test to qualify for a good school that won't charge her family a high tuition. If she gets a low score, she will have to attend a lower-quality high school or pay a lot of money to buy her way into a better school. Mei doesn't want to put this kind of financial burden on her family. In addition to the expenses of living in the city, Mei's parents try to send as much money as possible back home to their parents. They don't have the money for high education fees, so Mei works hard to earn good grades.

Whenever Mei worries about schoolwork and sprouts wrinkles on her forehead, her mother is there to smile and smooth them away. She tells Mei that God—whom they call *Shangdi*, or "Emperor Above"—has a plan for her life and will provide everything she needs. After all, who is richer than the Creator of the universe? Her mother's life has not been easy, yet she manages to remain serene and strong, trusting day by day that God has everything under control. Mei wants to demonstrate the kind of trust and joy in her life that she sees every day in her mother. She thanks God for her mother's quiet faith and her father's integrity as examples of how to live a Christian life and bring glory to the Lord.

Skyline of Tianjin. Photo: flickr user kilroy238.

Mei likes living in Tianjin, which most locals just call Jin. Although it is still a very big city—the sixth largest in China—it is only half the size of Beijing and much smaller than Shanghai. On weekends during the hot, humid summers, Mei loves to picnic at the Tianjin Water Park, with its many gardens and lakes. Young Lin's favorite is the Tianjin Zoo, where she insists on spending most of their time watching the pandas and cries when it is time to go home. Once their father took Mei on the Beijing-Tianjin train, one of the fastest passenger trains in the world. Built just before Beijing hosted the Olympics in 2008, the train races between the two cities at 330 kilometers an hour, or 205 miles per hour, cutting the trip from over an hour to just thirty minutes. Mei enjoyed being with her father, but she isn't sure she'd want to travel that fast all the time.

Classes at Mei's new middle school are longer than she is used to, so she's tired when she gets home at night. But she knows her parents have been working hard all day too, so she jumps in cheerfully to help with things that need to be done. Mei especially likes cooking. Using the fresh ingredients her mother has purchased on her way home from work, Mei helps prepare a simple stir-fry recipe with chicken, seafood, and vegetables seasoned with ginger and garlic. Another family favorite is fried rice with eggs. Mei's mother mixes up spicy sauces to put over everything! Mei is practicing making more complex dishes, like homemade dumplings stuffed with meat, called *bao*, so that she can become as good a cook as her mother. Mei has been eating with chopsticks since she was small, and now she is trying to teach little Lin to use them too.

After the simple meal is finished, Mei's father brings his Bible out of its hiding place inside one of the walls of their home and reads to them. Mei and her family feel very blessed to own a Bible. They know, however, that owning a Bible means they could be arrested and sent to jail if the Chinese authorities ever find out. Believers in China have to be very careful and very brave. Many meet secretly in homes or basements, but others are determined to meet in public no matter

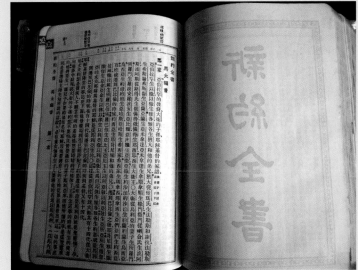
A Chinese translation of the Bible. Photo: myself.

what the cost.

Mei's father has friends in Beijing who attend Shouwang Church, a group of a thousand people who meet to worship every Sunday. The Chinese government knows all about them, and officials do what they can to stop the church from meeting. Police detain the pastors on Sunday mornings, interrogating them for hours so they cannot lead the others in worship. They block the church from renting meeting space and close public parks to keep the members from gathering. The government repeatedly denies the church's applications to be registered as an independent church, and they even sabotage the church's website so that its members and other Chinese people can't find information about the church, its activities, or the message of the gospel. Although the government is creative and thorough in its persecution of the church, Chinese officials have not been able to stop Christians from meeting together or sharing the good news of their faith. Their joy and zeal for God and His Word are contagious, and many more Chinese become Christians every day because of their witness.

Tianjin apratments. Photot: flickr.com user Jakob Montrasio.

Mei and her family are members of a "house church," a small group of believers in Tianjin. Sometimes they all crowd into a small apartment, and sometimes they meet in parks or other public places, trusting that God will keep them safe. Often Mei and her family don't know until Sunday morning where that day's service will be held. Mei's father says that *people* are the church, the body of Christ, and it doesn't matter if they have a building of their own. She is grateful to be part of a close-knit church family.

Despite the dangers, when Mei's house church meets, the atmosphere is one of celebration and joy. They sing and worship together and study teachings from the Bible. They also devote much of their meeting time to prayer. Prayer means a great deal to Chinese Christians because every day they see the need for God's power in their lives and their nation. As children of the living God, the believers in Mei's church expect to see signs and wonders and miraculous answers to prayer. Mei has seen many people healed of sickness and injury during their meetings, and she has no doubt her Father in heaven is stronger than sickness and death and even the communist government.

Many underground churches in China do not have an official pastor, but Mei's church is blessed to have one. However, their pastor is quick to step aside and let others in the congregation speak or lead during prayer times. He knows he may not always be free to lead, so he wants as many people as possible to be prepared to take his place. Last year, Mei's pastor was arrested by the Chinese police and imprisoned for two months while they questioned him about his activities and teachings. While he was in prison, Mei's father led the church for a few Sundays until he too was arrested. For two weeks, her father was questioned about his involvement with the underground Christian church. Mei and her mother prayed for hours every day, asking God to protect him and send him home.

Two weeks later, her father was returned. He had been questioned for long hours each day, but miraculously he had not been hurt. When the police decided he did not have any useful information for them, they sent him home with a strong warning never to attend services or preach again. But the next Sunday, he stood up in church and spoke to the people about how God had protected him in prison, the miracles he witnessed there, and the things he learned about faith while under arrest. Listening to her father, Mei was never more proud of his courage and determination to follow God.

Despite the persecution Christians endure from the communist Chinese government—sometimes because of it—there are many strong believers in China. Mei knows that Christians around the world are helping the Chinese churches by sending money, training Chinese pastors, smuggling Bibles into China, and praying for protection for Chinese churches and for many more people to be saved. She is very grateful that strangers would give their time and money to help their brothers and sisters in the Lord in a faraway land. Knowing there are people around the world who care about her and Christians like her helps Mei trust God more each day.

WHAT'S THE DIFFERENCE?

- How is the way Mei lives different from the way you live? How are your lives similar?

- How is Mei's church different from yours? How is it similar?

- Is a church that meets in someone's home still a church? Why?

- Why does the Chinese government persecute its citizens who follow Jesus? Why do you think a communist government might consider Christianity to be dangerous?

THE HOUSE OF TRUTH: THE EIGHTH PILLAR

Throughout this book, you have been building a new wall in your House of Truth to help you remember what God says in the Bible about who you are and how God expects you to live. This wall, the Image-Bearing Wall, represents your relationship with yourself as you become more like Jesus Christ.

Over the last few lessons, you erected the fourth and final pillar in this wall:

BIBLICAL TRUTH 12:

Jesus died to restore harmony within me.

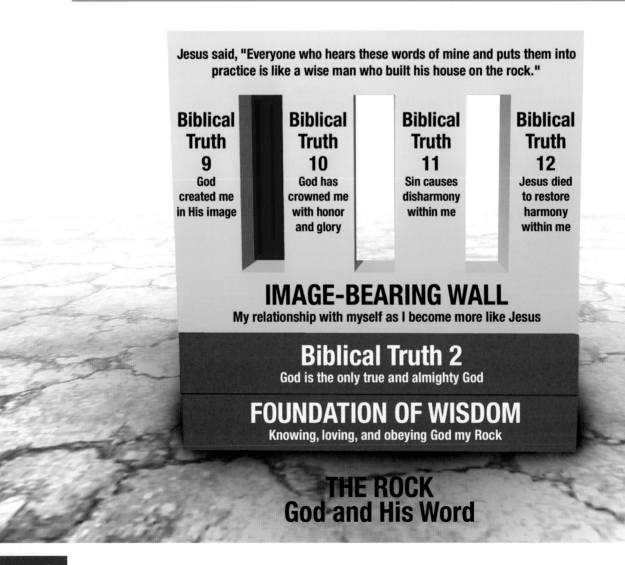

Jesus said, "Everyone who hears these words of mine and puts them into practice is like a wise man who built his house on the rock."

Biblical Truth 9
God created me in His image

Biblical Truth 10
God has crowned me with honor and glory

Biblical Truth 11
Sin causes disharmony within me

Biblical Truth 12
Jesus died to restore harmony within me

IMAGE-BEARING WALL
My relationship with myself as I become more like Jesus

Biblical Truth 2
God is the only true and almighty God

FOUNDATION OF WISDOM
Knowing, loving, and obeying God my Rock

THE ROCK
God and His Word

INDEX

ACKNOWLEDGMENTS

Our gratitude and appreciation go out to several individuals, without whom this book could not have been written. Thank you first of all to Dr. David Noebel and John Stonestreet of Summit Ministries and Davis Carman of Apologia Educational Ministries whose vision and commitment to worldview studies made this series possible. Thank you to Zan Tyler, director of Apologia Press, for her unwavering support and tremendous encouragement from the project's inception through the lengthy writing and production process.

Thank you to our loving wives, Nancy and Peggy, for their invaluable assistance and remarkable patience during the writing of this book. We greatly appreciate your reading and re-reading of the text. Nancy, you have a remarkable eye for catching the smallest typographical error and graciously correcting our grammar. Peggy, thank you for compiling the index, contributing to several of the sidebar articles, and tolerating an insomniac's crazy work schedule.

Thank you to Doug Powell, not only for his outstanding creative design work, but also for his insights into Christian apologetics and the Greek lexicon. And our very special thanks to Amanda Lewis, who contributed much of the Worldviews in Focus content in addition to several of the sidebar articles. We couldn't have done it without you!

Soli Deo Gloria!

CELEBRATE YOUR CHILD'S SPIRITUAL JOURNEY

The What We Believe Series is a wonderful way to build a foundation of faith. Now your children can personalize and capture what they learn along the way in a keepsake they will want to revisit as they grow in Christ. These beautiful spiral-bound notebooking journals from Apologia include lesson plans, study questions, artful graphics, imaginative writing and drawing prompts, puzzles, activities, and full-color mini books. There's even a place on the cover for the child to write his or her name as the author of the journal!

NATURE'S FOOTPRINTS

Read a book about tracking animals, then plan a nature hike with a parent. Bring equipment to draw or photograph any animal prints you find. Record your findings here.

132

MAKE A NOTE OF IT
WHY DID GOD MAKE ME THIS WAY?

In the story "Sasha's Choice," Sasha learned that he was created by God to be unique and that neither his birth nor his lame foot was an accident. What is it about the way you were made that you've sometimes wished you could change? Have you ever considered thanking God for making you this way?

LET WISDOM BE YOUR GUIDE

WORD LIST

King Kong	anger	Judas
King Solomon	deceitful	Salt Lake City
The Last Supper	Gethsemane	genealogy
impulse	Vulcan	temple recommend
fishermen	praise	polygamy
Ichthus	grief	tithing
emotions	Lazarus	Mormon Church
anxious	temper	

ACROSS

1. The Christian "fish" seen on millions of car bumpers
7. Put on "a garment of _____ instead of a spirit of despair" (Isaiah 61:3)
11. Giant ape who "fell" for an actress
13. Leonardo da Vinci's famous mural of Jesus and His disciples
    He betrayed Jesus to the authorities
    Deep sorrow usually brought on by the loss of a friend or loved one
    Profession of Peter, James, and John
    Star Trek planet where inhabitants are taught to suppress their emotions
    "The heart is _____ above all things" (Jeremiah 17:9)
10. Also known as the Church of Jesus Christ of Latter-day Saints

DOWN

2. You must have this special pass to enter a Mormon temple
3. The study of a family's history
4. "Controlling your _____ is better than capturing a city" (Proverbs 16:37, NCV)
5. Olive grove where Jesus prayed the night of His arrest
6. A sudden or spontaneous urge to do something you hadn't planned to do
8. He wrote that there's "a time to weep and a time to laugh" (Ecclesiastes 3:4)
9. Elihu's home town
12. The practice of having more than one wife or husband
15. "Do not be _____ about anything" (Philippians 4:6)
16. The Lord is "slow to _____ and rich in love" (Psalm 145:8)
18. They're a gift from God
20. Jesus wept at the death of this brother of Mary and Martha

100 / 101

Notebooking Journal

Who Am I?

And What Am I Doing Here?

NORMAN ROCKWELL

Written By

Notebooking Journal

Who Is MY NEIGHBOR?

And Why Does He Need Me?

Written By

ENCOUNTERS WITH JESUS
THE WEDDING FEAST

1. Read the biblical account of the wedding at Cana in John 2:1–11 and compare it to the story you've just read. What did the authors of your book add to the story as told in the Bible? Did they leave out anything important? How would you have told the story differently?

2. With Miriam getting married, what do you think life at home will be like for her sister Rachel?

3. Why do you think hospitality was such an important part of a Jewish wedding?

4. Why was Miriam so distressed that the wedding party was running low on wine? What might people have said if the wine had run out so early in the festivities?

5. According to the apostle John, this was the first of the miraculous signs Jesus performed. So why do you think Mary came to Jesus with this problem? What did she expect Him to do? Why?

6. Although the time for Jesus to reveal Himself to the world as the Son of God had "not yet come," He chose to turn the water into wine. Why do you think Jesus made this decision?

7. How did Jesus serve this young bride? What need did He meet? Whom else did He serve through this miracle?

8. What is your favorite story from the life of Jesus? Why?

MAKING A DIFFERENCE

volleyball
China
cargo
freighter
social triune

interdependence
servanthood
trusting God
companionship
helper

buddy system
NASCAR
make a difference
two by two
safety in numbers

two are better than one
be all that you can be
change the world
mustard seed

17

Notebooking Journal

What on Earth CAN I DO?

Written By

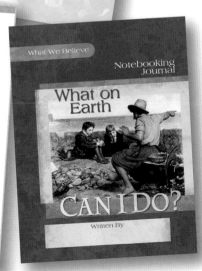

I Know What I Believe, Too

Introducing What We Believe coloring books for those who learn best when their hands are active! These 64-page coloring books are lovingly illustrated by award-winning artist Alice Ratterree. Every drawing depicts a story or teaching from the companion textbook, so even the youngest member of the family can follow along!

IMAGE LICENSE INFORMATION

Creative Commons Attribution-Share Alike 3.0
    Tannenberg, 16
    Alex Zelenko, 50
    Stanislav Traykov, Niabot, 62
    Peter Kammer, 80
    Donovan Govan, 82
    Henry Flower, 104
    Ondřej Žváček, 115
    Diliff, 135
    Myouzke, 229
    Concord, 251

Creative Commons Attribution-Share Alike 3.0 Unported
    Steindy, 67
    Wolfgang Sauber, 79, 86, 119
    Yan Schweizer, 81
    Chris 73, 101
    CenkX, 106
    Tevaprapas Makklay, 108
    Mufunyo, 123
    Mistereze, 143
    Yann Forget, 166
    Matthias Juchem, 174
    Jonathan Oldenbuck, 182
    Jmex60, 183
    Grombo, 221
    Gilad Rom, 226
    BrokenSphere, 256

Creative Commons Attribution 3.0 Unported
    Taty2007, 78
    Tedder, 196
    thddbwnd, 228
    myself, 259

Creative Commons Attribution-Share Alike 2.5 Generic
    Introvert, 17
    Matthias Prinke, 40
    Malene Thyssen, 53
    Ben Schumin, 59
    Bresson Thomas, 98
    Lior Golgher, 193
    Siddhasana, 197
    Lenepveu, 244

Creative Commons Attribution-Share Alike 2.0 Generic
    woody1778a, 83
    Tom T, 84
    Dean Franklin, 89
    Shelley Mannion, 104
    Andrew Dunn, 176
    Frederic Humbert, 182
    Jim Bowen, 189
    Clinton & Charles Robertson, 199
    Jeff Kubina, 209
    Rex Pe, 258
    kilroy238, 259
    Jakob Montrasio, 260

Creative Commons Attribution 2.0 Generic
    PhotoDu.de, 27
    omar_chatriwala, 42
    Pachango, 63
    Peter Duhon from New York City, USA, 67
    Daniel Martini, 91
    RebeccaPollard, 92
    Genvessel, 93
    DrGBB, 100
    chem7, 105
    randomduck, 190
    Mark Scott Johnson, 227
    John Pavelka, 228
    Kok Leng Yeo, 230

Creative Commons Attribution-NoDerivs 2.0 Generic
    Po Yang, 70
    Serdar Gurbuz Photography, 71
    Willy_G91, 150

Courtesy of Art Resource:
    John Pettie. *The Vigil*. Exhibited 1884. Oil on canvas,
    115.8 x 170.3 cm. Tate Gallery, London, Great
    Britain. Photo Credit: Tate, London / Art Resource,
    NY, 236